WORLD OF THE SPIRITS

World of the Spirits

*A Christian Perspective on
Traditional and Folk Religions*

DAVID BURNETT

**MONARCH
BOOKS**

First published by Monarch Books 2000

ISBN 1 85424 499 X

British Library Cataloguing Data
A catalogue record for this book is available
from the British Library.

Inset cover photos by David Barnett

Designed and produced for the publishers by
Bookprint Creative Services
P.O. Box 827, BN21 3YJ England
Printed in Great Britain.

CONTENTS

FOREWORD

Lotieng was an old headman living in Karamoja, a remote area of northeastern Uganda. Like many parts of Africa in the 1980s, this region had suffered from drought. It was another sunny morning with a clear blue sky when he welcomed me to a rainmaking ritual. I looked on somewhat incredulously as the little group of some hundred people who made up the homestead prepared for the ceremony. They sacrificed a black bull according to well-defined ritual, and whilst the meat was being cooked the elders began praying to Akuj, the name they used for their great high god. We ate and then people began to dance. As I filmed the celebrations, I noticed a small cloud appear on the horizon. Gradually it grew and spread across the sky, and by late afternoon it began to rain.

It was with this story that I commenced the book entitled *Unearthly Powers* published in 1988. The experience with Lotieng has continued to fascinate me, and raised for me some significant questions. I wrote *Unearthly Powers* with the aim of helping Christian workers appreciate the richness of societies that Western missionaries often consider primitive and barbaric. Frequently their beliefs have been dismissed as demonic and irrelevant. However, with Lotieng I saw a man who was concerned about his people, and was operating within the rationality of his particular worldview. I came to respect him

7

and wanted to appreciate his perspective on the world in which he lived. *Unearthly Powers* therefore sought to provide a framework for understanding the complex variety of beliefs and practices that Christian workers often face in such societies.

During the last 12 years much has changed not only for the Karamojong, but societies throughout the world. Many of the traditional societies have adopted one of the major world religions, and all have been affected by the relentless penetration of materialism and globalisation. Anthropologists have also continued to reassess their material and theories of religion and magic, and all this has influenced my own thinking. This book commenced as a revision of *Unearthly Powers*, but by the end there emerged an essentially new book that deserved a new title.

World of the Spirits differs from the previous book in two main ways. First it seeks to delve further into many of the same questions considered before, but now I have engaged more with the theoretical issues. I have changed from the use of the expression 'primal religions' to 'traditional religions' because it is an expression that has become more widely adopted amongst scholars. I have also commenced the book with a chapter that reviews how Western thinking about traditional societies has changed during the last two hundred years. This introduces some of the scholars and ideas that have influenced the subject during the period of the European missionary movement. Many of the questions I have considered have been of particular interest to anthropologists, but are equally significant for Christian workers. Why does witchcraft occur in some societies and not others? Why does magic continue to be practised? Why do new religious movements emerge? I also discuss the various approaches made by Christians to address these issues.

Second, *World of the Spirits* also differs from the former book by looking more at the relationship between world religions and traditional societies. It contains new chapters on the subjects of conversion, social demoralisation and religious syncretism. I have sought to address the question of why traditional societies have been particularly responsive to the world religions such as Islam and Christianity. The text therefore is not merely about 'traditional societies', but provides a guide to understanding 'folk' beliefs and practices in the world religions.

This book has benefited from the insights of many scholars who have influenced my thinking over the past years. However, it has been those people like Lotieng to whom I feel most indebted. They have allowed me to enter somewhat into their world. I hope they would consider that I have presented their views with understanding and respect.

Chapter One

STRANGERS ABROAD

The old chief made his way towards his village pondering the changes that he had known during his life. So much had changed. The British had long since granted independence to India, but his people seemed to have greater problems. He was of the Maltos people who live in the Rajmahal highlands over-looking the Ganges valley in the state of Bihar. In the broad valley there were farms and towns, railways and roads, schools and hospitals. In contrast, his people lived in small villages in the inhospitable hills where there were no roads, electricity, or schools. The Hindi-speaking people of the Ganges valley call them 'Paharias' meaning 'hill people'.

During the time of British rule a few white missionaries had come to them, but the Maltos had shown no interest.[1] Now new missionaries had come but this time they were Indians from the south. The native language of these missionaries was similar to their own, and they had come to live with them and learn their language. Two or three had even died in the difficult conditions of the Rajmahal hills, but more missionaries had come to replace them. They not only tried to help them by setting up a clinic and school for their children, but also told them about the supreme creator God.[2]

Maltos believe the world is full of spirits which they called *gosain*, usually translated into English as 'god'.[3] For generations

Maltos had offered sacrifices to appease the *gosain*, which they often represented by a pile of stones. As long as anyone could remember they had always worshipped these spirits, but now with all the sickness and poverty in the village the old chief wondered if it was worth bothering any more with the *gosain*. What help were they to his village now? Here he was walking along a path where some of the same stones hindered his path. Why should he set up some stones and regard them as his gods, whilst others he trod underfoot? Some of the other villages had become Christian, and he wondered if it would not be the best for his village. He knew that some of the people had been saying this, so he decided to raise the issue with the men.

A few days later at a meeting of the older men they discussed the question as to whether the village should become Christian. Some expressed apprehension due to fear of the spirits, but all agreed that the spirits were now of little assistance. They decided to ask the Indian missionaries to come, and tell them how they could become Christians.

* * *

The story of the old chief and the Maltos people is illustrative of many communities around the world who at one time or another have converted to a major religious tradition such as Christianity, Islam, Hinduism or Buddhism. These religions have variously been called 'Primitive Religions', 'Animism', 'Primal Religions', 'Pre-literate' or as they will be called in this book, 'Traditional Religions'. Most scholars acknowledge the limitations of all these terms. However, if the religious expressions of indigenous people are to be discussed academically alongside religious traditions such as Islam, Hinduism and Buddhism, some such term must be adopted. It is these so-called 'primitive' societies that have been the particular focus of study by anthropologists, and amongst whom the missionary has found the greatest response to the Christian message.

Today, writers like Adam Kuper have expressed the concern that the idea of 'primitive society' is essentially a construct of Western contact with a world that was for them both strange and exotic.[4]

> In the second half of the nineteenth century, Europeans believed themselves to be witnessing a revolutionary transition in the type of their society ... [They] conceived the new world in contrast to 'traditional society'; and behind this 'traditional society' they discerned a primitive or primeval society.[5]

The Europeans' belief in their own superiority, coupled with their ideas as to how the transformation of their own society was achieved, provided the context for what Kuper calls the 'invention of the primitive'. As Kuper further contends, 'The anthropologists took . . . primitive society as their special subject, but in practice primitive society proved to be their own society (as they understood it) seen in a distorting mirror'.[6] In other words, primitive society was the antithesis of modernising European society, and it is in that sense that it is an invention. As Tienou has pointed out, the anthropological ideas of primitive society have had a great influence upon Christian missionaries, and as such cannot be ignored.[7] This first chapter explores the ways that Westerners as strangers abroad have thought about primitive societies, and seeks to provide an introduction for a sympathetic and meaningful understanding.

Understanding others

The study of the religious beliefs of indigenous people has passed through various phases which may be simply classed into three: travellers and missionaries, academic anthropologists, and African historians.

Explorers

The description of traditional religions began in the reports by traders, slavers, missionaries, administrators and soldiers as Europeans began to explore the world in the sixteenth century. Some of these travellers proved to be accurate and reliable reporters. Willem Bosman, for example, lived at Elmina Castle on the Gold Coast from 1688 until 1702, and made an extensive and accurate description of the Akan and Guan societies.[8] Other travellers tended to be more critical, and revealed their cultural bias. In 1867, Sir Samuel Baker wrote of the Sudanese:

> Without any exception, they are without a belief in a Supreme Being, neither have they any form of worship or idolatry; nor is the darkness of their minds enlightened by even a ray of superstition. The mind is stagnant as the morass, which forms its puny world.[9]

Similarly in 1864, Sir Richard Burton referring to West Africa:

> The negro is still at that rude dawn of faith – fetishism – and he has barely advanced to idolatry . . . He has never grasped the ideas of a personal Deity, a duty in life, a moral code, or a shame of lying. He rarely believes in a future state of rewards and punishments, which, whether true or not, are infallible indices of human progress.[10]

Such reports affected the attitudes of Colonial Governments who saw their role in part to civilise these primitive societies as well as bringing them into the economic system of the West. This was to be 'the white man's burden'. The writing of explorers also stimulated Christian concern, and missionaries responded to the perceived need of these so-called 'primitive' people. These missionaries often stayed longer than the explorers, and so often became more knowledgeable and sympathetic towards the indigenous people. For example, David Livingstone had a famous debate with a 'rain-maker', in which he records the man as saying:

I use my medicines, and you employ yours; we are both doctors, and doctors are not deceivers. You give a patient medicine. Sometimes God is pleased to heal him by means of your medicine: sometimes not – he dies. When he is cured, you take the credit of what God does. I do the same. Sometimes God grants us rain, sometimes not. When he does, we take the credit of the charm. When a patient dies, you don't give up trusting in your medicine, neither do I when rain fails. If you wish me to leave off my medicines, why continue your own?[11]

These reports stimulated new theories concerning the origin and evolution of human culture. As early as 1760 Charles De Brosses proposed the theory that religion originated with a phenomenon he called 'fetish', from the Portuguese word 'fetico'. In Portugal it referred to amulets and the relics of saints, but the meaning was extended to certain objects venerated by the inhabitants of the Guinea coast. De Brosses regarded religion as having originated in fetishism and his views were widely accepted until the mid-nineteenth century. August Comte made fetishism the first of his three-fold scheme in the development of religious ideas: fetishism, polytheism, and monotheism. In such a scheme, fetishism represented individualistic rather than organised religion, and to a large extent corresponded to what later writers described as magic.

In 1883, Sir Edward B. Tylor rejected Comte's use, and coined the more specific term 'animism' as a belief in souls (*anima*).[12] This became a turning point in the study of anthropology, when a vast amount of material collected from missionaries and travellers was set forth in analytical style. Tylor's theory of animism focused on the belief that not only human beings and animals, but also inanimate objects have life and personality. Tylor's theory had two aspects, the first of which accounted for the origin and the second the development of religion. Tylor argued that as primitive people reflected on experiences such as death, trance, vision and dream, this led to the conclusion that there was some immaterial entity apart from the body. By considering the soul as somehow independent from its material form, Tylor argued that it was then a simple step to the notion of spiritual beings. The belief in spiritual beings led to reverence of ancestors who eventually developed into gods. This evolution then moves from polytheism to monotheism.

The other great Victorian anthropologist was Sir James G. Frazer who from Cambridge University kept up a great correspondence with people around the world. Much of this work was brought together in his massive work *The Golden Bough*, which is a systematic collection of beliefs and rituals from around the world.[13] According to Frazer religions everywhere evolved through three stages of intellectual development: from magic to religion, and then from religion to science.

In 1898 Andrew Lang published *The Making of Religion,* in which he challenged the notion of animism as the first human religion.[14] He argued the case that the existence of high gods was common in the religion of primitive peoples. Lang's conclusion was not based upon new material, but on a different way of interpreting the existing information. The Catholic ethnologist Father Wilhelm Schmidt later supported Lang in his twelve-volume work *Der Ursprung der Gottesidee* which was published over a forty-three year period (1912–1955). In this text he traces the various monotheistic ideas found in traditional societies. Although most anthropologists initially rejected his idea it did lead to an appreciation of the widespread belief in a Supreme Being as will be discussed in the following chapter.

The first World Missionary Conference was held in Edinburgh in 1910 with twelve hundred missionary leaders and administrators in attendance. Twenty-five missionaries contributed to a report on 'Animistic Religions', and this reflected much of the current study of the religion of traditional societies during that period. The animistic theory of the origin of religion as presented by Tylor was generally accepted as self-evident by Westerners, even though the few African representatives rejected it. The Africans considered the evolutionary model as derogatory and paternalistic to their cultural heritage.[15] Tylor's views were however moderated by those of the missionary Bishop Henry Callaway who had worked among the Zulus of southern Africa. From a study of Zulu myths Callaway concluded that the religious sentiment is common to and shared by all human beings. The 'human mind is to religious matters not a mere passive *tabula rasa*, but a prepared *tabula*, like photographic film-prepared to receive the impression of light.'[16] Callaway therefore saw the movement to Christianity as a matter of exposure, and an educational process that built upon what was already present in the African religious experience. These views had an on-going influence upon missionary strategies.

Academic anthropologists

While amateur ethnographers continued to contribute in various ways, the first decade of the twentieth century saw a more academic approach to the study of traditional societies. Colonial governments perceived the need, for various reasons, for more reliable information on the indigenous societies which they governed, and began to appoint 'government anthropologists' to supply them with the information. They allotted these posts at first to suitable political officers in their own service. A notable example is R. S. Rattray who was appointed by the British in 1921, and who had a great linguistic ability and knew the language of Akan people of the Gold Coast. His books on Asante society provided detailed descriptions of Akan culture, even though they have little theoretical discussion.[17]

In the late 1920s, colonial governments began to use academic anthropologists in addition to government anthropologists. Most had been trained in the new method of 'fieldwork' by participant observation following the ideas and practice of the anthropologist Bronislow Malinowski (1884–1942) who though born in Poland became a significant figure in British anthropology. They tended to stay longer in an area and also learnt the language of the community. Initially these anthropologists followed the ideas of Malinowski and were more interested in the function of religious rituals and beliefs within the social system. Mythology, for example, was considered to serve as a 'charter' that legitimated social and political institutions within society.

One of the most prominent of the academic anthropologists was E. E. Evans-Pritchard who was invited by the government of the Anglo-Egyptian Sudan in 1926 to research the Azande, and in 1930 the Nuer. Evans-Pritchard examined the nature of logic of such societies, and explored the question as to whether it was rational to believe in witchcraft. As such he sought to understand Zande and Nuer behaviour according to a system of ideas within their own universe of thought (worldview).

> I have tried to show how some features of their [Nuer] religion can be presented more intelligently in relation to the social order described in earlier volumes but I have tried also to describe and interpret it as a system of ideas and practices in its own right.[18]

This move from 'function' to 'meaning' among British anthropologists stimulated many studies of African people. John Middleton made an important study of the Lugbara, and Godfrey Lienhardt of the Dinka. This approach also led to a greater respect for indigenous people. This was seen in the prolific writings of Geoffrey Parrinder, among which was the influential book *African Traditional Religion*.[19] His avoidance of terms such as 'primitive' and 'tribal' and his choice of the term 'traditional' suggested that African religions are worthy of respect. He finally put African Tradition Religion on a par with Christianity and Islam in his book entitled *Africa's Three Religions*.[20] This comparative approach, however, emphasised more what African traditional religions had in common than how they differed, thereby homogenising them as a single religious phenomenon. This is shown in the use of the term religion in the singular rather than in the plural. It also put emphasis on what they had in common with Christianity and Islam so shaping them after the template of Christian doctrine. As will be shown later, this had a major affect on how the study of traditional religions was to develop.

As anthropologists learnt the language of the people and sought to understand the world in the way their informants did, they concentrated more upon ritual symbols in an attempt to exegete their meaning. Victor Turner was a leader in this line of inquiry during his time among the Ndembu of Zambia. He argued that it was necessary to see how the meaning of a symbol is derived from its relationship to the totality of symbols which comprise the society's worldview.

The term 'primal religions' was introduced as an alternative classification by John V. Taylor in 1963 in the influential book *The Primal Vision*.[21] By 'primal' Taylor referred to that which is basic or fundamental to all religions. The expression was popularised in Britain by Harold Turner in the 1970s who defined it as 'meaning those religions that both anteceded the great historic religions and continue to reveal many of the basic or primary features of religion'.[22]

African writers

The third period of reflection on traditional religions has come from members of their own societies. The major discussions and writings have arisen in the African continent south of the Sahara. The earliest African authors produced essentially descriptive accounts of their religious experience, but later academics from departments of religious studies began to produce more theological works.

Joseph B. Danquah (1895–1965) was the first to mount a criticism on the anthropological interpretation. Danquah was a member of the Akim-Abuakwa royal family of the Gold Coast and read law and philosophy in London in the 1920s. In the book *The Akan Doctrine of God*, first published in 1944, he sought to expound an African idea of the Supreme Being in Western terms. In response to the European tendency to reduce African religions to mere polytheism he contended that Akan religion already believed in only one God.[23] Jomo Kenyatta (1897–1978) was also of an African royal family, and both his father and grandfather had been leaders in Kikuyu society. Kenyatta studied anthropology with Malinowski at the London School of Economics from 1935 to 1937, and made a study of Kikuyu society and religion.[24] His classic book, *Facing Mount Kenya*, was published in 1938. The frontispiece of the book has a picture of him dressed in traditional attire with a spear in his right hand, while feeling the sharpness of the point with his left hand. There was certainly political inspiration in the romantic picture that he presented of traditional Kikuyu society, which eventually expressed itself in the nationalist movement.

The greatest contribution to the study of traditional religions has recently come from African University departments of religious studies. Bolaji Idowu, for example, in 1973 argued for a monotheistic interpretation of Yoruba religion in which traditional religions were 'the (indigenous) religion (of Africans), which resulted from the sustaining faith held by the forebearers of the present Africans.'[25] The title of his book *African Traditional Religion: A Definition* illustrates the homogeneity assumed by his approach. He also built upon Schmidt's suggestion of 'primitive monotheism', and introduced the notion of 'diffused monotheism' to convey the idea of a Supreme Being who is partially diffused throughout other deities. The primary function of his writings seems to have been the indigenisation of the Western Christianity of the mainline churches of Nigeria. Culturally it also helped restore a respectable religious past, thereby giving self-respect to the educated African.

Idowu's writing stimulated more theological books from

African writers such as John Mbiti who tried to lay the basis of a distinct African theology. In the book *Concepts of God in Africa* he presented a synoptic survey of African supreme beings in almost three hundred different societies, and argued that the African concept of supreme deity came from an independent reflection upon the One Supreme God recognised in the Christian tradition.[26] These writers created what may be considered an authorised version of the African religious experience under the title 'African Traditional Religion' in which African Traditional Religion is discussed in the same analytical approach as Western Christian Theology. The result was that in the analysis much of the great diversity of religious experience was lost, and the emphasis was placed upon what people believed rather than what they did.

Through each of these three phases writers tried to describe and understand a wide range of religious phenomena under one rubric. By so doing they have often imposed a foreign analytical structure upon the people's beliefs often to such an extent that these become unrecognisable. The religious traditions were discussed and described as through an alien lens, which often denigrated and sometimes westernised. A continuing issue in the current study of traditional religions is how to discuss the complex range of religious phenomena without imposing too much of an assumed analytical structure.

Characteristics of traditional religions

The late nineteenth century saw the categorisation of religious traditions into major collections labelled as Hinduism, Mohammedism (later more respectfully Islam), Buddhism, etc. Islam remained somewhat distinct from the others because it was the religion that had been in closest contact with Christianity, and was appreciated as monotheistic. But what about China, and India? Both had great civilisations, literacy and religious philosophers. The religion of the people of the

Indian sub-continent was initially considered 'primitive', but during the nineteenth century Western scholars began to translate the great Indian texts. Max Muller opened major areas of scholarship that amazed European scholars, and the religious tradition of India was eventually called 'Hinduism'. These religions of major civilisations were therefore considered as 'world religions', partly out of respect for these civilisations and the literature of the religious tradition.

However, such categories create gaps, and into these gaps were gathered heaps of intransigent phenomena. Rosalind Shaw argues that in religious studies, these residual categories were classed as 'tribal religion'; later the more respectful terms 'traditional religion' and 'primal religion' were employed in this typology.[27] Textbooks on religious traditions label their material under categories such as Christianity, Islam, Judaism, Hinduism, and Buddhism. The variety found in the religious expressions covered by each term is great, and stretches such classification. The category Traditional Religion therefore tends to be the catch-phrase for all other religious expressions from whatever part of the world they may originate. No wonder it has become accepted to use the plural form 'Traditional Religions'. The problems of this categorisation are illustrated by the problems librarians often face in cataloguing books into various sections of a library. There may be a section on the various world religions, but what about those books on religions that fall outside these sections?

Shaw also writes: 'Primal religions are defined in contrast to the great religious systems, and are accorded a positive evaluation solely on the basis that they have contributed historically to and overlap with the latter.'[28] Harold Turner made deliberate use of such a distinction when he defined primal religions as those that 'have preceded and contributed to the other great religious systems'.

What is therefore a so-called 'world religion'? Four characteristics have generally been used to distinguish between 'World

Religions' and 'Traditional Religions'. First, a world religion proposes to be universal, and relevant to all humanity. In contrast, traditional religions are perceived as relating to a local community. Second, a world religion generally has written texts, one or more of which is regarded as a particularly holy text such as with the Bible or the Qur'an. In contrast, traditional religions have no such texts, and depend on oral transmission. Third, world religions have explicit doctrines, which have emerged as a result of scholarly consideration. No such clear doctrine is found among traditional religions, but this does not mean that wise people have not given thought to the issues raised. Finally, world religions have centres of authority based often upon a priestly hierarchy and association with state sponsorship. In general, no such authority exists in traditional religions, and it is usually the teaching of the elders that hold the greatest respect.

However, certain aspects of these characteristics can be found within so-called Traditional Religions, but in so doing they hide much of the diversity. Baylis recognises this and she has stated that 'there are as many primal religions are there are primal societies, each with its own unique history and development . . . ideally each primal religion should be studied in its entirety in terms of its social context'.[29] Nevertheless, she concludes that 'there are sufficient similarities between them to make some valid generalisations possible'.[30] One of the main factors put forward by most scholars, including Harold Turner and Baylis, as a criterion for identifying traditional religions is that they are local religious expressions that possess no missionary intent. Shaw challenges this criterion by questioning the consistency of the use of the concept of 'universal' religion. Why, for example, is Judaism usually regarded as a 'world religion' when it applies mainly to an ethnic community? Hinduism is essentially an expression of Indian culture and social structures within which there is a wide diversity of religious expression. A similar comment could be made about the universality of classical Chinese and Japanese religions such as Taoism, Confucianism and Shintoism.

Another characteristic that is claimed to distinguish World Religions from Traditional Religions is their reliance on oral or non-literary forms of communication. Because traditional societies are generally pre-literate they do not have a codified statement of belief. However, even in literate societies with World Religions, oral communication is still of great importance in preaching, story telling, prayer, and even meditation. It would be wrong to argue that written scriptures imply a higher form of religion than those which are exclusively oral in character. These points illustrate many of the problems that recent writers on the subject have had to face, and will be seen within this book. How may one describe the religious features in these societies without imposing foreign classifications and assumptions?

Wilfred Cantwell Smith suggested that all terms for classifying any cluster of religious phenomena such as 'Buddhism', 'Hinduism', or 'Christianity' are inadequate because they are subject to innumerable qualifications. Smith preferred the term 'cumulative traditions' because he wanted to stress that traditions are never static but developed in response to various internal and external forces. Cox argues for a similar awareness to be kept in the study of 'primal religions', and suggests the use of the expression 'the religions of *indigenous* peoples'.[31] To this he would argue that appropriate geographical, ethnic and linguistic qualifiers should be used, such as Shona-speaking Karanga peoples of Zimbabwe.

As Cox notes, this scheme of classification does not prevent the identification of universal religious themes. However, when such generalisations are made care must be taken by referring back to the specific practices upon which such generalisations are based, at the same time noting the nature and context of such practices. In this way the tendency to impose an artificial unity will be reduced though perhaps never eliminated.

The present study

This book has several aims. The first is one of building respect for all societies including those that have previously been called 'primitive'. All humans have stereotypes of other groups, and although stereotypes contain elements of truth, they generally take the form of the binary opposites of 'us' and 'them'. As Tienou writes:

> In mission, the missionized have developed stereotypes of missionaries, and missionaries have theirs about the missionized . . . Where can one find sources that demonstrate stereotypical representations of missionized people? One need not look far, for descriptions of missionized people are found in the various forms of mission ideological literature: magazines, biographies, hymns, travel diaries, journals, letters to supporters, international and national conference proceedings, and scholarly treatise.[32]

This book therefore does not seek to be judgmental, but to explain what they believe and do. In this way an attempt is sought to retain respect for all human societies. For Christians, and missionaries in particular, this approach raises some additional problems based upon their own assumptions, and it is therefore important for Christians to recognise the nature of these assumptions. This brings us to the second aim of this book. Christians consider the Bible an authoritative document as the basis of their faith, and as such presents certain distinct doctrines. The first would be the existence of a Supreme Being who created all things out of nothing. The second would be that this creation consists of what the Bible calls the 'visible and invisible' (Col. 1:16), or in other words, there exists a reality beyond the empirical. These beliefs have profound effects on the way that Christians seek to understand the nature of traditional religions. For example, Christians do not merely assume that spiritual beings are the cultural constructs of another community because their own belief-system means that such entities may have an inherent existence. The nature of this existence may be subject to cultural interpretation, but the possibility of their reality may not be discarded. For this reason missionaries have often equated, rightly or wrongly, the spirits of other societies in terms of the demons mentioned in the Bible.

Similarly, an indigenous people may believe that religious artefacts are the focus of spiritual power. If the Christian believes in some non-empirical reality then these items may in fact be endued by an 'unseen power' (or demon) that may affect the Christian observers (missionaries) themselves. Yet another example is that of possession which may be understood in cultural or psychological terms, but for Christians this does not remove the spiritual nature and possible influence of a spiritual being. Christians are therefore continually faced with the question of how they understand these manifestations in terms of their own belief system. As will be shown, some of the postmodern scholars are facing similar questions as they are 'experiencing ritual'.[33]

The third aim of this book is to show the continuing movements not only within traditional societies, but the patterns of transformation that they have experienced in the last hundred years especially. As people have moved from the jungles to the urban slums, many of their traditional beliefs have moved with them. The possession rites of West Africa are now expressed in similar ways in the growing cities of Latin America. Although many people have changed their allegiance to the major world religions, many traditional notions are expressed in what loosely may be called 'folk religion'. The world of the spirits is still of significance to many millions in the modern world.

Notes

1 Rev. F. T. Cole had worked among the tribal people of that region for forty years before his death in 1917.

2 Raj, M., 'Christianity and the Social Transformation of the Maltos People of Bihar, India' (MA thesis, ANCC, 1997).

3 Sankar, S. S., *The Malers of the Rajmahal Hills* (Calcutta: Model Printing Works, 1974).

4 Kuper, A., *The Invention of Primitive Society* (London: Routledge, 1988).

5 *Ibid.* p. 4.

6 *Ibid.* p. 5.

7 Tienou, T., 'The invention of the "primitive" and stereotypes in mission', *Missiology* 19 (1991), pp. 293–303.

8 Bosman, W., *A New and Accurate Description of the Coast of Guinea Divided into the Gold, the Slave, and the Ivory Coasts* (London: Frank Cass, 1969). Original English edition published in 1705, and the Dutch edition in 1704.

9 Quoted in Evans-Pritchard, E. E., *Theories of Primitive Religion* (Oxford: Clarendon Press, 1965), p. 7.

10 Burton, R. F. *A Mission to Gelele, King of Dahome* (London: Tinsley Bros., 1864), p. 231.

11 Livingstone, D., *Missionary Travels and Researches in South Africa* (New York: Harper & Brothers, 1958), pp. 26–27.

12 Tylor, E. B., *Primitive Culture* (London: John Murray, 1871).

13 Frazer, J., *The Golden Bough* (London: Macmillan Press, 1978).

14 Lang, A., *The Making of Religion* (London: Longman, 1898).

15 Friesen, J. S., *Missionary Responses to Tribal Religions at Edinburgh, 1910,* (New York: Peter Lang Publishing, 1996), p. 137.

16 Quoted in *ibid.*, p. 66.

17 Rattray, R. S., *The Ashanti* (London: OUP, 1923).

18 Evans-Pritchard, E. E., *Nuer Religion* (New York: OUP, 1977), p. 320.

19 Parrinder, G., *African Traditional Religion* (London: Sheldon Press, 1962).

20 Parrinder, G., *Africa's Three Religions* (London: Sheldon Press, 1962).

21 Taylor, J. V., *The Primal Vision: Christian Presence and African Religion* (London: SCM Press, 1963).

22 Harold Turner, lecture 1979.

23 Danquah, J. B., *The Akan Doctrine of God* (London: Lutterworth, 1944).

24 Kenyatta, J., *Facing Mount Kenya* (Nairobi: Heinemann, 1982).
25 Idowu, E. B., *African Traditional Religion: A Definition* (London: SCM, 1973), p. x.
26 Mbiti, J. S., *Concepts of God in Africa* (London: SPCK, 1970).
27 Shaw, R., 'The invention of African traditional religion', *Religion* 20 (1990), pp. 339–53.
28 *Ibid.* p. 341.
29 Baylis, P., *An Introduction to Primal Religions* (Edinburgh: Traditional Cosmology Society, 1988), p. 2.
30 *Ibid.*
31 Cox, J. L. 'The classification "Primal Religions" as a non-Empirical Christian Theological Construct' *Studies in World Christianity* 2 (1996), p. 74.
32 Tienou, *op. cit.* p. 300.
33 Turner, E., *Experiencing Ritual: A New Interpretation of African healing* (Philadelphia: University of Pennsylvania Press, 1992).

Chapter Two

GODS AND SPIRITS

Within traditional societies beliefs are preserved in the form of myths, rituals, songs and images. Myths of creation and origins of the community, for example, are told and enacted in song and dance as people relax at the end of the day. It is essentially from this oral tradition that Westerners have sought to understand the religious beliefs of traditional societies. It is not surprising that Western scholars have too often formed these oral accounts into a pattern that reflects a Western analysis rather than the dynamic accounts of the people themselves. Horton argues that the study has often been made through what he calls 'Judaeo-Christian spectacles'.[1] By this he means that the study has generally been in the long tradition of comparative studies of religion carried out by Christian theologians.

Generally, academics have recognised two fundamentally different forms of divinity in traditional religions: the one creator god, and the many lesser gods and spirits. This contrast raises some key questions concerning the religious experience of traditional societies which have caused much debate in academic circles. Does the widespread belief in a creator mean that all traditional religions are essentially monotheistic, or does the predominance of the lesser spirits in everyday life mean that traditional religions are essentially polytheistic? Some writers have tended to take one stance or the other, but, as will be shown, more complex approaches have also been proposed.

The Supreme Creator

The status of the Supreme Being in pre-colonial traditional African thought has been subject to much discussion.[2] As mentioned in chapter 1, Father Schmidt argued that monotheism was the earliest form of religion. He considered that belief in additional gods and spirits was nothing but functional 'differentiations' of the Supreme Being. This interpretation was later adopted by Evans-Pritchard, in his study of the Nuer of the Sudan. He noted that when the Nuer had been in contact with foreign people, they did not regard them has having a different God from their own, but merely a different name and rituals to communicate with him. Evans-Pritchard therefore concludes, 'The Nuer attitude in this matter shows clearly the markedly monotheistic tendency of their religious thought. It is polyonymous, but not henotheistic. The inference we can draw from this in considering the spirits of the air is that they are not thought of as independent gods but in some way as hypostases of the modes of attributes of a single God.'[3]

Many scholars therefore assumed that there was a concept of a Supreme Being in all traditional societies even though it was very hazy. The discussion would proceed as follows. Throughout Africa there are stories of a Supreme Being who is the creator of all and who is known by various names. The Nuer call him 'Kwoth', the Ibo 'Chukwu', the Krobo 'Mau', the Yoruba 'Olorun', and the Karamojong 'Akuj'. The Akan of Ghana use the name 'Onyame' meaning 'a shining being living beyond the ordinary reach of man, but revealed through his own light'. They believe that God made the universe in an orderly fashion – first he made the sky, then the earth, rivers, waters, plants and trees. 'Then he made man, and for man's use he made animals. In order to keep the animal alive, he ordered them to eat plants, which men were also to eat in addition to eating the animals. Then God made spirits of the water, forests, and rocks, in order to protect man.'[4] The myths of creation have been passed on through oral tradition from one generation to another. They provide explanations of how the world came to be as it now is, but they also reveal the Creator as being the one who also created the established social order.

An example is given in a story recorded of another Sudanese people, the Dinka, recounted by Pater Schmidt:

> The creator created people in the East under a tamarind tree – or others say, on the bank of a great water. Their names were Abuk and Garang. He made them so small – only half the length of a man's arm – of clay, and laid them in a pot which he then covered. When he uncovered it, the two stood up and were complete and full-grown. In the morning, Garang was grown and carried the spear (penis), and the breasts of Abuk were big, and they married. And they bore children. And the creator said 'Your child will die, but after only fifteen days he will return.' Garang disagreed and said, 'If people return again they will be too numerous. Where will they build their homes? There will not be enough land.'[5]

One may expect that the Supreme Being would be at the very centre of Dinka religion, but this is not the case. Generally within traditional societies, the Supreme Being usually has neither temples nor priests, and is regarded as too exalted to be concerned with the affairs of human beings. Myths also provide explanations of how the original contiguity of divinity (and the sky) and people (and the earth) was spoiled.

For example, among the Dinka, the story is told of how the earth and heaven were formerly connected by a rope, stretched parallel to the earth and at the reach of a man's outstretched arm above it.

> By means of this rope men could clamber at will to Divinity. At this time there was no death. Divinity granted one grain of millet a day

to the first man and woman, and this satisfied their needs. They were forbidden to grow or pound more. The first human beings, usually called Garang and Abuk living on the earth had to take care when they were doing their little planting or pounding, lest a hoe or a pestle should strike Divinity, but one day the woman 'because she was greedy' (in this context any Dinka would view her 'greed' indulgently) decided to plant (or pound) more that the permitted grain of millet . . . In order to do so she took one of the long-handled hoes (or pestles) which the Dinka now use. In raising this pole to pound or cultivate, she struck Divinity who withdrew offended, to his present great distance from the earth, and sent a small blue bird (the colour of the sky) called *atoc* to sever the rope which had previously given men access to the sky and to him. Since that time the country has been 'spoilt', for men have to labour for the food they need, and are often hungry. They can no longer as before freely reach Divinity, and they suffer sickness and death, which thus accompanied their abrupt separation from Divinity.[6]

Usually several different stories have been recorded in these societies that convey a similar concept. Among the Dinka, Lienhardt was also told the story that 'there was once a wall in the sky, which held a man in until he ate part of the wall, and was therefore pushed below by Divinity'.[7] The common themes of these stories are that people originally felt confined and restricted by the closeness of God and wanted freedom, but this brought toil and suffering.

Many missionary Bible translators have used the vernacular name for the Supreme Being in their translation of the English word 'God'. They argued that this was what the apostle Paul had done when using the Greek word *theos* as a translation for the Hebrew name *Yahweh*. Through teaching, the Greeks came to appreciate the character of God as revealed in the Old Testament within the designation of *theos*. Missionaries assured themselves that a similar process occurred with the English word 'god', which originated from a name of one of the Teutonic hierarchy of gods. A Biblical content was therefore given to each of these names which mixed a familiarity of the term with a newness of interpretation.

Several African theologians, however, went further and argued that long before the arrival of Christian missionaries the peoples of Africa believed in a supreme creator god who possessed very similar characteristics to those of the Christian God. In 1944, the Methodist J. B. Danquah in his *The Akan Doctrine of God* tried to expound the African idea of the Supreme Being in Western philosophical terms.[8] John Mbiti also accepted the concept of a common monotheism within African traditional religions. In *Concepts of God in Africa* Mbiti studies the idea of God in three hundred African languages, and concludes that the concept of one Supreme God has 'sprung independently out of African reflection on God'.[9]

This view has been taken up by African theologians such as Idowu who described the attributes of Olodumare – the Supreme Being of the Yoruba of Nigeria. 'The Yoruba do little abstract thinking. Their picture of Olodumare is, therefore, of a Personage, venerable and majestic, aged but not ageing, with a greyness which commands awe and respect.'[10] Idowu argues that Olodumare is perceived as creator, king, omnipotent, all wise, all seeing, judge, immortal, and holy. 'Thus, if we speak of "The religion of the Yoruba", we can only do so in reference to the fact that Olodumare is the core which gives meaning and coherence to the whole system . . . For this purpose of a descriptive label, we would like to suggest such a startling thing as "Diffused Monotheism": though it is a monotheism in which the good deity delegates certain portions of His authority to certain divine functionaries who work as they are commissioned by Him.'[11]

In contrast to this view, there are those like Okot p'Bitek who argue that these scholars have generated this concept of a Supreme Being out of non-reality, and have done so, in part, to defend Africa from the intellectual arrogance of the West. Okot

p'Bitek called this school of thought the 'Devout' and contrasted it with what he called 'De-Hellenist'.[12] Horton later proposed the terms 'Devout' and 'Devout Opposition', which is
perhaps clearer.[13] The Devout are those like Idowu and Mbiti
who propose that there existed among all African peoples,
before contact with Islam or Christianity, a Supreme Being
with similar attributes to those currently associated with the
God of monotheistic religions. In p'Bitek's words, African
scholars robed their deities in 'awkward Hellenistic garments
[in order] to show to the world . . . that the African deities are
but local names of the One God who is omniscient, omnipres-
ent, omnipotent, transcendent and eternal'.[14] Unfortunately
much of p'Bitek's criticism has been a verbal assault on the first
wave of African scholars.

Robin Horton has offered an alternative explanation of the
African concepts of a Supreme Being. He argues that before the
coming of Islam and Christianity, the majority of Africans
were not concerned with 'ontological definitions' of a transcendent being, but with the practical aspects of living life in the
here and now.[15] This argument does not deny the fact that some
African cultures did indeed have a concept of a Supreme God
who created the world and sustains it. Rather it is argued that
the attributes accorded to this being were not necessarily those
associated with the God of Islam and Christianity. For
example, John Middleton, in his study of *Lugbara Religion*,
shows that the Lugbara supreme being is associated as much
with evil as he is with good. Among the Ijo-speaking people of
the Niger Delta the supreme being is considered female, and is
referred to as 'Our Mother'. How far may these deities be
ascribed attributes revealed in the Bible?

In 1982, S. N. Ubah, an Igbo historian, returned to his home
community to gather data on its traditional religion.[16] He took
particular care to distinguish the views of those who, especially
in their formative years, had little or no exposure to
Christianity, and those who were brought up as Christians.

First, he found that for those who were less influenced by Christianity the lesser spirits were autonomous agencies and not intermediaries of the Supreme Being. Second, he found that 'the ancestors, who had little to do with the supreme being here on earth, appear to have found him no less withdrawn in the other world'. He concludes that it was only in the thought of those with much exposure to Christianity that there is anything like the 'Devout' version of the Igbo worldview.

Horton therefore concludes that there were two mutually reinforcing processes:

> On the one hand, missionaries busily engaged themselves in extracting from the peoples they were attempting to evangelise names for the supreme being. Sometimes, it seems, the peoples involved could only produce the names of lesser spiritual forces, and it was the missionaries who deceived themselves into thinking that they were in possession of indigenous names for the supreme being . . .
>
> On the other hand, the peoples on the receiving end of missionary activity found themselves in an era of rapidly expanding horizons for whose comprehension their parochially oriented cosmologies were not fully satisfying. Some responded to this situation by entering the Christian fold . . . Many others, however, were unwilling to go so far . . . they found certain elements of the missionary message concerning the supreme being particularly congenial to their purpose, and used them freely to create new though still unmistakably indigenous syntheses. In the course of such reworking, ironically, they often took back from the missionaries items of religious vocabulary that were subtle transformations of items which the missionary themselves had earlier extracted from them.[17]

Sandra Greene has added to the discussion by showing that the concept of the Supreme Being was continually subject to reinvention as the result of economic and political changes in a region.[18] For example, during the seventeenth century in West

Africa, the inhabitants of Whydah called their supreme deity by the name *Mawu*. They regularly traded with the people of Dahomey who called the Supreme God *Nana Buluku*. Greene writes: 'From the eighteenth century on, when Dahomean king Tegbesu (1740–1774) associated himself with the worship of *Mawu,* the god – first introduced as a lesser deity or *vodu* – gradually gained the attributes of a Supreme Being. This elevation appears to have altered its defined position vis-à-vis *Nana Buluku*. *Mawu* was no longer described as the creation of the latter; rather *Nana Buluku* and its powers became one of *Mawu's* attributes as the Supreme Deity.'[19]

There therefore seemed to be a tendency to merge conceptualisations of the Supreme Being with the worship of specific deities. When the powers of a particular deity that had previously been defined as a Supreme Deity seemed to decline, the people would redefine the Supreme Deity by associating it with another god. When Tegbesu accepted Mawu as a deity associated with the royal family, its patronage naturally increased. Greene therefore concludes that the conceptualisation of the Supreme Being was deeply influenced by the politics of the local situation, and so was continually subject to reinvention.

On another continent, Jane Simpson has shown in her study of Moari religion, that it was not until 1876 that there occurred the first textual conjunction of the words 'Supreme Being' and 'Io'.[20] She states that it was about this time that a chief is said to have confided that the Moari believed in a Supreme Being whose name was so sacred that it was kept secret. Today, however, the standard view of Moari cosmology follows that of James Irwin, who describes three realms: the realm of ultimate reality, the realm of humans, the realm of the dead. The highest realm is that of Io the Supreme Being.[21]

The mists of time probably mean that a true perception of the cosmology of many traditional societies before the coming of Islam and Christianity will never be fully understood. However, most Christians from such societies are usually convinced of the remarkable similarity between the God of the Bible and the notion of a Supreme Being common in the beliefs of their people. This assumption is probably the most relevant issue for today.

Lesser gods and spirits

Whilst one aspect of traditional religions is that of the Supreme Being, the other is the many lesser gods and spirits that are constantly part of everyday life. While the supreme creator generally remains distant as far as daily life is concerned, the lesser gods and spirits are immanent. Their very nature is bound up with human experience, so they require shrines, images, priests and rituals. Some of the spirits are regarded as of greater importance than others. These may range from powerful spirits, which must be treated with respect, to relatively insignificant spirits of the forest, field or water who may merely cause a nuisance to humans. The water nymphs of Roman mythology would be an example of this, as would fairies, goblins, and elves in traditional English beliefs. These gods and spirits may cause sickness or even possess people, as will be described in following chapters.

These deities are sometimes believed to form a hierarchical order depending upon their local importance and power. They are often related to a particular aspect of nature, or some area of life over which they rule. The pantheons of Greece and Rome are examples of these patterns of belief. Neptune was the god of the sea; Apollo the god of medicine and the fine arts; Venus the goddess of beauty, love and marriage, and Pluto the god of death and the underworld.[22] For this reason these beings have often been called 'nature spirits'.

Returning to the description of 'Olodumare', the Supreme Being of the Yoruba, his position is often seen to be like that of a traditional king who works through his ministers. The general name for the subordinate gods is *orisha*, which means 'head-source'. 'Orisha-nla' or 'Obatala' is the chief *orisha* and executes the creative functions of Olodumare. He is the shaper and former who moulds the baby in the womb each of which he creates for a purpose. He is the one who gives a man riches or poverty, strength or deformity. His colour is white, and he favours an offering of pure water brought to his sanctuary by a pure virgin or an old woman. There are many other deities, but it will be sufficient here to describe the four most important: Sango, Ogun, Esu, and Ile.

Sango was an early king of the city-state of Oyo about which the Yoruba tell many stories. According to one story his wives and people were forever quarrelling, so he went up into the sky and rules by using thunder and lightning. According to another legend he was a tyrant who was deposed and sent into exile where he hanged himself. If lightning kills a person, this is believed to be divine retribution. Sango is sometimes represented in human form along with three smaller people, who may be his wives. Art forms associated with him are the double-headed axe, rams, gourd rattles, and inverted food mortars. Shopona is the power of smallpox and most fevers including boils and other skin eruptions. The German scholar Frobenius at the beginning of the twentieth century was amazed at many parallels between Sango and the Norse god Thor.

Ogun is more like a Yoroba equivalent to Mars, the Roman god of war. He is feared because of his power to kill and destroy even his own people. He is also patron of the hunter and wanders through the forest. He is also connected with iron, and is particularly worshipped by blacksmiths. Blacksmiths have in the past been given a special position in society, and were required to live on the edge of society. Their work of handling metal was considered a religious rite and was subject to several restrictions such as refraining from sexual relations before their work. Iron provided an important role in helping both the warrior and the farmer tame the African forest.

Esu is considered as the power of mischief, and has been aligned by some Christians and Muslims with Satan. However, within traditional Yoruba tradition there is no duality between good and evil, and gods have subtleties not easily understood by humans. Esu is the messenger to the world above, and is everywhere observing and reporting to the divine. He may deceive people into doing wrong, so necessitating them to offer sacrifices in order to regain the favour of the gods. He is often represented in the form of a human figure with horns and a nearby club or knife.

Ile is the earth, and as such stands apart from the previous deities. She is one of the primordial beings. When people are born they rest on her, and at death they are placed in her womb. At every meal the ancestors who dwell in her are honoured with a few drops of drink poured on the ground. These Yoruba deities will be referred to later when the Afro-American religious movements are examined in chapter 15.

The Ga of southern Ghana believe in dozens of gods, called *kple*. These include some of the traditional deities of the area worshipped before the coming of the Ga tribes. Chief of these are the gods of the lagoons which are found along the coast. In addition there are nature gods, and war gods who are worshipped with singing and dancing and the offering of food at feasts. The worship of the *kple* has traditionally been focused upon Labadi which is now a suburb of modern Accra.

Whereas nature spirits have no direct kinship with people, there is a strong belief in many traditional societies concerning humans who for various reasons have taken their place amongst the gods and permanent spirits in the world. The subject of ghosts and ancestors will be dealt with in chapter 4, and there a distinction will be made between ghosts and spirits. Spirits are those supernatural beings who have always existed in that form, whilst ghosts were formerly human beings who after death have taken on a different form of existence. Together with the class of deified ancestors, there is that class of humans whose lives have been so meritorious that they did not become mere ghosts, but have taken their place among the permanent spirits in charge of the world. Often the nature spirit has become merged with the human aspect.

Describing cosmologies

As with the description of the divine, traditional cosmologies may be also be distorted by viewing them through Western, and usually Christian, perspectives. This can show itself in several ways. The following three examples illustrate how preconceived ideas affect the explanation of the cosmology of a society.

The first is the debate concerning monotheism and polytheism in traditional beliefs. As mentioned previously, Idowu has argued that these *orisha* are the emanations of God's power and activity as understood by humans. The fact that the Yoruba recognise hundreds of *orisha* does not make them polytheists, but show the richness of religious thought in what Idowu calls 'diffused monotheism'. The problem with such an analysis is that one is bounding the discussion with categories that in practice are not recognised by most ordinary Yoruba.

In contrast, Maupoil recorded his conversations with a particular diviner called Gedegbe, and recorded all he said even if it was contradictory.[23] This was not general knowledge, but the ideas of one man and his personal knowledge of *Ifa* divination. Gedegbe's cosmology was that of two bowls (literally calabashes), one inverted over the other as the sky is over the earth. This presents a more realistic representation of indigenous belief than the formal analysis in Western categories.

A second assumption is the tendency to view beliefs and rituals as being distinctive of a particular community. This idea was introduced into mission thinking by Donald McGarvan in his writings in the 1970s who used the term 'homogeneous unit'.[24] The people group model tends to consider societies as bounded entities with their own distinctive religions. The implication is that the religion of a people group can be clearly described as a fixed system of unchanging beliefs and practices.

Anthropologists have shown, however, that there has historically been considerable interaction and interchange between traditional communities. Common myths and stories are found across vast areas of Africa, and as was noted by Greene, names for gods may be borrowed from neighbouring communities. The borrowing of names and concepts is shown in Figure 1, which compares the religious cosmology of the Yoruba-speaking people and the nearby Fon-speakers.

	Yoruba	Fon
Supreme Being	Olodumare	Mawu-Lisa
Lesser deities **Thunder** **War and iron**	Sango Ogun	Xeviso Gun
Divination **Trickster**	Ifa Esu	Fa Legba
Diviners	Babalawo ('father of secrets')	Bokon ('keeper of secrets')

Fig. 1 Comparison of the cosmology of Yoruba and Fon of Nigeria

There are clear similarities between the names of Ogun with Gun, Babalawo and Bokon, Ifa and Fa. There are also similarities in the characteristics of deities as seen with 'trickster' who is the messenger of the gods. Elements of belief and practice have diffused across language boundaries, and may spread across great areas. This is not merely a matter of the diffusion of ideas, but the spread of what have been called 'Regional Cults' or 'Religious Movements'. In 1976, three leading experts on Central Africa, Willy de Craemer, Jan Vansina and Renee Fox, wrote a groundbreaking paper on Congo religious movements based on their extensive field research. [25] They argued that movements spread as neighbouring settlements become convinced that the new movement seems to offer better protection against misfortune. These movements will be discussed further in chapter 16. It is necessary here merely to point out the frustration of these writers with earlier anthropologists who held to what might be equated to the people group approach:

> The concept of culture that emerges from this study differs significantly from the assumptions of most anthropologists. Culture in Central Africa is less homogeneous and less particularistic than has generally been supposed. One culture does not exist for each ethnic group, for each shares part of its cultural makeup, especially the fundamental aspects of its religion, with many others. These aspects are the core of the common Central African culture.[26]

An associated problem with the people group concept is that it tends to produce a static view of traditional societies and their religions. It is almost as if these societies have remained unchanged until the coming of the 'white man'. Throughout history communities have migrated, and in settling they have often either displaced the indigenous people or mixed with them. As Craemer, Vansina and Fox have shown religious ideas travel along trade routes sometimes over vast areas. Traditional societies have their history of change. However, it is quite correct that the coming of the European traders and Christian missionaries has brought about a radical change to traditional societies as will be discussed in later chapters.

Third, missiologists, like Peter Wagner, have proposed that spirits have distinct geographical territories that they are believed to control.[27] It is therefore possible to map such territories. Certainly many deities and spirits are perceived as being located in a particular region or social activity. It is common to hear people speak of the deity of a particular shrine who is

GODS AND SPIRITS 43

responsible for a particular local area or activity. In many parts of West Africa deities are associated with particular rivers, and if they are not shown due respect they may cause a boat to overturn. When people move to another area they often join in the rituals to the deity of that village or area.

There are some examples, such as the Dande of Zimbabwe, where there are territorial domains. According to David Lan, the Dande believe that when a chief dies he is transformed into a *mhondoro* and becomes the source of fertility of the land itself.[28] He provides rain for the fields and protects the crops as they grow. He writes:

> One of the most unusual features of the *mhondoro* is that each is thought to rule over a specific territory which he is believed to have conquered or been given when he was alive. Following Kingsley Garbett's pioneering lead, I refer to these as 'spirit provinces'. No part of Dande is unclaimed. Every square centimetre is part of one spirit province or another. They vary enormously in size. Some contain no more than a scattering of villages, some spread out for fifty-odd kilometres containing hundreds or thousands of people. Their borders which are usually rivers, cross the boundaries of chieftaincies and administrative districts and some spill over into Mozambique.[29]

However, Lan's comment that this notion of 'spirit provinces' is a most unusual feature should be noted. Wagner's assumptions of territorial spirits cannot therefore be applied to all, or even most, situations. As I have tried to show previously, it is all too easy to describe other religions in terms assumed by the outsider that have little relevance to indigenous reality. Even so, ideas such as territorial spirits have sometimes been adopted by some Christian converts to describe the spiritual reality in alternative ways.

* * *

The debate between 'monotheism' and 'polytheism' in traditional religions depends much on the perspective taken. Supreme Beings have characteristics both similar to and different from those of the Christian God, and should best be understood as variations upon a common theme of transcendence and creation. Although the gods and spirits appear of greater concern for the majority of the people, the underlying notion of the Supreme Creator is common. Among the Bantu, the people usually only turn to the Supreme Being as a last resort when the other spiritual beings have failed. John V. Taylor tells of the story of a hunting expedition in Malawi, which had no success for two weeks. In desperation the leader of the hunt exclaimed, 'I am tired of asking the shades (ancestors), let us pray to God.'[30]

Notes

1 Horton, R., *Patterns of Thought in Africa and the West* (Cambridge: CUP, 1994), pp. 161–93.

2 *Ibid.*

3 Evans-Pritchard, E. E., *Nuer Religion* (New York: OUP, 1977), p. 49.

4 Parrinder, G., *African Mythology* (London: Paul Hamlyn, 1967), p. 44.

5 Quoted in Linehardt, G., *Divinity and Experience: The Religion of the Dinka* (Oxford: Clarenden Press, 1987), p. 36.

6 *Ibid.* pp. 33–4.

7 *Ibid.* p. 35.

8 Danquah, J. B., *The Akan Doctrine of God: A Fragment of Gold Coast Ethics and Religion* (London: Lutterworth, 1944).

9 Mbiti, J. S., *Concepts of God in Africa* (London: SPCK, 1970), p. xiii.

10 Idowu, E. B., *Olodumare: God in Yoruba Belief* (London: Longmans, 1962), p. 39.

11 *Ibid.* pp. 203–4.

12 p'Bitek, O., *African Religions in Western Scholarship* (Nairobi: Kenya Literature Bureau, 1971).

13 Horton *op. cit.* p. 162.

14 P'Bitek, *op. cit.* p. 47

15 Horton, R., 'Judaeo-Christian spectacles: boon or bane to the study of African religions?' *Cahiers d'Etudes Africaines* 24 (1984), pp. 392–436.

16 Bah, C. N., 'The Supreme Being, divinities and ancestors in Igbo traditional religion: evidence from Otanchara and Utanza', *Africa* 52 (1982), pp. 91–103.

17 Horton, o*p. cit.* pp. 174–5.

18 Greene, S. A., 'Religion, history and the Supreme Gods of Africa: a contribution to the debate', *Journal of Religion in Africa* 26 (1996), pp. 122–38.

19 *Ibid.* p. 132.

20 Simpson, J., 'Io as supreme being: intellectual colonization of the Moari', *History of Religion* 37 (1997), pp. 50–85.

21 Irwin, J., *An Introduction to Moari Religion* (1984).

22 Guerber, H. A., *The Myths of Greece and Rome* (London: George G Harrap & Co, 1925).

23 Maupoil, B., *Le geomancie a l'ancienne Cote des Esclaves* (Paris, 1943).

24 McGavran, D., *Understanding Church Growth* (Grand Rapids: Eerdmans, 1970).

25 Craemer, W. de, Vansina, J. & Fox, R. C., 'Religious Movements in Central Africa: a theoretical study', *Comparative Studies in Society and History* 18 (1976), pp. 458–75.

26 *Ibid.* p. 475.

27 Wagner, P., *Territorial Spirits* (Chichester: Sovereign Word, 1991).

28 Lan, D., *Guns and Rain: Guerrillas and Spirit Mediums in Zimbabwe* (London: James Curry, 1987).

29 *Ibid.* p. 34.

30 Taylor, J. V., *Primal Vision* (London: SCM Press, 1963), p. 80.

Chapter Three

HUMAN NATURE

When Lia was about three months old, her older sister Yer slammed the front door of the Lees' apartment. A few moments later, Lia's eyes rolled up, her arms jerked over her head, and she fainted. The Lees had little doubt what had happened. Despite the careful installation of Lia's soul during the *hu plig* ceremony, the noise of the door had been so profoundly frightening that her soul had fled her body and become lost. They recognized the resulting symptoms as *qaug dab peg*, which means 'the spirit catches you and you fall down.' The spirit referred to in this phrase is a soul stealing *dab*; *peg* means to catch or hit; and *qaug* means to fall over with one's roots still in the ground, as grain might be beaten down by wind or rain.[1]

The Lee family were members of the Hmong people, many of whom fled Laos in 1975 when the communist forces finally seized power. From their home village they had come as refugees to California, a land of technology, schools and hospitals. When they took Lia to the local hospital the doctor made a thorough diagnosis and diagnosed the illness as epilepsy and she suffered a grand mal episode. During the three days Lia spent in hospital she underwent a spinal tap, a CT scan, an ECG, a chest X-ray, and extensive blood tests. It is not known how much was explained to the Lee parents. The doctor did not know that the family had already diagnosed their daughter's problem as the spirit catches you and you fall down.

Fadiman's fascinating book shows in the life of the Hmong child and her American doctors the collision of two cultures. Human nature is a cultural category, which is understood in vastly different ways – as the previous story illustrates. The understanding of human nature expresses itself in many aspects of everyday life and behaviour. As will be shown in the following chapters, it has a great bearing on the nature of the after-life, pollution, and healing. It also makes important contributions to the notions of misfortune and sickness, and especially witchcraft and sorcery. This is why in the study of religions it is essential to explore assumptions about human nature.

The contemporary Western understanding of human nature emerged out of the Enlightenment period, and the Cartesian assumption, 'I think, therefore I am.' A clear duality has therefore emerged between the material body and the mind. The result is a very individualistic and self-contained understanding of the 'self' that contrasts with most other societies, which have more sociocentric and holistic concepts of the human nature. Morris writes: 'The "self" structure of Western culture has thus been widely described as individuated, detached, separate and self-sufficient, and as involving a dualistic metaphysic.'[2]

In order to illustrate the variety of views found within traditional societies on this subject, I want to briefly describe the beliefs of three societies from different regions: the Asante of Ghana, the Buryat of Mongolia, and the Gahuku-Gama of Papua New Guinea. A problem in making such a study is to simply equate the terminology of Western psychology with the notions held by another society. Because of the need to use the English language, related words have to be used – but the meanings must be seen within the particular cultural context.

The Asante of West Africa

The Asante live in the forest region of southern Ghana, and established a powerful state around their capital city of Kumasi during the nineteenth century. They are the largest of a number of Twi-speaking people in the region who are generally known as Akan. The Asante remain an important community in Ghana, and have been leaders in its development. Today, the great majority of Asante would call themselves Christian, and the following description relates primarily to the beliefs of the Asante in the early twentieth century.

Apart from the physical body (*honam*) the Asante speak of three different aspects or faculties that make up a human being.[3] Although these are complex and interrelated it is best to describe them separately. First, the *okra* constitutes the guiding spirit of a person, and is often translated by the English word 'soul'. Busia describes it as 'the small bit of the creator that lives in every person's body'.[4] The verb *kra* in Twi often means saying goodbye, or giving a gift or message at a time of departing. Thus, the Supreme Being will '*kra*' the person when they are about to be born. At birth the *okra* of a person appears before god and words are spoken that will indicate the destiny of the individual from birth to death. The *okra* is therefore like a person's double linking them with God, and acting like a guardian spirit. The destiny is not a predetermined set of occurrences as may be expected from a Western understanding of destiny, but it is like a guardian spirit offering good advice to keep the person out of trouble. The *okra* also provides the person with protection, and the person will give offerings in what is known as 'soul-washing'. This occurs when a person has recovered from a serious illness and wants to thank his or her guardian spirit for help in the time of crisis. If the *okra* gives bad advice and fails to guide the person, the Akan say *Na kra apa n'akyi*, 'His soul failed to guide him.'

Only human beings can have an *okra*, and this leads to certain rules of etiquette that apply specifically to humans. When the Akan describe the height of an animal they place their hand prone, but when referring to the height of a child the palm faces upwards. After a child is born, it is usually kept indoors until the eighth day, when the family performs the 'out-dooring' ritual and the child is given a name called the *kradin*. The name corresponds to the name of the day in Twi, one for the male child and one for the female child. During life the *okra* never leaves the person, but at death the *okra* returns to God and gives an account of its earthly life.

The second element is the *sunsum*, which is the spiritual aspect of the person, and must be seen as a part of the wider category of the *ntoro*. The terms *sunsum* and *ntoro* are often used synonymously of the inherited characteristics. This is derived not from God, but from the biological father through the semen. The *sunsum* is associated with personality and moral character, so has often been translated 'spirit'. Training is the father's responsibility, which is why the father today is expected to pay school fees. A mother is expected to train her daughter in domestic and social skills, but if her daughter misbehaves the father is to blame. Personality and morality are passed on through the semen as *sunsum*, and reinforced after birth by the behaviour of the father.

Unlike the *okra* the *sunsum* may leave the body momentarily during life as during sleep when it is able to roam about. During dreams the *sunsum* is the actor of the person's dreaming, so that if in a dream one commits an offence the act has actually been done. Dreams may therefore be used as evidence in the traditional court. For example, if a man dreams he has committed adultery with another man's wife, he is liable to pay the same fine as for an offence committed whilst awake. The *sunsum* is also subject to illness and is vulnerable to sorcery (as will be discussed in chapter 9). Men are considered to have 'heavier' *sunsum* than women, and if a man is retarded, cowardly, or effeminate, he is considered to have a 'light' *sunsum*. A person with a 'light' *sunsum* is frequently suspected of witchcraft, which consequently means that women are most likely the guilty parties (as considered in chapter 8).

Families, lineages, and whole nations have a *sunsum*. This is especially important for the Asante nation that has a common *sunsum* enshrined in the Golden Stool. What happens to the stool happens to the nation. It was in March 1900 that Sir Frederick Hodgson visited Kumasi and foolishly sought to claim the Golden Stool as a symbol of British rule over the Asante. Hodgson thought of the stool as a kind of Stone of Scone upon which the kings of Asante were seated at their accession and a symbol of supreme authority.[5] Hence, as representative of Queen Victoria he naturally expected to have it brought to him. In actual fact no king of Asante ever sat on the stool as it was acknowledged as far more important in being the very soul of the people. Within a week the Asante nation was at war with Britain and Governor Hodgson was besieged at Kumase by tens of thousands of Asante warriors.

The third element is *mogya*, meaning blood. The Asante recognise that a human being is formed from the blood of the mother and the *ntoro* of the father. *Mogya* is bestowed by the mother, and forms the basis of the clan (*abusua*) system. In this matrilineal society the *mogya* determines the inheritance, status, and royal succession from the mother's line. Among all the Akan there are eight clans with one or two corresponding subdivisions. Members of the same clans regard themselves as brothers and sisters no matter where they come from, and are not allowed to intermarry. At death the person is escorted to the abode of the ancestors, but the *mogya* remains to become the person's *saman*, or ghost with a bodily form. The *saman* can influence the living either for good or bad.

To summarise, the Asante believe that human beings are formed from the blood of the mother, the spirit of the father, and derive fate from God. The dichotomy in Asante culture is not between spirit and matter, but between two spiritual forces that reflect different aspects of Asante social life. The matrilineal aspect is represented by the *mogya*, maternal blood, and the paternal by the *sunsum* and *ntoro*.

The Buryat of Central Asia

The Buryat are a nomadic people living in the former USSR near the border with China.[6] They have been subject to acculturation by Lamanist Buddhism and Russians, and currently number somewhere in the region of 300,000. The Buryat tend to divide the cosmos into threes, such that the spirits are divided into higher spirits, middle and lower. This triple division in Buryat cosmology is reflected in the triple division of human nature. The first part is known as the *beye*, the physical body, the second, the *amin*, the breath, and the third, the *hunehen*, the soul of the person. The soul is in turn divided into three hierarchical levels.

The first is the lowest soul that is housed within the whole skeleton of the person, and may be regarded as an invisible copy of the skeleton. If a bone is broken, the soul is also injured, and the *beye* disintegrates after death, as does the skeleton. Animals also possess such a soul, and at a sacrifice great care is taken to avoid breaking the bones, as the deity would reject the offering.

The second soul (*amin*) has the form of a little person resident in the body around the region of the heart, lungs, liver, and even the larynx. This soul not only corresponds to the likeness of the person, but to the physical activity of the body. If a man is riding a horse, the second soul rides the same horse, and wears the same clothes. It may also leave the body in a form like that of a wasp or a bee. This second soul can easily be alarmed and may flee from danger. For example, a child may lose its soul when frightened by a barking dog, and the soul has to be encouraged to return. It is the loss of this aspect which results in sickness, and the healer, called 'shaman', needs to retrieve this lost soul if the person is to be healed (as will be described in chapter 11). After death this second soul also continues wandering the world. At night it amuses itself by frightening people, but generally it is harmless.

The third and highest soul is similar to the second, except it is the chief soul that determines the character of the person. At death the chief god calls this soul to the afterworld, and the leaving of this soul marks the end of the life span of the individual. Among some of the Buryat tribes, this soul lives in the afterworld for some time, and then returns and is born again. This element of reincarnation found among some of the tribes may be a result of Buddhist influence, as suggested by Krader.[7]

The Gahuku-Gama of Papua New Guinea

The Gahuku-Gama are a collection of communities living in the Eastern Highlands of Papua New Guinea, and although they have a common language and culture they have no centralised political system. Their villages are situated along the mountain ridges, and their main cultivation is sweet potato. The activity of the men focuses upon the men's house, resulting in a marked separation between men and women. Kenneth Read in his study of the Gahuku-Gama writes of both men and women being volatile and abrasive in character.[8]

The Gahuku-Gama concept of personality emphasises that the individual is a complex of physical and physiological elements. Of particular importance is the word *gupe*, meaning skin, which is used in a variety of contexts to express information about moral feelings and personality traits. Read says that they denote a specific concept of individuality that does not recognise any sharp distinction between the physical and psychic constituents of a person's nature. This is illustrated in their preoccupation with the body, and the many ceremonies associated with the growth and development of children.

The Gahuku-Gama do, however, recognise a psychic aspect to the person known as *meni*, which is associated with the neck. It is the whole self or personality, and is the basis of consciousness and continuous individual existence. Read stresses that this concept is fundamentally different from the Christian concept of the soul, for the *meni* is the 'breath soul' which animates the physical body and at death simply ceases to exist. The Gahuku-Gama therefore does not have any notion of personal survival after death. The *meni* simply departs. What does remain is neither the body nor the *meni*, but rather a 'shade', which lacks positive characteristics and has no fixed abode. For the Gahuku-Gama self is embodied, and death means the virtual end of personality.

For the Gahuku-Gama human nature is primarily social, and moral behaviour is linked to various social roles. Although they do acknowledge that all human beings have a common humanity, the Gahuku-Gama do not consider that this involves them in identical moral duties. Read contrasts this with the Western view of a person as an entity endowed with intrinsic and unique value and individuality that is distinct from the social roles they occupy. In other words, the Gahuku-Gama do not recognise the person as an ethical category, but as part of society. Although there are many differences between the Gahuku-Gama and the Asante there is a common notion of the person as an integral part of community.

Patterns of human nature

These three case studies illustrate the wide differences in the conception of human nature within traditional societies, but they also show some common features.

The first is the emphasis upon community. The example of the Asante reveals the way that each person is inherently part of, and dependent on, others in the community. The social significance of the Golden Stool as the 'soul of the nation' provides a focus of unity that is both spiritual and political. John Mbiti writing of African societies in general comments:

> In traditional life the individual does not and cannot exist alone except corporately. He owes his existence to other people, including

those of past generations . . . He is simply part of the whole . . . whatever happens to the individual happens to the whole group, and whatever happens to the whole group happens to the individual. The individual can only say: 'I am, because we are; and since we are, therefore I am'.[9]

Absent is the integrated view of self, which makes the Westerner feel as though he is a distinct isolated being. Instead one finds related people forming integrated communities with a strong sense of historical continuity. The individual is part of nature, and part of the tribe as a whole. As John Taylor has said: 'In Africa "I think, therefore I am" is replaced by "I participate, therefore I am."'[10]

The sense of community can however result in a dichotomy between us and them. Many years ago Ruth Benedict noted that many tribal names, Zuni, Dene, Kiow, for example, are not only the names by which the communities are known, but are also the vernacular for 'human beings'.[11] Thus, although other people may be classed as 'human' only the Zuni, Dene, or Kiow, are real persons. Levi-Strauss similarly observed that for 'savages' humanity ceases at the boundary of the group, which implies that strangers somehow pertain to the domain of the extra-human. He illustrates the universal reciprocity of this attitude with an anecdote:

In the Greater Antilles, some years after the discovery of America, whilst the Spanish were dispatching inquisitional commissions to investigate whether the natives had a soul or not, these very natives were busy drowning the white people they had captured in order to find out, after lengthy observation, whether or not the corpses were subject to putrifaction.[12]

The general point of this story is that the Indians, like the European invaders, considered that only the group to which they belong incarnates humanity. Strangers are on the other side of the border that separates humans from animals and spirits, culture from nature. Sometimes this can result in an ethical duality. Killing and theft may not be considered a crime if done to the other group, but it is a horrendous crime if done within social group itself. The answer of Jesus to the question 'Who is my neighbour?', has important implications in such cases.

A second feature that is common in many traditional cultures is that the soul is viewed as a complex entity. The different emotional, intellectual and social aspects of human nature are attributed to different faculties or components of the total person. None of the conceptions of person fit easily into the Western ideas of the body-soul that derive from Plato, or are presented by Christian theologians, and psychologists. In traditional societies there is therefore a degree of permeability with the wider environment. This is especially seen in the case of the Asante and the Buryat when a faculty is considered to leave the body in certain situations.

Within African concepts of personhood this provides an explanation of dreams, and, as will be discussed in later chapters, of sickness. In the case of the Asante it is believed that a person's *sunsum* may leave a person during sleep, and dreams are considered real experiences encountered by the *sunsum*. Dreams therefore are taken far more seriously than by Westerners, and one may often hear Asante discussing the possible meaning of a particular dream. When the *sunsum* does leave the body it is supposed to travel along an invisible cobweb. If a person is woken up suddenly his *sunsum* may not be able to find its way back and the person may become ill. Among the Buryat the notion of the soul leaving the body provides an explanation not only of sickness, but also of the role of the healer – the shaman. The shaman is able to use the power of the spirits to succeed in recovering the soul of a sick person.

The contemporary Western view of a body-soul distinction has not always been the case as Lyndal Ropal has shown in her study of sixteenth-century German concepts of the body. She comments:

> The body is not so much a collection of joints and limbs, or a skeletal structure, as a container of fluids, bursting out in every direction to impact on the environment . . . it is also a state in which the boundaries between the self and others, the bounded self and the fluids which spill into the surrounding world, have become melted, as if one could approach the state in which there is no longer distinction between self and the world.[13]

This view has great importance for the issue of witchcraft and evil, and Ropal explains. 'Here again, the insides of the bodies are of crucial importance, for it is in the bodily interior that the demons are housed. The demon must be brought out of the body and into the light, expelled from the body cavity, if the sufferer is to be cured.'[14]

A third feature that emerges from the previous discussion is what former writers call 'soul-stuff' for lack of a better term. Many societies have the belief that in some way the very personality of the individual is contained in those elements of the body such as the hair, fingernails, spittle, or even the name of the person. Hair and nails are looked on as containing 'soul-stuff' in surpassing measure, because they are constantly growing, a proof of their indestructible power. Blood and the sex organs are frequently regarded as being rich in 'soul-stuff'. Care is therefore taken with the disposal of such items least an enemy gets hold of them and uses them for harm. There is a concern amongst some in Ivory Coast that the spittle used to seal envelopes can be used for sorcery. Some traditional societies even regard the perspiration of an individual as containing soul-stuff, and so clothes which have become saturated with it have gained soul-stuff. Footprints can even be used as a source of sorcery by means of the sweat that adheres to them. When the Government of Papua New Guinea was planning to establish a blood bank they found a great hesitancy amongst the people. The rumour was that when you gave blood the government would have power over you. Only after an extensive education programme were some people willing to give blood. Other people have a fear of the camera because they believe that the camera may catch something of their soul, and so could be used to give others power over them.

* * *

Within traditional societies people do not perceive humans as protected within some impervious wall that gives an impression of the person being a distinct isolated being. Instead there is a sense of inter-relatedness not only with other human beings, but also with the wider cosmos. The soul may be lost from the physical frame and alien spirits may intrude. The boundaries between life and death are also relatively porous. After death, elements of the former being may continue to exist as ghosts and ancestors in the complex world of the spirits.

Notes

1 Fadiman, A., *The Spirit Catches You and You fall Down* (New York: Noonday Press, 1999), p. 20.

2 Morris, B., *The Anthropology of the Self: The Individual in Cultural Perspective* (London: Pluto Press, 1994), p. 16.

3 Bartle, P. F. W., 'The Universe has three Souls', *Journal of Religion in Africa* 14 (1983), pp. 85–112.

4 Busia, K. A., 'The Ashanti of the Gold Coast' in Ford, D. (ed.), *African Worlds* (Oxford: OUP, 1954), p. 197.

5 Smith, E. W., *The Golden Stool* (London: Holborn Publishing House, 1926).

6 Krader, L., 'Buryat religion and society', in Middleton, J. (ed.), *Gods and Ritual* (Austin: University of Texas Press, 1967), pp. 103–32.

7   *Ibid.* p. 110.

8   Read, K. E., 'Morality and the concept of the Person among Gahuku-Gama' in Middleton, J. (ed.), *Myth and Cosmos* (New York: AMNH, 1967), pp. 185–229.

9   Mbiti, J., *African Religions and Philosophy* (London: Heinemann, 1969), pp. 108–9.

10 Taylor, J., *Primal Vision* (London: SCM Press, 1977), p. 93.

11 Benedict, R., *Patterns of Culture* (London: Routledge & Kegan Paul, 1934), p. 5.

12 Levi-Strauss, C., *Structural Anthropology* (Harmondsworth: Penguin, 1973), p. 384.

13 Roper, L., *Oedipus and the Devil: Witchcraft, Sexuality and Religion in Early Modern Europe* (London: Routledge, 1994), p. 23.

14 *Ibid.* p. 24.

Chapter Four

GHOSTS AND ANCESTORS

Death is a tragedy that affects all. It disrupts the family, and raises many questions that even modern science is unable to answer. A people's understanding of what has happened usually is set in some form of afterlife, which is associated with the concept of human nature. The English words ghost and ancestor convey two common ideas.

Ghosts

The belief in what may loosely be called ghosts is found in every culture. The character and formation of such beings may vary, but the idea of some ongoing existence of the dead that has an influence upon this world is common to all. This was the very point that led Sir Herbert Spencer to argue for an evolutionary development in religious thought, originating with a belief in ghosts, then a belief in ancestors and finally spiritual beings.[1] Ancestor worship was in the nineteenth century therefore considered the definitive mark of 'primitive religion'. However, even Western society with its strong adherence to materialism still retains some belief in ghosts. As the African writer Idowu comments about Western society,

Modern sophisticated man may wish . . . to dismiss as puerile stories of experiences of ghosts and of haunted places; but deep down in the minds of thousands of men and women of every level of spiritual or intellectual attainment is the . . . persistent notion, that the deceased still have a part to play, for better or worse, in the lives of the living.[2]

Although the concept of ghosts is one which is surprisingly common, the way in which it is understood varies. One therefore needs to be careful in understanding the term *ghost*. First, it is useful to make a distinction between ghost and spirit (or god). A spirit has always existed in the form of a supernatural being, whilst a ghost had, at one time, been part of a natural living being. Second, the concept of a ghost relates to the concept of the nature of the soul and to that element which continues to exist beyond biological death. Third, the possibility of a kinship link with the deceased person leads to a special relationship with the ghost which is specified by using the term *ancestor*. It is important to retain a distinction between ghost and ancestor as the concept of a kinship link implies the continued interest of the ancestor in the well-being of the family, whilst if a ghost is unrelated to a particular person it may seek to cause mischief and harm.

The idea of a ghost resulting from a 'bad death' is another common belief, and especially so amongst the peoples of Africa. This is similar to the Western notion of ghosts as being those who have died as a result of murder or execution. In Africa today, there is still great concern at a 'bad death'. This may lead to considerable fear in which a man's house may be abandoned in case the ghost will return and cause harm. It could be that a whole village will move to another locality. However, more usually a diviner would be called in to identify the cause of death – especially if it is feared that it could be as a result of witchcraft. Once the cause has been identified some offering may be necessary to pacify the ghost and encourage it to leave and cause no more harm to the people. Amongst the Bimoba of Ghana one of the worst forms of bad death is that of a woman dying during childbirth with the baby undelivered. In this case 'the woman's room is broken down, every trace of it is cleared, and all her belongings are thrown away. No funeral ceremony can be performed in such cases, for the (ghost) refuses to go to god; it just wanders about, and is called *kpeey-iok* (literally meaning "dead person without an owner").'[3]

Many societies do believe that ghosts may materialise in some form which can be seen by the living. In northern India for example, the *bhut* are believed to be able to appear at night in the form of human beings. There are two notable differences: first, they do not cast a shadow, and secondly, their feet point backwards. In the villages of India the fear of ghosts is strong and a person would avoid being in isolated fields when night has come. It is easy to consider this a result of superstitions and a lack of education, but many Western people have similar fears in dark and isolated areas. Another common belief is the possibility of a person becoming possessed by a wandering ghost. A *bhut* may lay hold of any passer-by who may have unwittingly trespassed within its domain, or may have roused its interest. The ghost is said to 'lay hold of' the person and the victim has to resort to exorcism for deliverance. This can take various forms, but a discussion of this topic will be left until chapter 10 when the subject of possession will be considered.

Ghosts may be considered to have varying degrees of human characteristics. Not all are considered to be harmful and wanting revenge. Some, such as those of traditional Chinese mythology, are delightfully human. They have stories about female ghosts who come to a poor scholar in his mountain retreat, to live with him and minister to him in his sickness. Other stories tell about a female ghost who returns to her lover and bears him children. The period of cohabitation may last from a few weeks or for a generation until she has born him children and they have reached adulthood. These children after they have succeeded in their examinations return to their mother – only to find that the gorgeous mansion of their youth has disappeared and in its place is an old grave, with a hole underground, where lies a dead mother fox. Sometimes she leaves behind a note saying that she was sorry to leave them, but that she was a fox and only wanted to enjoy human life, and now that she has seen them prosper she is satisfied, and asks for their forgiveness.[4]

Amongst the Cheyenne Indians, ghosts or *mistai* are spirits derived from the dead, but are not the actual ghosts of particular people. The *mistai* are really poltergeists who make their presence known by whistling and making strange noises in dark and isolated places. They tug at one's clothes, and make strange creaking noises. The soul of a person is different in that the spiritual nature of the body travels to the home of *Heammawihio* via the Hanging Road.

Ancestor concepts in Africa

The variety of beliefs in ancestors has been mentioned already and, to illustrate this, focus will now be placed on the different pattern of these beliefs in Africa and in the Orient. In both these regions ancestors have a significant role in the daily lives of the people.

Anthropologists have made various suggestions as to why the veneration of ancestors has played such an important part in the life of Africans. With the rejection of evolutionary models of religion, the functionalist developed theories relating to the social role of the ancestors. Fortes argued for a general pattern claimed to occur in most African societies in which the ancestors are considered vested with mystical powers and authority.[5] The relationship between the living and the dead is ambivalent, as both punitive and benevolent and sometimes even capricious. Ancestor benevolence is assured through the offering of sacrifices to propitiate any anger. Busia in his study of the Asante kingship recounts a typical story.

I was dangerously ill, I became dumb and could not speak. For two weeks I had not spoken. I could not eat or drink. I could only drink a little soup, which had to be pushed down my throat. One night I became very stiff. It took six strong men to hold me down. Then I went off to sleep. I dreamt I saw my brother, the late chief. He looked very angry. He told me he had always warned me about my bad temper, and that I should show proper respect to my elder sister, who was now the head of the house and served food to the ancestors. I had been afflicted with sickness because the ancestors were displeased with me. He threw me a medicine-ball (*dufa*), and asked me to give it to my sister in the morning, and direct her to dissolve a little in water for me to drink. Next morning, when my sister came, I could not speak to her. But I lifted my pillow. The medicine-ball was there. I gave it to her, and showed her by signs what she was to do. When I drank it, I became well. I have still got the rest of the medicine-ball.[6]

Ancestors are intimately involved with the welfare of the kin-group, but the nature of the linkage may not be the same with every member. The linkage is first through the elders, and the elders' authority is related to their close association with the ancestors. In some ways the elders are seen as representatives of the ancestors and the intermediary between them and the kinship group. Among the Asante, for example, each lineage has its own blackened stool kept at the shrine of the ancestors. During ritual ceremonies the elder places sacrifices on the stool, and pours libations on it, and prays for the welfare of the clan. When a new chief is installed he is led to the shrine where after various sacrifices the chief is then lowered and raised three times.[7] He is then enstooled and acts as intermediary between his royal ancestors and the tribe.

Fortes also clarified some of the structural features by noting the relative lack of interest among Africans in the cosmology of the afterworld in which the ancestors reside. The emphasis is not on how the dead exist, but on the manner in which they affect the living. Different ancestors are recognised as relevant to different contexts, and only certain ones are worshipped as ancestors. As illustrated with the Asante, it is not the individual personalities of the ancestors, but their particular legal status that is important. The family must therefore perform the correct observances so that the deceased reaches the abode of the ancestors (*samando*). The ancestors provide the basis for the unity and authority of the Asante people.

In 1971, Igor Kopytoff presented the controversial idea that African societies draw no significant distinctions between ancestors and living elders.[8] According to Kopytoff the phrases 'ancestor cult' and 'ancestor worship' were misleading when speaking of African societies. These terms set up a conceptual separation between living elders and ancestors, which he said was not found among the Suku of south-western Congo. The Suku have no term that can be translated as 'ancestor'. These dead members of the lineage are referred to as *bambuta*, meaning 'old ones', which is also used of the ruling elders. Eldership is not an absolute state of being old, but is always relative to someone else. My *bambuta* collectively are all the members of the lineage who are older than I am, whether they are alive or dead. By introducing Western connotations of ancestors, he argues, anthropologists have created paradoxes of their own making. The elder's social role does not radically change when he crosses the line dividing the living from the dead, and the African 'ancestorship' is but an aspect of the broader phenomenon of 'eldership'.

This view has been challenged by various writers, and most notably by James Brain.[9] Brain has demonstrated that most African societies do indeed make a clear linguistic distinction between 'elders' (both living and dead) and 'ancestral spirits'. Walter Sangree has shown that among the Tiriki of Kenya, a distinction is made between the fairly recently deceased paternal and mother's parental ancestors (*baguga*) and the generalised ancestral spirits (*misambuwa*).[10] It is the latter collectively rather than the recent dead who are perceived by the Tiriki to be important for the well-being of life. A ritual elder does not expect the ancestral spirits to hear his supplications directly, and he can only reach them through the recently dead elders who in turn act on his behalf. The genealogical relationship between children-parents-grandparents is extended with living elders, recently dead forebears (*baguga*), and the ancestral spirits (*misambuwa*). Although the ideas of Kopytoff are now not accepted it is generally considered that he has made a significant contribution by stressing the cultural continuities between elders and ancestors.

Mendonsa examined this when studying the Sisala of northern Ghana.[11] There are two important terms in the language: *zila*, and *fa*. *Zila* is politeness or mutual respect, which every junior should show to a person senior to him. However, some elders have the direct responsibility of protection for the individual, and it is thought important for the guardian to install *fa*, or fearful respect. A child must fear (*fa*) both his father and the ancestor. The father-son relationship therefore becomes a model for the relations with living elders and ancestors as reflected in the following statements of a Sisala elder:

> While a man's father is alive, it is his father (father's father) who watches over the family. When the father dies, he (the father) watches over a man and his offspring.

In all sacrifices the heir therefore addresses the former custodian of the shrine, who in turn acts as a go-between with the other ancestors. When a person dies he, as the most recently departed, becomes the ancestral representative demanding continued interest and charged with the protection of the living family. For this reason Mendosa agrees with Kopytoff that ancestor worship is not a suitable term, and should be dropped. However, the African data does warrant the retention of the term 'ancestral cult', as there is a distinction between the world of the living and that of the dead ancestors.

The period of ancestorhood tends to be conceived of in one of two ways: linear or cyclic. In the linear model the ancestor is supposed to have an existence for a period, but it does not return to have further human existence. The cyclic model assumes the possibility of a reincarnation of the ancestor in the form of a new-born child.

For those societies believing in a linear view of ancestorhood one could see that with time the number of ancestors would become multitudinous. For this reason there is some form of limit on the number of ancestors with which one must reckon, and the most common is the limit resulting from the loss in remembrance. So long as the ancestor is remembered by some living person the ancestor has some existence, but with the death of the last person to remember the ancestor the ghost ceases to have the same existence. The ghost may wander lost or congregate with other ghosts in the world of the ghosts. Exactly what is the final state of the ghost is often unclear.

Many African peoples do in fact believe in a form of reincarnation of the ancestor. This is an important belief amongst the Ga, who consider that the dead will only be reborn in their own families, a grandfather as a grandson, or a dead first child as a second child. Therefore, it is a great curse to be childless. The Ga word for this reincarnation is the same as that used for a vine twining round a post so that it reappears again and again all the way up the post. This is an important aspect in the ancestral beliefs of the Nilotic peoples of Eastern Africa such as the Maasai or Karamojong. The whole of the Karamojong view of adult life is seen as being a cycle made up of various age-sets which make up four generations of which about half the members are ancestors at any particular time.[12]

Frequently when a child is born people will study the child to see which of the ancestors he or she resembles. When a child dies at birth it may be persuaded to be born again, and this time to stay with the living. The Ga provide us yet again with an example of this.

When a couple lose a child, both father and mother were traditionally shut up together for seven days fasting and mourning. During
these days they were supposed to focus their thoughts on the child,
and tell him aloud that they wish for his return. On the eighth day
they are taken to the beach and purified. The woman is thereafter
assumed to become pregnant and the child born again.[13]

Thus, in African society the dead are not forgotten but are considered to be sociologically alive, at least for a period of time.
They are remembered by offerings and respect, and the ancestors in turn are considered as helping the living.

Chinese concepts of ancestorhood

Ancestorhood is not limited to Africa. It is found in many parts
of the world, and no more so than in the Orient. In China, the
ancestor cult was known as far back as Shang and Yin dynas-
ties (before 1000 BC), and remained strong mainly through the
rationale given to it by Confucius (551–479 BC) by his teaching
on filiality. As the Confucianist classic states: 'When one lives
one should think of his ancestors, and when one drinks one
should think of the spring from which the water comes.' Or, in
a more direct translation, 'To live, one should not forget one's
origin; to drink, one should remember its source.'

In ancient times the Chinese had a notion of two souls: the
hun soul, which might reside in the memorial tablet and would
eventually revert to heaven; the *p'o* soul which at death decom-
posed with the body, and could become angered if disturbed.
The *hun* was considered to be able to leave the body during life
and wander freely. Death occurred when the *hun* permanently
left the body, and it was then that the *hun* was invited to inhabit
the ancestral tablet. The invitation of the soul to inhabit the
tablet was ritually similar to inviting a god to inhabit a statue in
a temple. It allowed the relatives to pay their respects, express
their grief and include the ancestor in the life and business of

the family. Food and drink were placed in front of the tablet to symbolically include the deceased in the family meal.

After death the *p'o* was considered to decompose with the body, and for this reason great care was taken of the corpse. There were elaborate instructions to discourage the leakage of the *p'o* or the entrance into the body of foreign souls seeking a home. From early history the Chinese seemed to use many resources to slow down the process of decay. Strong watertight coffins were used, and care was taken to place them in the most auspicious place. When misfortunes occurred after the death it might indicate that the ancestor was not satisfied and a ritual specialist would be called in for advice. Coffins were sometimes realigned, bones cleaned, and even painted to restore the comfort of the ancestor. Today, on 5 April the Ching Ming festival is held in Hong Kong when thousands of people visit the graves of their families to clean them and present them with food offerings and yellow paper money.

After Buddhism acculturated with folk Chinese beliefs in about 600–900 AD a more coherent concept of heaven and hell began to emerge. Heaven, like the imperial court, watched over the activities of human beings on earth, and took responsibility for maintaining order. Hell, in contrast, was perceived as a penal system where one paid for past sins with the eventual hope of release. Later Buddhism and Taoism introduced the notion that the living could lighten the suffering of their dead ancestors by the transference of merit. The living could provide the dead with various aids to help them on their journey. Today, Chinese stores sell 'Hell Bank Notes', or visa papers, that are taken by the family to be burned at the temples and so conveyed to the ancestor. More recently paper mobile phones, pagers and cars have also offered to assist the difficult journey through the afterlife.

The journey in hell and the time of purgatory terrified many Chinese. It is an unforgivable breach of filial piety to fail to make offerings to one's ancestors, and it is a great tragedy for a couple not to have a son to do this for them. Daughters marry out of the family, and if there is no son to make them offerings they may become 'hungry ghosts', lost and homeless. For this reason many Chinese parents have objected strongly to their children becoming Christians. The importance of ancestor veneration within Oriental society means that for many first-generation Christians a major question they must face is that of how should they participate in their family ancestral rituals. Many young Christians have faced great social pressure or even violence because they have refused to participate in the family rituals.[14]

Christianity and afterlife

Christians have tended to make two assumptions about ghosts, namely that the dead are unable to contact the living and that materialisations are evil spirits in disguise. The first assumption is based on verses such as Job 7:9, '. . . so he who goes down to the grave does not return'. However, it must be realised that some of Job's statements question the traditional Hebrew religious views, and some would say border on blasphemy (e.g. Job 9:14–35). It would therefore be unwise to base any doctrine totally on his statements. Another text is the parable of the rich man and Lazarus in Luke 16:19–31, but even so, it cannot conclude that ghosts are unable to communicate with the living. A careful reading shows that Abraham does not tell the rich man that it is impossible for the dead to return, but that it is spiritually useless. 'He (Abraham) said to him, "If they do not listen to Moses and the Prophets, they will not be convinced even if someone rises from the dead"' (Luke 16:31).

There is some evidence in the Bible that would support the argument for the reality of ghosts. In the story of the so-called witch of Endor, 1 Samuel 28, the medium was surprised that Samuel actually rose from the dead. Her surprise seems to have come from the unusual nature of this occurrence, as she was more used to using trickery and personal insights in her role as a medium. The New Testament also recounts the story of Moses and Elijah conversing with Jesus on the Mount of Transfiguration. Although these are unique cases, they do not discount the possibility of ghosts. It may therefore be concluded that the Bible leaves open the question of whether the dead may communicate with the living. Scripture, however, is emphatic that any attempt to communicate with the departed is sin. In Israel there was to be a total ban on anyone who 'consults the dead' (Deut. 18:11). One of the sins of Israel condemned by Isaiah is that the people tried to consult with the dead. 'When men tell you to consult mediums and spiritists, who whisper and mutter, should not a people enquire of their God? Why consult the dead on behalf of the living?' (Is. 8:19). One must conclude that it is absolutely forbidden for Christians to communicate with ghosts even if they are ancestors.

Veneration or worship?

Many practical questions occur for Christians coming from a background where ancestral beliefs are accepted. How may one answer the African Christian who affirms that it was his deceased father who spoke to him in a dream and so saved him from harm? These may easily be considered as hallucinations due to emotional stress, but could they just as well be warnings from God in the same way as they are found in the Bible? As Robert Cook has written when he paraphrased the seventeenth-century philosopher, Thomas Hobbes, 'When a man claims that an ancestor spoke to him in a dream, this is no more than to say that he dreamed that an ancestor spoke to him.'[15]

Some theologians have attempted to use the concept of ancestors to make Christianity more relevant to the African context. The Roman Catholic scholar Mutiso-Mubinda writes, 'Christ is our "Ancestor" par excellence, because he plays this role of mediation, and because he has preceded us in "passing-over".'[16] Charles Nyamiti has taken on his ideas further in his book *Christ as our Ancestor* in which he speaks of four types of ancestors that the African Christian will discover.[17] First, those that he will expect to meet are his own traditional ancestors. The second type is all the heavenly saints and those in purgatory who are without natural ties to the individual. Then above all these there will be Christ himself, the divine Brother-Ancestor of all humanity. Finally, Christianity will offer him God the Father Himself as the divine Parent-Ancestor. After discussing the strengths and weaknesses of the assumption Nyamiti concludes, 'In any case, we hope to have shown that the African teaching on ancestors is an excellent preparatory road for the Christian doctrine on Christ and the saints.'[18]

In contrast to ghosts, the subject of ancestors raises the issue of family ties. Protestants have generally taken the view that the Bible exposes death as being a radical break with life. The Asian Consultation on Ancestor Practices therefore makes the statement:

> 'Ancestors' spirits' have no supernatural power either to bestow blessings or to inflict curses upon the descendants. We, therefore, encourage Christians confronted with the problems of ancestor practices not to be controlled by a sense of fear, trust, or adoration of the ancestors nor create an impression of such to the surrounding society and to fellow Christians.[19]

On the other hand, the Asian Consultation recognised the need to stress the obligation of children to 'honour your father and your mother . . .' (Ex. 20:12). This Consultation has shown the necessity for Third World Christians to reassess the Scriptures in the light of their own cultural heritage. This is a complex subject, and the Westerner must approach it with humility. It may be easy for him to condemn the ancestral shrines of the peoples of the Orient, but where does the line fall between that and his own acts of placing flowers on the grave of a departed loved one, or even a Christian memorial service?

Another issue of importance in the conversion of people from traditional societies is the concept of the afterlife. Both Christianity and Islam introduce a new concept of a division in the afterlife into two abodes that are dependent upon an individual's moral behaviour in this life. This is a strikingly new concept for most traditional societies, as they usually perceive the afterlife as a single place to which all the ancestors go. For example, the Cheyenne had no concept of hell or punishment of any sort in afterlife.[20] Although the Cheyenne do commit sins in this life, the punishment is expiated here and now. There is therefore no problem of salvation. Goodness is sought for its own sake, and for the approval of one's fellows. At death the soul is free to travel along the Hanging Road to dwell thereafter in the proximity of the Great Wise One. Only those who commit suicide are barred from this peace. When these souls travel the Hanging Road they are diverted along a fork in the road which leads not to heaven, but to nothingness.

The Tonga of the Zambezi Valley had a concept of the afterlife that contained neither the idea of a divine judgement nor a reward or punishment of the dead. With the coming of Methodist missionaries in 1905 a different perspective was open to them, which was that those who prayed and lived 'in the right way' would live with God, while those who failed to do so would 'go to the fire'. The notion of divine judgement of the dead and the teaching of hell as a place of eternal damnation and suffering hit the core of Tonga religion and social organisation. The ritual intercourse between the living and the ancestors (*mizimu*) was a basic feature of Tonga culture and religion. This was to have a radical effect on the Tonga as Ulrich Luig writes:

> The conversion of a single member of a lineage was surely a blow to the family but it left the kin group as a whole intact. The notion, however, that the spirits of the believers in the *mizimu* would be burnt after death implied that those who had joined the 'European way of prayers' and 'worshipped *Leza* (God) in the right way' were

saved while those who remained with their *mizimu* were lost. The Christian dogma of the divine judgement of all mankind meant, in fact, the introduction of a divided cosmos.[21]

The coming of World religions to traditional societies therefore introduced radically new concepts that undermined family ties. Often belief in the ancestors continues irrespective of the change of allegiance, but there was generally a gradual decline in the practice of the ancestor cult. This often corresponds with a shift from lineage solidarity to that of the nuclear family. Whatever approach the Church has taken to the subject of ancestors, it is one that is of great significance around the world among traditional societies. It is an issue that cannot be neglected, and continues to require an answer among those who would call themselves Christian.

Notes

1 Spencer, H., *The Principles of Sociology*, vol. II & III (New York: Appleton, 1880–1896).
2 Bolaji, I. E., *African Traditional Religion* (London: SCM Press, 1973), p. 178.
3 Barker, P., *Peoples, Languages, and Religion in Northern Ghana* (Accra: GEC, 1986), p. 164.
4 Lin Yutang, *My Country and My People* (London: Heinemann, 1962), pp. 90–1.
5 Fortes, M., 'Some reflections on ancestor worship', in Fortes, M. & Dieterlen, G. (eds.), *African Systems of Thought* (London: OUP, 1965), pp. 122–42.
6 Busia, K. A., *The Position of the Chief in the Modern Political System of Ashanti* (London: Frank Cass & Co., 1968), p. 25
7 *Ibid.* p. 26.
8 Kopytoff, I., 'Ancestors as elders in Africa', *Africa* 43 (1971), pp. 129–42.
9 Brain, J., 'Ancestors as elders in Africa: further thoughts', *Africa* 43 (1973), pp. 122–3.

10 Sangree, W. H., 'Youths as elders and infants as ancestors: the complementarity of alternative generations, both living and dead, in Tiriki, Kenya, and Irigwe, Nigeria', *Africa* 44 (1974), pp. 65–70.

11 Mendonsa, E. L., 'Elders, Office-holders and Ancestors Among the Sisala of Northern Ghana', *Africa* 46 (1976), pp. 57–61.

12 Lamphear, J., *The Traditional History of the Jie of Uganda* (London: Clarendon Press, 1976).

13 Field, M. J., *Religion and Medicine of the Ga People* (London: OUP, 1961), p. 202.

14 Bong Rin Ro, *Christian Alternatives to Ancestor Practices* (Taiwan: ATA: Taichung, 1985), p. 4.

15 Cook, R. R., 'Ghosts', *East Africa Journal of Evangelical Theology*, 4 (1985), pp. 45–6.

16 Mutiso-Mubinda, J., *Anthropology and the Paschal Mystery* (Eldoret: Gaba Publications, 1979), p. 52.

17 Nyamiti, C., *Christ as our Ancestor* (Gweru: Mambo Press, 1984).

18 *Ibid.* p. 149.

19 Bong Rin Bo, *Christian Alternatives to Ancestor Practices* (Taichung, Taiwan: ATA, 1985), p. 9.

20 Hoebel, E. A., *The Cheyennes: Indians of the Great Plains* (Orlando: Holt, Reinhart & Winson Inc. 1978), p. 92.

21 Luig, U., *Conversion as a Social Process: A History of Missionary Christianity among the Valley Tonga, Zambia* (Hamburg: LIT, 1996), p. 191.

Chapter Five

FORBIDDEN THINGS

Following his journey around the Polynesian Islands it was Captain Cook who first reported the word 'taboo' in Europe in 1777. The word 'taboo' originated from the Polynesian word 'ta' meaning 'to mark' and 'pu' meaning 'exceedingly', so 'taboo' meant something marked thoroughly. His sailors realised that the word designated a prohibition, and they used it themselves when they wanted to keep visitors off the ship. The word quickly became absorbed into the English language because it matched the existing category of prohibition in a more expressive manner.

Sir James Frazer later gathered an impressive arrangement of taboos in his famous volume on Taboo in *The Golden Bough*. He draws these from many parts of the world, and associates them with primitive forms of religions. He talked about positive and negative magic, meaning by the latter taboo. Margaret Mead makes an effort to define taboo in her article on the topic in the *Encyclopaedia of the Social Sciences* published in 1937.

> Tabu may be defined as a negative sanction, a prohibition whose infringement results in an automatic penalty without human or superhuman mediation.[1]

The word taboo has therefore been applied from the original Polynesian context to all societies. It is therefore necessary first to examine how the word was used in Polynesia.

Taboo in Polynesia

Taboos were so many in Polynesia that every author who has tried to describe them has resorted to some form of classification. I shall here use Lehmann's divisions because they show something of the breadth of taboo. He divides taboos into three classes related to: a) society, b) the human body, and c) religion.

Under sociological taboos Lehmann lists six groups. The first are those connected with persons holding high office, who have the power to declare taboos. The second group relates to those applying to women and result in a segregation of gender. The third are those that apply to economic activities and crafts. Fourth are wartime taboos. Fifth are those that are a sign of legal claim. Finally, are those relating to the custom of *tapa-tabu*.

The second main division relates to the human body. These Lehmann grouped into three classes. The first are those that relate to head and dorsal taboos. Second those associated with special bodily conditions such as the temporary ritual impurity connected with childbirth and menses. Third are those connected with illness and death.

The third class is those relating to religion. This is surprisingly only a small group, mainly because Lehmann has classed many taboos connected with the priests under the first class. Although the listing of taboos in this sort of way is helpful it does not explain the context. What is important in Polynesia is the way in which taboo is related to the notion of *mana*, which reveals the political-ritual meaning of both terms.

A former missionary working in the Pacific Isles, R. H. Codrington was the first to define the concept of *mana*.

> The Melanesian mind is entirely possessed by the belief in a supernatural power or influence, called almost universally *mana*. This is what works to affect everything that is beyond the ordinary power of men, outside the common processes of nature; it is present in the atmosphere of life, attaches itself to persons and to things, and is manifested by results which can only be ascribed to its operation.[2]

The definition first draws a distinct difference between the concept of *mana* from the technical powers. In Fiji, for example, there are two quite distinct words for power. *Calwa* refers to physical strength, and *mana* refers to spiritual power that may be possessed by an object or a person. If a person were conspicuous by his particular success in hunting, fighting, or powers of leadership, such would be considered proof that the person possessed *mana*. It is appreciated that the yams will grow naturally when planted in the earth, but they will not be very large unless *mana* comes into operation. Similarly a canoe will not be very swift unless it possesses *mana*, nor will a hunter be very successful unless he possesses *mana*. Writing about the Melanesian concept, Codrington sought to define *mana* in the following way. 'It is a power or influence, not physical, and in a way supernatural; but it shows itself in physical force, or in any kind of power or excellence which a man possesses. This *mana* is not fixed in anything, and can be conveyed in almost anything . . .'[3]

Mana may generally be understood as being an impersonal force much like high-voltage electricity. Although this is a useful illustration, care must be taken not to take it too far. The way that the term is used implies that *mana* is descriptive of the possession of the power rather than the power itself, and so it is always connected to some person or spirit that may activate its effect. In other words, the measure of a person's political authority is the taboos he can impose, and these can only be overruled by a higher official. Captain Cook mentions the taboo of a Tongan food controller. It was his office to tell people what not to eat, and once he had made this declaration it could not be eaten until the next harvest.

Mana is also conceived of as intrinsically amoral. Whether it brings good or evil depends upon the possessor. A healer may use his *mana* to cure the sick, whilst a sorcerer may use his to cast a curse upon a person. It is the intentions of the person that give to the power its moral quality in much the same way as drugs may be used to heal or to kill. *Mana* may increase a person's prosperity, preserve a man from danger, and enable a barren woman to bear children. A charm has power to protect a person from danger because it bears the name of a powerful spirit or god upon it, or it has been made in a particular way such that the spirit has transferred *mana* to the article. Most Polynesian men had at least one disease-bearing taboo, which is similar to the notion of spell to be discussed in chapter 9. The slight difference between the two is that a taboo has the social function of protection. An example is the death taboo:

> This was made by pouring some oil into a small calabash and burying it near the tree. The spot was marked by a little hillock of white sand. The sight of one of these was also effectual in scaring away a thief.[4]

Mana has something of a qualitative element about it. *Mana* can be built up within an object or person by use of suitable rituals. In pre-Christian Solomon Islands, the taking of heads was one way of building up *mana*. The heads of slain enemies were offered to the skull of the honoured ancestor and in so doing the latter's *mana* was increased, and so its effectiveness to protect the tribe increased. Tippett, writing of the Malaita bushmen, recounts the following scale in which the heads have an increasing *mana* value, from pig as the lowest ascending to woman, warrior, chief, and ultimately white man.[5] A man could therefore rise in power, gaining more and more *mana*, and extending his power of imposing taboos.

Although there is danger in applying the concept of *mana* universally the notion is found in many societies in one form or another. The Iroquois of North America have the term *Orenda* that particularly refers to the mystic power derived from a chant. The Inuit (Eskimos) have the notion of *Sila*, a force watching and controlling everything. The Chinese have the concept of *Fung Shui* which particularly refers to the powers inherent within the contours of the earth and sea. Within village Islam the term

Baraka, usually translated holiness or blessing, embraces many of these concepts.[6] It is interesting to draw a comparison with the English meaning of the word luck which derives from a Teutonic background. A businessman may consider his promotion to chairman as being the result of his hard work and intellectual abilities, but he may also recognise that he was 'lucky' to be at the right place at the right time. A person who has just won a lottery will reckon himself to be lucky.

Among the Asante a taboo (*akyiwadie*) are things forbidden or required because they are offences against the ancestors or a deity. For example, it is taboo to till the soil on Thursday because this is the day holy for the earth goddess Asase Yaa. They also have a prohibition against sex in the bush, or even on the bare floor, because Asase Yaa is believed to bring her wrath upon the whole community by destroying the crops. Elders recognise this as a sensible restriction as it is clearly meant to issue a stern warning to men who may be tempted to rape a woman in the fields.

Frazer, in *The Golden Bough*, joined the two terms of *mana* and taboo together into a common category of 'contagious magic'. Van Gennep staunchly rejected this animistic theory following his studies of taboo (*fady*) in Madagascar first published in 1904.[7] He saw taboo as an expression of a sense of pervasive, non-dualistic power, known in Malagasy as *hasina*. If *hasina* (*mana*) is likened to high-voltage electricity, taboo may be likened to electrical insulation. Taboos therefore act like a sign warning of high-voltage electricity running through overhead power cables. However, taboos are not merely symbolic representations of a boundary, but act as boundaries between persons or groups. Van Gennep would argue that in delimiting and differentiating persons and bodies they actually help to constitute them.

In Malagasy taboos are distinctive at every level of social inclusion from society to individual.[8] Some taboos differentiate relationships between men and women, young and old, members of a specific locality, or a particular descent group. Taboos also mark people undergoing specific rites of passage or healing rites. Usually women observe more taboos than men do. Thus, it is the mother rather than the father that is subject to birth taboos. There are many taboos that are individual, and are only discovered by means of astrology. Once these are identified they are spoken about in ways not dissimilar to how Westerners talk about having allergies. The totalities of an individual's taboos provide a summary of his or her current social status.

Pollution

Mary Douglas followed van Gennep in linking boundary transgression with pollution and danger.[9] European notions of dirt are bound up with concepts of bacteria and hygiene, but these ideas only entered the secular worldview in the last century. Even before that time cleanliness and holiness were part of the European life. In traditional societies, the notion of pollution can be far ranging, and is seen primarily as a religious offence. This is a concept interwound with that of the concept of sin, and yet it retains its own character in the practical living of many peoples. Evans-Pritchard writes of the Nuer, 'Adultery, besides being a wrong done to the husband by infringement of his rights, is a further wrong to him in that he is polluted.' The husband who discovers his wife's immorality demands not only compensation from the man, but also the giving of an ox called *yang kula*. This is paid to protect the husband from the consequences of the adultery. 'All three persons are polluted, but if sickness results it falls on the husband, and it is most likely to fall on him if the adultery took place in his home.'[10] The *yang kula* is sacrificed to wipe out the pollution.

It is very common to find that all bodily emissions are considered polluting, and once they are discharged from the body they become both dangerous and polluting. The Gypsies, for example, consider all emissions from the top half of the body to be clean and curative and all emissions from the lower half to be polluting. Saliva is considered to have curative properties especially with regards to the 'evil-eye'. On the other hand, contact with menstrual blood, urine, faeces and semen can cause illness and result in social exile.

The Law of Moses made a clear distinction between the clean and the unclean. 'You must distinguish between the holy and the common, between the unclean and the clean.' (Lev. 10:10). This ceremonial defilement was contracted in several ways, and for each, provision was made for cleansing.

The first class of defilements are those resulting from bodily discharge: 'A woman who becomes pregnant and gives birth to a son will be ceremonially unclean for seven days, just as she is unclean during her monthly period' (Lev. 12:2). A man with a bodily discharge is unclean (Lev. 15:1–15), as are those things which he touches. A man who has a discharge of semen is unclean till evening (Lev. 15:16–18). Washing with water is a common purification from this pollution. Secondly are those relating to skin diseases, and especially leprosy (Lev. 14). The person, his clothes, and his house were all polluted. A third group was that of touching a dead body (Num. 19:11–22). In this case a person was unclean for seven days, and he had to bathe on the third and seventh days to become ceremonially clean. A fourth class of defilements is those of clean and unclean foods. Leviticus 11 contains an extended list of creatures, which may or may not be eaten for reasons of ritual purity. The most popular theory amongst critical scholars is that advanced by W. Robertson Smith who considered the system to be based on Semitic tribal taboos, and the worship of clan totems.[11]

An analysis of the 'Abominations of Leviticus' in *Purity and Danger* by Mary Douglas is one of the best known attempts to interpret an extremely complex system of rules and restrictions. The list of animals that are prohibited in Leviticus according to Douglas must not be considered piecemeal, but within the context of creation laid out in Genesis. Creation has a threefold classification into the earth, the waters and the firmament. Living beings that reside in each medium are described according to their type: flesh, fish and fowl respectively, and each has an appropriate means of locomotion. On the earth there are four-legged animals that hop, jump or walk; in the water are fish with fins, and in the sky two-legged birds with wings. Those creatures that are forbidden do not fit into this system of classification. It includes four-legged creatures that fly, and creatures with two hands and two feet who move about on all fours. If the proposed interpretation of the forbidden animals is correct, the dietary laws would have been like signs which at every turn inspired meditation on the oneness, purity and completeness of God. By rules of avoidance holiness was given a physical expression in every encounter with the animal kingdom and at every meal.[12]

This theory recognises various social boundaries. Within those boundaries things are orderly, and therefore regarded as pure. However, at the boundaries there is an area of ambiguity and so the danger of pollution. People who are in these marginal states, although they may have done nothing morally wrong, are defiled because of their status. 'Take, for example, the unborn child. Its present position is ambiguous, its future equally. For no one can say what sex it will have or whether it will survive the hazards of infancy. It is often treated as both vulnerable and dangerous.'[13]

These concepts of clean and unclean must not be relegated to some historical discussions with no importance for today. Many people on becoming Christian are concerned about these very issues. I have often been asked by those involved with the independent churches of Africa whether a woman can attend church during her monthly period. Whilst Westerners tend to limit pollution to matters of hygiene, those from a traditional worldview see pollution as having an important religious meaning.

Douglas has interpreted taboos relating to menstruation, which are very widespread, as often manipulative devices for controlling women. An example is that of the Kwaio people who live on the Solomon Islands in Melanesia, and illustrate how the symbolic division of the cosmos expresses lines of cleavage in the social structure and is reflected in the rituals and spatial arrangements. This is in spite of the fact that they have been in contact with Christian missionaries since the beginning of the twentieth century.

For the Kwaio the ancestors move in a realm where sacredness prevails, and communicating with them is dangerous and done only by men.[14] All the men of a decent group will take part in purification rites in which pigs are sacrificed and eaten. Women are excluded from these events, because the bodies of women are considered polluting. There is a scale of pollution from urination, to menstruation, and most polluting of all is childbirth.

A major preoccupation of Kwaio rituals are with keeping sacred realms properly demarcated from the mundane activities such as eating, gardening, talking and sleeping. Following Mary Douglas' analysis the symbolism is expressed in a series of dualistic opposites:

Female	Male
Polluted	Sacred
Down	Up

Thus, men and women eat and drink out of separate cooking vessels. The symbolic model is mapped onto a spatial form in the structure of the village (see figure 2). At the upper margin of the clearing in which the village is sited is the men's sacred house close to the shrine. This is off-limits to women. At the bottom margin of the clearing is the menstrual hut, which is polluted and taboo to men. An invisible line runs across the clearing where the domestic houses are sited. The upside of the clearing is essential for men and the downside for women. A man may move freely between the dwelling house and the men's house, and the women between the dwelling house and the menstrual hut. Women are allowed to cross the line for particular purposes such as scraping the clearing, picking up pig droppings, and carrying firewood.

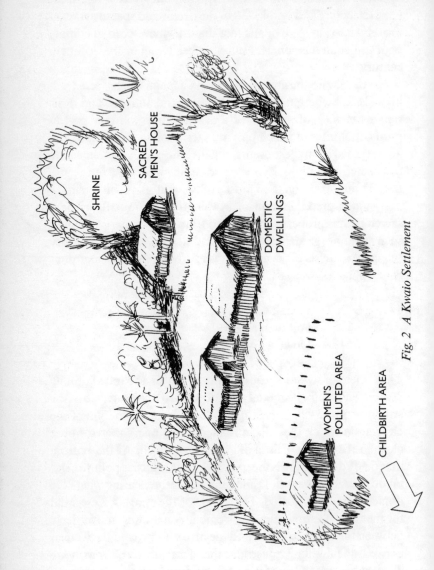

SHRINE

SACRED
MEN'S HOUSE

DOMESTIC
DWELLINGS

WOMEN'S
POLLUTED AREA

CHILDBIRTH AREA

Fig. 2 A Kwaio Settlement

A woman about to give birth will retire to a hut in the forest below the menstrual hut, out of all contact with men, and attended usually by a young girl. In contrast the priest who offers sacrifices retires to the men's house near the shrine, out of all contact with women, where a young boy attends him. Transitions from one realm to another are carefully observed. If a woman takes firewood from the house, she must first light an intermediate stick before lighting a fire in the menstrual hut.

Sin

Sin is frequently regarded by many as a concept which is brought, or imposed (depending on your view), by Western missionaries to traditional societies. Whilst this may be true in part, it is necessary to recognise that the notion of sin is generally universal. The list of offences denoted as 'sin' may vary from one culture to another, but the concept is common. It can be seen that the concepts of pollution merge with those of taboo, which in turn overlap with those of sin. The relationship between pollution and morals is far from straightforward, but pollution beliefs frequently uphold a people's moral code.

Alan Tippett from his work in the Solomon Islands has proposed three classes of sin, which provide a useful framework for discussion.[15] First there are anti-social sins which are offences that are made against the kinship group, tribe, or any member of the tribe. These rules recognise a strong sense of group solidarity and group cohesion. Incest is frequently the most serious sin, as amongst the Nuer. Failure to respect authority is a sin especially if a son disobeys his father; so is the use of sorcery against one's own people. As this class of sins relates to the group they do not therefore apply to members of another group unless they are bound by some ceremonial agreement. Thus, a dual moral code can emerge, one relating to insiders and another to outsiders. An offensive act against a member of another tribe may not be a sin, except in so far as it may bring reprisals for which the group as a whole is held responsible.

Second there are theological sins which are offences against tribal god(s) or ancestors. These may occur as a result of neglecting to correctly perform some ritual, which will cause offence to the god or ancestor. They may result from a failure to observe a taboo, or offer a sacrifice. A society depends for its cohesion not only upon inter-personal relations, but also upon the support of their deities and ancestors. If a person sins against the gods or ancestors, the support of these deities will be withdrawn and the whole community will suffer. Thus, for example, when a member of a community becomes a Christian he is in fact committing a 'theological sin', because he no longer practices the established rituals. Repercussions could come upon the whole tribe with fearful results.

Tippett's third class of sins is those against forces outside the normal life of the community. Many of these offences are committed unwittingly because the person does not know the rules or taboos of a particular deity, or even know of the existence of this 'unknown god'. For this reason a shrine may be built to an 'unknown god' (see Acts 17), and sacrifices made, just so as to avoid such a danger. It is when a person is outside his home territory that he is in greatest danger. He does not know the abodes of the spirits, and the taboos of the local deities. The people settled in Israel by Nebuchadnezer were said to have been attacked by lions because they did not know the laws of the god of the land.

For this reason one finds in all societies a wide range of charms and rituals to protect the unwary traveller by land or by sea. Within folk Islam charms are common. The distinctive 'Hand of Fatima' is common in North Africa and the Middle East. The Sufi orders of Islam often turned the granting of *baraka* (holiness in the form of power) to travellers into a highly profitable commercial venture with agents to collect the payment from the traveller who successfully completes his journey. In a similar way some Christians wear a St Christopher medallion when they are travelling.

All societies tend to have an informal classification of the degree of seriousness of various sins. In Western society the worst sins are usually conceived as being murder, or rape, followed by theft, and much lower down the list one will find sins such as lies, lack of hospitality, and meanness. In many traditional societies the order is transformed. Being mean and inhospitable to your own people is a great sin because it touches the very solidarity of the group. On the other hand, murder or rape of members outside the group is of little significance.

Does this variation mean that there are no universals with regards to sin? Prohibitions against stealing, murder, and adultery tend to be almost universal, but the way in which they are actually defined varies from one culture to another. Thus, through a personal, culturally conditioned conscience, every person has an awareness of what is right and wrong. Wayne Dye saw the reality of this as he was doing Bible translation among the Bahinemo of Papua New Guinea.

> I tried to translate Jesus' list of sins in Mark 7. As each sin was described, they gave me the local term for it. They named other sins in their culture.
>
> 'What did your ancestors tell you about these things?' I asked them.
>
> 'Oh, they told us we shouldn't do any of those things.'
>
> 'Do you think these were good standards that your ancestors gave you?' They agreed unanimously that they were.
>
> 'Well, do you keep all these rules?'
>
> 'No,' they responded sheepishly. One leader said, 'Definitely not. Who could ever keep them all? We're people of the ground.'
>
> I took this opportunity to explain that God expected them to keep their own standards for what is right, that He was angry because they hadn't. Then I pointed out that it was because they fell short of their own standards that God sent His Son to bear their punishment so that they could be reunited with Him.
>
> This was a crucial step towards their conversion.[16]

Taboo, pollution and sins are all part of boundary formation for a society. These are regions of danger, but they may be passed through by means of rituals.

Notes

1 Mead, M., 'Tabu' in *Encyclopedia of the Social Sciences* (London: Macmillan, 1937), vol. VII, pp. 502–5.

2 Codrington, R. H., *The Melanesians: Studies in their Anthropology and Folklore* (Oxford: Clarendon Press, 1891), pp. 118–20.

3 *Ibid.*

4 Steiner, F., *Taboo* (Harmondsworth: Penguin, 1967), p. 45.

5 Tippett, A. R., *Solomon Islands Christianity* (Pasadena: William Carey Library, 1967), p. 9.

6 Douglas, M., *Purity and Danger* (London: Routledge & Kegan Paul, 1966) p. 109.

7 Van Gennep, A., *Tabou et totemisme à Madagascar: étude descriptive et théorique* (Paris: Ernst Leroux, 1904).

8 Lambek, M., 'Taboo as cultural practice among Malagasy speakers' *Man* 27 (1992), pp. 245–66.

9 Douglas, *op. cit.*

10 Evans-Pritchard, E. E., *Nuer Religion* (New York: Oxford University Press, 1977), p. 185.

11 Robertson Smith, W., *Lectures on the Religion of the Semites* (London: A & C Black, 1927).

12 Douglas, *op. cit.* p. 57.

13 Douglas, *ibid.* p. 95.

14 Keesing, R. M., *Kwaio Religion: The Living and the Dead in a Solomon Island Society* (1981).

15 Tippett, *op. cit.* pp. 16–19.

16 Dye, T. Wayne, 'Towards a Cultural Definition of Sin', *Missiology* 4 (1976), pp. 26–41.

Chapter Six

RITUALS FOR LIVING

Ritual is a word with a broad meaning, and can be defined as any formal behaviour prescribed by a society, but it also carries a more specific meaning related to beliefs in spiritual beings. It is in this more restricted sense that the term is applied to religious rites. A well known definition is that of Victor Turner:

> Prescribed formal behaviour for occasions not given over to technical routine, having reference to beliefs in mystical (or non-empirical) beings or powers regarded as the first and final causes of all effects.[1]

Anthropological study of ritual has undergone major changes in recent years, but a significant starting point is found in the views of the Dutch anthropologist Arnold van Gennep who in 1908 wrote, 'The life of an individual in any society is a series of passages from one age to another.'[2] He saw society as like a house divided into rooms and corridors, and people move from one room to another. These transitions he termed 'rites of passage', and they provide a useful framework for understanding the place of ritual in traditional religions. These rites are simply considered in three categories: the passage of status, the passage of time, and the passage of situation.

Transition of status – lifecycle

This first category includes a wide range of transitions when the individual moves from one status to another and includes birth, puberty, marriage and death. The process of transition entails the crossing of social boundaries, and at that point a person is neither of one status or the other, so there is a confusion of roles and possible danger for the individual and the society as a whole.

Van Gennep argued that all transition rites have a three-phase structure. The first is when the person is separated from his or her initial role. This may involve the physical removal of the person from the village, a change of clothing, or ritual washing to remove any pollution from the earlier phase. The second stage is the period of transition that may last from a few hours to a few months during which the person is subject to pollution so is kept apart from ordinary society. In the third phase, the person is brought back into normal society, and ushered into his or her new role. The actual proceedings of the final stage are often similar to those of separation but in reverse.

Birth rituals

In all societies there is great joy when a wife finds that she is expecting a child. This is essential for the continuity of the tribe, and the child that is born is thought to belong to the whole group. As soon as the woman knows she is expecting she may be required to observe various regulations and taboos. For example, a woman may stop sexual relations with her husband, avoid certain foods, or wear charms which are believed to protect her and her baby from harm. At birth both mother and child may be required to undergo various rituals.

The Minahasa are one tribe amongst the many thousands in Indonesia. For them the cutting of the umbilical cord is of great importance. At that very instant the baby will gain the power of life. The witch-doctor ties the cord with a thread using three knots. The husband or the father-in-law gives the child a name from one of the ancestors of the family. The witch-doctor whilst holding the child prays in the fashion, 'We give you the name . . . so that you may have the attributes of him/her. Oh, ancestor here is your grandchild. Take care of him/her because he/she is your existence right now.'[3] After praying the umbilical cord is cut and the child is given to the grandmother. The placenta with the cord is then placed in a pot with the words, 'I am so sorry that you have to be separated from your friends.' The pot is then buried near the entrance of the house.

The Minahasa often place a mirror above the head of the baby when it is asleep. This, it is believed, will keep the ghosts away as they do not like to see their faces. Forty days after birth, another ritual is held in which the hair of the child is shaved because to do otherwise will mean the baby will become sick. The witch-doctor will make a charm for the child, and the grandmother will feed the baby with a small portion of liver which has been dedicated to the ancestor. In this way the child will have a long and successful life like the ancestor, and so is brought into the social life of the community.

Puberty

Puberty initiation rites mark the transition from childhood to adulthood, and as such are celebrated amongst all traditional societies. They separate the person from one life in which the child is dependent upon his mother, into another where he is a man, or a woman with the opportunities of marriage and the procreation of children. These rituals show the characteristic three-phase structure of a rite of passage, and often include the following:

- Separation and seclusion from the normal life of the society.
- Testing to show that the person is worthy to be a man or a woman. This often involves the need to respect one's elders.

- Instruction in both the religious mythology of the people and in the accepted behaviour of an adult.
- Marking as a sign of adulthood. Circumcision is common, but there may also be tattooing or scarification.

A great variety of initiation rites could be described for both males and females from many parts of the world. Some are kept secret from outsiders, whilst others are willing to speak about them. Basically, initiation provides the bridge by which the child becomes an adult member of the society. Some initiation rites include the dedication of the person to a particular spirit or deity, and in some cases this has even lead to spirit possession. For this reason most Christian missionaries have objected to initiation rites, and discouraged their converts from taking part. Whilst recognising this danger it is also necessary to realise the fact that if a person fails to go through such rituals, according to the tribe, that person is no longer regarded as an adult member of the community. The convert may therefore become a non-person with regards to his own society with little social influence.

Marriage

One of the primary aspects of adulthood is that the person should marry and have children. In this way human life is preserved, propagated and perpetuated. Marriage therefore comes at the very centre of human life and signifies the formal transition from single to married status. Because of the importance of the tribe and the family, marriage is not seen so much as the binding of two individuals, but as an association of two families.

As with the other rites of passage, the first step is the setting apart of the individual from his or her usual activities. This procedure can be seen within Western society where immediately before the wedding, the bride and groom are separated. The groom is taken out by male friends for a 'stag party' in which they may indulge in excessive drinking and sexual joking. It is regarded as 'bad luck' for the bride to see the groom on the day of the wedding before she actually arrives at the church. Special clothes are worn for the ceremony which is rich in symbolism. The bride is dressed in white symbolic of purity and virginity. Finally, the couple must be incorporated into social life again, but this time in their new status as a married couple. In contrast to being set apart from each other, now the couple are set apart as a unit from other people during their honeymoon.[4]

Death

The rituals surrounding death are often long and complex as one might expect from a fear of the ancestors and spirits. As was shown in chapter 4, in traditional societies death is often seen as the initiation of the person into a new stage of existence – ancestorhood. Funeral rites must include the practical aspects such as the disposal of the body, but must also deal with any evil or pollution that has occurred as a result of this transition. The ghost of the person must be placated, and any malice dealt with by sacrifice or punishment of the guilty. These rites must also deal with the grief and the social dislocation caused by the death.

The Ilongot, before they became Christians in the 1970s, were head-hunters. They believed that the death of a relative made one's heart 'heavy and distraught', and it was only through killing and taking the head of an enemy that the men, at least, were able to 'cast off the weight of grief and pain'. In the 1960s, head-hunting was no longer politically possible in the Philippines, and one of the reasons advanced for their conversion is that Christianity was able to calm their grief.[5]

Associations

In addition to these distinct rites of passage which apply to all members of a community, there are also rites of initiation into a voluntary association. An example is the Moba secret society known as Kondi, which conforms to the patterns described by van Gennep.[6] The Moba live in north-eastern Ghana and north-western Togo. Kondi is a mutual support group, which instructs its members in accepted norms of behaviour within the large Moba society. It is open to all post-puberty men and women, regardless of family or clan affiliation.

The initiation begins with a three-month period of seclusion during which the initiate receives rigorous training in Kondi language, dance and customs. Although all initiates move away from the homestead, male and female seclusions are held in different places. Male initiation is communal and takes place in a thatched house a short distance away from the supervisors compound, whereas the women's rites are individual events held in the family compound. Male initiates are kept in a sort of drugged state for much of this period. At the beginning of the period when the young person is in a state of semi-consciousness they receive the scars. When they regain consciousness they are told that they have been led into the world of Kangbewolare, the supreme Kondi spirit, by the elders and brought back again. Initiates of both sexes remain naked throughout the three-month training, and during the first two months the only people they can meet are members of Kondi. The seclusion is concluded with a brief cleansing ceremony, held the day before the exit, to remove the dangerous forces associated with the initiate's training. About mid-morning the drums sound and the initiates come out of seclusion with their heads shaved and their bodies well oiled, and wearing a belt of cowrie shells. The elaborate rituals continue all day. The 'new born' Kondi is finally integrated in his, or her, new role in society.

Transition of time – calendar rituals

Most societies have rituals that regularly mark the passage of time. As with rites of passage which mark transition through life, calendar rites regularise in social form natural cycles through the time of earth and moon. Thus, the year is divided in various ways depending on the local climate, and is often associated with the stages of the harvest in agricultural communities. In traditional societies these rites often relate to the activities of various local deities. Because they are scheduled long in advance there is a growing sense of anticipation for the coming of the festival. This usually leads to a considerable degree of preparation, which may develop over time to make these rituals some of the most elaborate held by the society.

Chinua Achebe describes something of the occasion of the New Yam festival among the Igbo of southern Nigeria.

> The Feast of the New Yam was held every year before the harvest began to honour the earth goddess and the ancestral spirits of the clan. New yams could not be eaten until they had been offered to these powers. Men and women, young and old, look forward to the New Yam festival because it began a season of plenty-the new year. On the last night before the festival, yams of the old year were all disposed of by those who still had them. The new year must begin with tasty, fresh yams and not with shrivelled and fibrous crops of the previous year. All cooking pots, calabashes and wooden bowls were thoroughly washed, especially the wooden mortar in which the yam was pounded. Yam foo-foo and vegetable soup was the chief food in the celebration.[7]

With the coming of a major world religion people usually conform to the wider practice of the confessional community. An obvious example is the adoption of the major festivals of Christianity with the celebration of Christmas, Easter and Pentecost. The major festivals of Islam differ from those of Christianity in that they follow the lunar and not the solar calendar. As the rituals of most traditional societies follow the solar calendar, this means the Muslim festivals remain distinct from the traditional rituals. However, many of the traditional rituals often continue to remain in some form even though they are regarded merely as superstitions or traditional customs. Calendar rituals may with time also grow or decline in importance. The celebration of Ascension Day was once an important festival in the Christian calendar, but today it passes almost unnoticed even amongst Christians in Britain.

In pluralistic societies each community tends to celebrate their own religious rituals resulting in a diverse series of festivals through the national calendar. Modern nations may also celebrate distinct days that have little religious significance, such as the celebration of Independence Day or some important event in the life of the 'founder of the nation'. This type of ritual has often been called 'civil religion', and seeks to transcend ethnic and religious boundaries. Their significance lies in the process of nation-building that produces in the lives of its citizens a sense of solidarity and identity as a people.[8]

In his little essay 'Time and false noses', Edmund Leach looks at the way people dress and behave during calendar rites.[9] He identifies three seemingly contradictory types of behaviour. First, there are those rites where people adopt more formal dress and differences of status are clearly defined. Attendance at church on Sunday often used to be associated with wearing one's 'Sunday best'. Second, there is the fancy dress type where the individual instead of emphasising personality and official status seeks to disguise it. Participants wear masks and the formal rules of daily life are abandoned. The festivals of Latin America are a notable example. Finally, there are the relatively rare instances where participants play-act the opposite role. Men dress like women, kings act as beggars, and masters as servants. The European pantomimes during the Christmas period are one example, when the 'Dame' is played by a man, and the 'handsome prince' by a young woman. Leach suggests that rituals have both a formal and a masquerade dimension as two contrasting opposites. Thus the formalities of holy days, or holidays, also have a fun side that may even involve role-reversal. The students' Christmas dinner may, for example, be served by the staff dressed as waiters! Although this may seem obvious and reasonable to people of one society, their behaviour may appear bizarre and even immoral to foreigners.

Transition of situation – rites of crises

Calendar rituals and the rites of passage are, in some way, predictable. However, there are a variety of other events which are not: sickness, disease, war, accident, drought and unexpected death. Secular society deals with these by giving explanations as to how they have occurred. For example, a man is killed in a car accident, and the enquiry shows that it was due to poor brakes on the car. Within a traditional or folk society the question of the cause would be taken further, 'Why was it that this particular man was killed?' 'Why was it him who was walking across the road at this time?' Secular society has no real answer to this type of question apart from that of probability or coincidence that results in a terrible accident. It is an unfortunate situation of two pieces of material trying to occupy the same space at the same time, and no real attempt is made to explain why it occurred but only how.

Traditional and folk societies, on the other hand, seek also to address the question of *why* it was that this particular man was the one killed in the accident. The answer may be that some deity or powers caused his harm, or it may be attributed to witchcraft, sorcery, or some other anti-social activity. If this is the case, balance and harmony must once more be brought to the system, and this can only be achieved through ritual. It is at this time that a religious specialist must be called in who is particularly proficient in handling powers in order to restore the situation. This topic will therefore be explored at greater length when the shaman and witch-doctor are considered in following chapters.

Magical practices are often closely related to religious beliefs and often it is not easy to distinguish between magic and religion. One attempt to distinguish magic from religion was proposed by William Goode. While recognising that there is no sharp dividing line between them, Goode listed eleven criteria by which magical aspects can be distinguished from religious.[10]

1. Magic is more instrumental, aiming at end results of a concrete and material kind.
2. Its goals are specific and limited.
3. It is more manipulative in its techniques.
4. It is directed at individuals rather than at group goals.
5. It is more a matter of private practice than a group activity.
6. It is more susceptible to substitution of techniques – if one does not work another is tried.
7. It involves less emotion.
8. Its practice is less obligatory.
9. It is less tied to specific times and occasions.
10. It is potentially more anti-social.
11. It is used only instrumentally and is not an end in itself.

The issue of magical rituals will be referred to again in chapter 9 when sorcery and magic are discussed.

Understanding ritual

Van Gennep thought that his idea of rites of passage was a universal phenomenon, and his model has certainly received wide acceptance. However, the model is essentially descriptive and does not provide an understanding of the actual function of ritual. A popular theory for the function of ritual has followed the ideas of Durkheim who saw religion as the reinforcement of collective sentiment that results in social integration. This theory provides an explanation of why specific societies hold onto their traditional rituals, and new nations develop civil religion. However, the theory does not fully explain rituals in all societies. Gluckman, who was born in South Africa, and followed in the sociological traditions of Durkheim, questioned whether this theory applied so neatly to traditional societies. It seemed to him that at times ritual did not express the cohesion of a group as much as reveal the conflicts going on within. He therefore undertook a major study of the Zulu of the Natal in the 1930s, and what he came to term their 'rituals of rebellion'.

He wrote of two examples he observed among the Zulu people. The first were agricultural rites traditionally performed by Zulu women at the beginning of the planting season. These rites were fulfilled in honour of the female spirit Nomkubulwana, who was associated with the rains and fertility. These local festivities were performed by local women, and contrasted with the national rites held communally by the kings. (The national festivals fell into disuse after the conquest by the British in 1879.) Gluckman writes that they 'required obscene behaviour by the women and girls. The girls donned men's garments, and herded and milked the cattle, which were normally taboo to them. Their mothers planted a garden for the goddess far out in the veldt, and poured a libation of beer to her. Thereafter this garden was neglected. At various stages of the ceremonies women and girls went naked, and sang lewd songs. Men and boys hid and might not go near.'[11] Gluckman pointed out the marked change in role with the temporary dominant role of women in a society that was strongly patriarchal, and the change of behaviour to lewdness in contrast to their usual modesty. This change of role was believed by the Zulu to be conducive to the social well-being of the community.

The second example was the ritual of *Incwala* that was an elaborate royal ritual extending over many days, and performed annually on the occasion of the first fruits. No-one was supposed to touch certain crops until the rites had been performed, and it was the king who was to touch the fruits first. What interested Gluckman was that during the ceremony many of the sacred songs ridiculed the king. During the rite the king also walked naked in front of the people, while the women wept. Gluckman suggested that this was not simply a ritual of national unity, but an expression of the rebellion against the king. Although Gluckman suggests that these examples may have a cathartic significance, he argued that the acting out of social tension actually enhances social unity. Gluckman's theory has been criticised mainly because he ignores the fact that similar lewdness and transvestism is found in male rituals.

Whilst these integrationalist theories give some explanation of the role of ritual in society, they neglect the actual details of the rituals. Victor Turner built upon the ideas of van Gennep and Gluckman, but moved from considering the mere function of ritual to study its symbolic nature. His major study was on the rituals of the East African Ndembu, and mapped the rich structure of their symbolism.[12] Turner stressed the importance of putting sets of symbols in the total context of the ritual in which they appear. For example, in the case of the Ndembu girl's puberty ritual the girl is lain under a tree for a whole day. The tree is called a *mudyi* tree, which is characterised by the fact that when the bark is scratched it exudes a milk-like fluid. Women explain that this liquid stands for breast milk, and represents the relationship between mother and child. However, whilst observing the ritual Turner realised that it also served to symbolise the separation of mother and daughter, women from men, and even certain groups of women. This was seen in the fact that the mother of the initiate was excluded from the group of women who dance around the motionless girl under the tree. Men were excluded from the ritual altogether, and the whole ritual was controlled by women. When the mother brings out food for the participants at the end of the dance, there is a kind of competition to be the first to take some, because the girl is said to marry into the family of the person who first takes of the food.

Victor Turner studied the transition stage in the rites of passage, which he called the *liminal* period. He argued that during this period people are thrown together as a result of the stress and change of identity, and they undergo a mutual experience he described as *communitas*. This realm is without clearly defined laws, and may be understood as a sort of 'other reality' – the realm of antistructure. Symbols are more than ritual markers or statements about the world, but rather triggers of the liminal condition. For example, in the language of the Kimbu of Tanzania the word *mpingu* has the significance of 'bead necklace'. During the girl's puberty rites, the word signifies not only the beads that are sought by women, but also the children desired by them. It is the context of female puberty and the expectations of motherhood that provide the clue for this symbol. Symbols are, therefore, essentially an appeal to experience. Although these explanations seem very convincing, there has been much discussion as to how far an outsider may interpret the rituals of other societies.

Victor Turner's most well-known study was the Ihamba affliction that was carefully documented in *The Drums of Affliction*.[13] Among the Ndembu of Zambia a tooth of a dead hunter is sometimes kept as an amulet helpful for hunting. However, if the tooth is neglected, so the Ndembu say, it enters someone's body and travels along the veins biting and inflicting a unique disease. This thing is both a spirit and a tooth. It is removed only after a lengthy ritual in which cupping horns are placed on the afflicted area to draw out the tooth. Victor Turner sought to understand ritual in terms of its social and psychological functions, but dismissed the Ndembu view that the real context of Ihamba is spiritual.

His wife Edith, who is also a trained anthropologist, returned to Zambia in 1985 some thirty years after their previous period of research. This time she actively participated in the ritual, and she records how she finally saw the Ihamba come out of a person. This was something that neither she nor her husband had observed before.

Clap, clap, clap – Mulandu was leaning forward, and all the others were on their feet – this was it. Quite an interval of struggle elapsed while I clapped like one possessed, crouching besides Bill amid a lot of urgent talk, while Singleton pressed Meru's back, guiding and leading out the tooth – Meru's face in a grin of tranced passion, her back quivering rapidly. Suddenly Meru raised her arm, stretched it in liberation, and I saw with my own eyes a giant thing emerging out of the flesh of her back. This thing was a large grey blob about six inches across, a deep grey opaque thing emerging as a sphere. I was amazed – delighted. I still laugh with glee at the realisation of having seen it, the Ihamba, and so big! We were all just one in triumph. The grey thing was actually out there, visible, and you could see Singleton's hands working and scrabbling on the back – and then the thing was there no more. Singleton had it in his pouch, pressing it in with his other hand as well. The receiving can was ready; he transferred whatever it was into the can and capped the castor oil leaf and bark lid over it. It was done.[14]

The difference this time was that she was not merely observing the ritual, but was actively taking part in the clapping. The discussion raises some important issues concerning subjectivity, as Edith Turner notes in her book *Experiencing Ritual*. Anthropologists are generally divided about subjectivity. Even those who have an experience will be uncertain about where such a sense impression comes from. Did the mind make it up? There have been a few writers who have tried to discuss the issue. Favret-Saada studied European witchcraft, and argues that in order for the anthropologist to understand the experience it is necessary for them the undergo the ritual.

To understand the meaning of this discourse [the 'gift' of unwitching, 'seeing everything'] there is no other solution but to practice it oneself, to become one's own informant, to penetrate one's own amnesia, and to try and make explicit what one finds unstateable in oneself.[15]

Christianity and traditional ritual

Rituals mark out social categories for a people, and give order and rhythm to life. The important role of ritual in most societies means that when a person converts to Christianity they are confused by a new set of rituals, and question whether they should continue to practice traditional rituals. The two theories of integration and symbolism provide some observations as to the Christian attitude to traditional rituals.

As we have seen, rituals have an important function of integrating a society. Christian rituals therefore not only bring the local community of Christians together, but also unite them to some degree with the wider Christian community. Throughout the world the celebration of Christmas and Easter become important expressions of people's identity as Christians. However, much of the symbolism that is meaningful to a missionary from northern Europe can appear strange and alien in tropical Africa. Major festivals of the world religions have therefore often been adapted by converts with the introduction of a symbolism that is significant for them.

It should not be forgotten by Christians that Christmas and Easter were originally traditional festivals that were transformed to become a central part of Western Christianity. It seems unlikely that Jesus was born on 25 December, but this was the traditional Roman festival celebrating the rebirth of the sun god during the darkest days of winter. With the Christianisation of the Roman Empire in the fourth century, this was a suitable time to celebrate the birth of the Son of God. Similarly, harvest festivals were held by the Angles and Saxons before the time that they were Christianised, and some aspects still remain – such as the corn dolls that are tied on the last sheaf of corn. Traditional festivals have often been transformed into a form more characteristic of the new religion, or the new religion arranged a parallel ritual which coincided with the traditional festivals.

Many Christian missionaries have realised the importance of establishing cultural substitutes with the local church. Amongst the Gonja of Northern Ghana the new yam festival has traditionally been an important festival to celebrate the beginning of the new harvest. This has been contextualized and made part of the life of the church, and Christians now give thanks to God for his gracious provision of a new harvest of yams. In seeking to find suitable substitutes Christians have usually sought to preserve three factors. First, the ritual must be an illustration of Christian teaching through the use of symbols that are relevant to the local culture. Secondly, although the coming of Christianity challenges many social issues, appropriate rituals can strengthen family and social relations. Finally, the rituals allow the people to participate in Christian worship in ways that are particularly relevant and meaningful to them.

Ritual is in some sense a performance or cultural drama. This is not to say that ritual and drama are the same: there are some notable differences, such as the fact that ritual does not just repeat a received script. Schechner classified performance as an axis with ritual and theatre at opposite ends.[16] At one end is 'efficacy' (the ability to effect transformation) and at the other 'entertainment'. The boundaries between ritual and theatre are not fixed, and movement can occur along the line. Ritual can therefore at times move towards entertainment. Ritual must also be appreciated as that which brings colour and enjoyment to life.

The question still remains as to whether Christian converts should participate in traditional rituals. In general, missionaries have usually advised converts to avoid such rituals even at the social cost involved. This has often been condemned by anthropologists, but is this because they have tended to dismiss the efficacy of spiritual powers? The back cover of Edith Turner's book makes a fascinating statement: 'Through her richly detailed analysis, she presents a view not common in anthropological writings – the view of millions of Africans –

that ritual is the harnessing of spiritual power.'[17] For those who actually participate in them, rituals may have more significance than social function and symbolic meaning.

Notes

1 Turner, V. W., *The Forest of Symbols: Aspects of Ndembu Ritual* (Cornell University Press, 1967), p. 19.
2 Van Gennep, A., *The Rites of Passage* (London: Routledge & Kegan Paul, 1977).
3 Personal account from Charlotte Peleake (1984), a missionary working among the Minahasa.
4 Sutherland, A., *Face Values* (London: BBC Publications, 1978), pp. 43–4.
5 Rosaldo, M. Z., *Knowledge and Passion: Ilongot Notions of Self and Social Life* (Cambridge: CUP, 1980).
6 Kreamer, C. M., 'Transformation and power in Moba (northern Togo) initiation rites', *Africa* 65 (1995), pp. 58–78.
7 Achebe, C., *Things Fall Apart* (Nairobi: Heinemann, 1958), p. 37.
8 Kertzer, D. I., *Ritual, Politics and Power* (New Haven: Yale University Press, 1988).
9 Leach, E., 'Time and false noses' in *Rethinking Anthropology* (New York: Athlone, 1971), pp. 132–6.
10 Goode, W. J., *Religion Among the Primitives* (New York: Free Press, 1951).
11 Gluckman, M., *Order and Rebellion in Tribal Africa* (London: Cohen & West, 1963), p. 113.
12 Turner, *op. cit.*
13 Turner, V. W., *The Drums of Affliction* (London: Hutchinson & Co. Ltd, 1981).
14 Turner, E., *Experiencing Ritual* (Philadelphia: University of Philadelphia Press: 1992), p. 149.
15 Fravret-Saada, J., *Deadly Word: Witchcraft in the Bocage* (Cambridge: CUP, 1980).
16 Schechner, R., *Performance Theory* (London: Routledge, 1994).
17 Turner, E. *op. cit.* Back cover.

Chapter Seven

DIVINATION IN A CHANGING WORLD

What happens when something goes wrong? Misfortunes are part of everyone's life, and they usually leave us perplexed and uncertain as to the cause and the appropriate actions to take. Finally a decision is made, and the results have to be accepted whether they be good or ill. How then do people make such decisions? First, common sense tends to be used to deal with the multitude of little matters which confront us every day. The difference between two options may be so small that we hardly feel as though there is a decision to be made because the answer is so obvious. Secular society has refined this approach through the use of management techniques so that people have ways of differentiating between two equal options. However, in most societies people often feel that they need to draw upon additional resources from some non-empirical source, and so turn to some means of divination.

Divination is the general term used to cover the ways in which people seek to determine the origin of a problem, and then to discover the appropriate answer. The important theme within divination, as Victor Turner has shown amongst the Ndembu, is that of 'bringing into the open what is hidden or unknown'.[1] Rose defined divination as 'the endeavour to obtain information about things future or otherwise removed from ordinary perception, by consulting informants other than human'.[2] Some forms of divination occur in all societies. At the simplest are those general customs used by people in daily life, such as a football referee who tosses a coin to decide in which direction the teams will play. In such do-it-yourself type divination, questions are answered almost automatically with a simple yes-or-no answer. At another level are specialists who are called in for the most important incidents, and are presented gifts by the client. The diviner's reputation will increase with his successful divinations, or decline if the people lose trust in him.

Methods of divination

The methods used for divination are many, but all involve some sort of ritual. What one society may use another would regard as being peculiar. However, for the people concerned the means used is taken seriously, and has been passed on from generation to generation. To illustrate the variety of techniques I want to consider those methods used by the Bunyoro of Uganda and carefully described by John Beattie.[3] He has grouped the actual techniques used by Nyoro diviners into three classes. The first involve mechanical means which make use of the manipulation of material objects. The second is the observation of animals under specially prepared conditions. Finally, there is divination by reference to 'spiritual' powers or forces with human attributes.

Mechanical methods

Most societies use some sort of technique that may be regarded as a chance phenomena. Beattie notes seven of these, but there are probably many more. By far the most common is divination by cowry shells (*nsimbe*). Cowries formerly served as currency in Bunyoro, as in many parts of Africa. They usually had their convex side levelled off, so that when they were used as currency a string could be passed through them. A consequence of this is that if they are thrown on the ground they are likely to fall with either side uppermost. The client would come to the diviner, and after the appropriate greetings, he or she would explain their troubles, and put money in the small bowl provided for the purpose. The diviner uses nine shells, which he holds in his left hand. He then holds the shells up to his mouth and asks the shells to divine well before scattering them on a mat spread on the ground between him and his client. Sometimes the client is asked to throw the shells himself. The shells are thrown a number of times, and the diviner interprets the pattern in which they fall at each throw.

There are conventional meanings associated with certain positions of the shells. It is considered good if they fall with the cut-off side up, and bad the other way round. One shell resting on top of another portends death. If they are widely scattered a journey is imminent. If three or more form a straight line the traveller will return safely. Usually the diviner gives his own interpretation, but he is open to clues provided by his clients.

A second method of divination is the throwing of small strips of leather onto a skin spread on the floor. These are about 10 cm by 7 cm, and are often decorated with cowries or beads on one side. Two or three are thrown at a time, and the diviner examines how they have fallen to interpret the answer to the question he has been asked. Third, some diviners use juicy leaves of a plant called *muhoko*. The diviner squeezes the leaves in his hands, and the amount and shape of the deposit are examined. A fourth method is called *Egonje* after a species of banana. The diviner cuts off the stem of a young plant, and places a grain of millet on the exposed surface. If the juice exuded from the stem displaces the grain the prognosis is unfavourable. Fifthly, some diviners use five small twigs, about 7 cm long with the bark peeled off. The diviner holds the bunch of sticks to his mouth and whispers for them to divine well, and then drops them into a basin containing a little water. Once again the pattern that is made is carefully examined.

A sixth method is the rubbing stick oracle. Here the diviner uses a short piece of wood, which he holds between his toes. The stick is moistened, often with the blood of a goat killed for the purpose, and the diviner holds it between his finger and thumb. He then runs his hand up and down the wood until his hand sticks. This indicates the oracle's answer to the question. Finally, a seventh method is a relatively recent innovation, and is said to be particularly practised by Muslims in cases of theft. One practitioner described by Beattie had a small oblong piece of wood that acted like a dice. On all six sides were inscribed Arabic characters. The client was asked to whisper the name of the suspect, and then drop it on the mat. Depending on the sign that falls uppermost, the diviner is directed to a particular passage of the Qur'an. He then reads the passage, and interprets the words as confirming or contradicting the client's suspicions. This method illustrates the appropriation of the symbolic power of a world religion by a society for its traditional purposes.

The theory of these methods is that by some means the 'non-empirical' affects natural aspects of the world order. The diviner is knowledgeable in these signs and so is able to 'read' these by various ritual techniques. This usually requires special knowledge, which is passed on orally, or in some cases is gathered into an elaborate written text. The Yoruba of Nigeria have a complex system of divination known as *Ifa* dependent upon the use of a set of sixteen palm nuts.[4] The diviner (*babalowo*) grasps the sixteen nuts in one hand and tries to transfer them to his other hand in a quick, throwing movement. He cannot throw them all, and some are left behind. If more than two are left behind the throw is discarded. If two are left, he makes a single vertical stroke with his finger in sand on a tray, and if only one is left behind, he makes two vertical strokes on the sand. He makes eight throws arranging his marks in two groups of four. The procedure is complex and varies from one region to another, but the diviner is asking assistance from the spirits.

Augury

In Bunyoro there are two types of augury, the first involving the behaviour of animals, and the second the examination of animal entrails. The first is illustrated by the movement of a small beetle. This is placed on a forked stick that is planted in the ground, and a little of the client's saliva is placed on one branch. If the beetle goes towards the saliva, it is a good sign, and if it moves away from it, bad.

The second form, the examination of animal entrails, is common in many parts of the world, and was used in the Middle East in ancient times. The method was used by the Babylonians as mentioned in the Bible. 'For the king of Babylon will stop at the fork of a road, at the junction of two roads, to seek an omen: He will cast lots with arrows, he will consult idols, and he will examine the liver' (Ez. 21:21). The Bunyoro currently use chickens, but they are said to have formerly used oxen as in other parts of East Africa. This is considered one of the most powerful methods and has to be handled carefully. The client will bring two young birds whose tail feathers have not begun to show. A small amount of the saliva of the client (or sick person if it is a matter of healing) is placed on the beak of the bird. The question is then asked before the diviner lays the bird on some leaves and cuts from beak to tail. The body is carefully opened and the intestines spread and examined. The diviner especially looks for white spots that are considered to present an unfavourable prognosis.

Spirit mediumship

Divination through possession by a god or spirit was known to the ancient Greeks. An outstanding example of this form of divination was seen in the classical oracle at Delphi in which a young virgin became possessed with a spirit and so was able to foretell the future. This is perhaps a similar case to that recounted of Paul in Philippi. 'Once when we were going to the place of prayer, we were met by a slave girl who had a spirit by which she predicted the future. She earned a great deal of money for her owners by fortune-telling' (Acts 16:16).

Bunyoro has a cult of spirit mediumship centred on a pantheon of hero-gods called the *Chwezi*, who are believed to have ruled the country in ancient times. In recent generations the more important spirits for divination have derived from outside Bunyoro and especially the Pastoral peoples who live to the north. One of the most famous of these non-Chwezi spirits is Irungu, the spirit of the bush and of wild animals. In this form of divination the medium becomes possessed by Irungu during a séance. The people congregate in a big semi-circle around the fireplace in the main room of the house waiting until the medium enters dressed in bark-cloth. The man enters and sits on the lap of the old lady who is a member of the spirit mediumship cult. He then begins to shake his rattle and sing some of the songs associated with spirit mediumship. All the people join in singing the songs to encourage the spirit to enter the medium's head. One of Beattie's informants described the séance as follows:

> Then his rattle began to shake very quickly and violently, and suddenly he fell off the old woman's knees where he had been sitting, and fell forward on the ground, where he lay face downwards, with his face buried in his hands. As he fell he flung his rattle away from him. Everyone stopped singing, and there was complete silence. After about ten minutes he began to utter small, high-pitched moans, still without moving from where he was lying . . . So people knew that the spirit had come into his head, and they began to ask him questions . . .
>
> A woman called Kaitamitano said 'my husband hates me, and I do not know why.' The spirit said, 'your husband has another wife besides you.' She agreed. The spirit went on, 'well then, she has made sorcery against you; if you don't take care she will kill you. You had better use your wits and leave your husband and go home,

if you want to be safe.' . . . The spirit which was in Binkamanyire's head answered many more questions, but after about two hours it became evident that it was leaving him. His voice and appearance were returning to normal.[5]

As will be discussed in chapter 10, the method by which possession occurs varies from culture to culture. Some mediums regard silence and meditation as being essential whilst others use dance, rhythm, and noise. A variation on this pattern is that in which a ghost or ancestor is called by the medium and allowed to communicate with the living.

The social context

The variety of methods found among the Bunyoro is not unusual in traditional societies, but it does raise the question of the social role of divination. It was mentioned earlier that divination often seeks answers to deeper questions than the mechanical cause of misfortune. This is illustrated in a discussion, which occurred some years ago, between an African villager and mission doctor.

African: This man is sick because someone worked sorcery against him.
Doctor: This man is sick from malaria because an infected mosquito bit him.
African: Yes, a mosquito bit him, but who sent the mosquito?

The conversation illustrates how the two men were working from two totally different sets of assumptions. An African diviner, however, would seek not only to suggest a cure but identify a cause that often has an origin in malice.

The sickness may be identified as resulting from sorcery, witchcraft or from an offended ghost or ancestor. As a result of

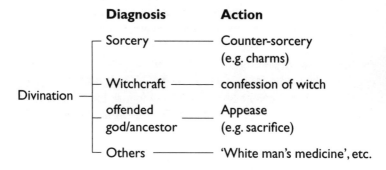

Fig. 3 The patterns of divination, diagnosis and action

the diagnosis the person would be recommended to visit a herbalist, or a witchdoctor, or even the missionary doctor if the sickness is diagnosed as being a 'white man's illness'. The diviner is concerned with an understanding of the total social context of the particular sickness. As Turner explains, 'He acts as a mechanism of redress and social adjustment in the field of local descent groups, since he locates areas and points of tension in their contemporary structures.'[6] In this way sickness is regarded not only as a physical phenomenon, but also as one with its origin within the social context and the wider unseen world. Divination is associated with the sense of danger, and often seems to provide relief. The diviner is therefore often regarded as a sort of primitive therapist who helps relieve the client's indecision and provides conviction that subsequent actions are endorsed in some way by spiritual forces.

Divination, however, is not merely a practical technique to aid decision-making. If it were simply this, it would be difficult to understand why people persist in practising divination when it is sometimes wrong. Divination is a ritual. The client and diviner become part of a ritual performance in which overt expressions of doubts, suspicions and fears are revealed. This can have dramatic quality that is especially striking in spirit possession where the medium takes on the character of the spirit. Beattie argues, 'A Western theatre-goer does not ask whether a play is "true." He asks rather, whether it aptly communicates what it sought to communicate. And, often, divination is a drama no less – perhaps more – than it is a technique.'[7]

For this reason writers such as George Park have proposed a 'sociological' interpretation of divination rather than one that is 'psychological'.[8] In this approach divination is seen as a kind of problem-solving expressing itself in a non-direct way. This is illustrated by an example of divination described by J. Abbink.[9]

> One morning, a woman collapsed in her hut. She had just come back from a small pond outside the hamlet where she had brought the family goats to drink and graze. After being struck down, she could neither move nor speak and in subsequent days she withered away. She was unable to eat or drink properly. Her frantic husband tried all sorts of medicines (traditional herbs and roots, some modern medicine from the nearby government clinic, magical prayers by Amhara people living in the area), but all to no avail.

Finally the husband, Berguwa, called an elder from a neighbouring village who was respected in the art of reading the entrails. When he arrived he immediately obtained a young black-and-white goat. Water was then drunk by the diviner, and sprayed over the goat. The remaining water was then poured over the left hand of the husband, which held the goat. The throat was then slit and the blood caught in a calabash for later use. The intestines were then taken out and carefully spread on the grass. The reading began. Abbink has carefully transcribed from a tape-recording the conversation that took place in Me'en.

Onyai: I see the intestines are clear.
Others: They are, there are no blemishes.
Onyai: Is this the road, is the road good? [pointing to the big arteria jejunale]

Others: This is good. What are these men? [=dark spots near lymphonodi jejunales and a lymphonodum coeliacum on the left side]. They come to here.

Onyai: Here it is clean and white [pointing to the large right side of the mucous membrane]. This must be the rain, the water. It will continue.

Others: It is rain, this is rain, it has not ended yet.

Onyai: The red ropes here [pointing to four red arteriae jejunales between the jejunum and the central part of the membrane], it is rope again, these people will be led away soon, they will leave the Me'en country.

Others: There are ropes, it looks bad, they are going.

Onyai: These three here [three small growths, probably lymphonodi jejunales again, near the small intestines, near the ileum entrance], aren't they good? Are these two [two white ones] the children, aren't they well?

Others: Where? They are white, they are white; and this one, the white with red?

Onyai: The intestines are clean, they are good. The red [pointing to the lymphonodus ileacus], isn't it the hearth [=of the family's compound]? There is no black.

Onyai: No black. It is the woman. The fire is burning.

Onyai: They are well, they are well. Here, this white, there is no evil in her. No bad words touched her [pointing to a fourth white knot, another lymphonodum jejunale, somewhat further from the other three, which might have indicated an eventual curse of a magician].

Others: Is it clean? It's good, no one wants to hit her.

Onyai: These small ones [probably the left jejunum] are they mixed? The white and dark, they are not mixed? No one had died.

Others: The small ones have no problems.

Onyai: The red spots here are very few, and there are none on the roads here [pointing to the largest two connecting arteria on the right side of the membrane].

Others: There is red there only. It is the fire-place isn't it? Is there something else? It may be good, it may be good.

Onyai: The entrails are clear (. . .) Let's proceed with the other things. Let's cast away the blood.[10]

The reading concluded with no clear interpretation made by the diviner Onyai. The general feeling was positive, but Onyai had raised some questions in people's minds. Five days later the woman died. She had never spoken again. Several people including Abbink himself were surprised. Were the entrails wrong? Onyai answered Abbink.

> Listen, I saw the three spots near the small intestines, the home-stead place they call it. One of them had a lot of red. I knew that was bad, but I didn't say anything. I was the only one responsible there. I knew how to 'see' them. I could not take it upon me to predict her death, at that moment. Why should I do that? There would be anger and unrest and people would turn against me. But didn't you see Berguwa's (the husband) reaction? He saw some-thing. The entrails were not lying?[11]

The diviner may have known that the woman was about to die, but he had tactfully left the conclusion to be drawn by the husband himself and others present. Although the acknowl-edged diviners take the lead in interpreting the entrails, they don't claim any firm authority based on their expertise. They allow the discussion to proceed, by so doing they raise pertinent questions, and encourage people to be prepared to take redres-sive action. As Abbink writes, 'They are part of an ongoing "social debate" about community matters, exploring and con-structing the bounds of social praxis.'[12]

Divination in the modern world

Divination is not limited to traditional societies, but is found even in the most sophisticated societies with advanced technol-ogy. Astrologers and various forms of fortune-tellers are common around the world and are an important part of the daily life of many people who would state their allegiance to a major world religion. Why does divination continue? Three reasons may be proposed which give some explanation for the effectiveness of divination. First, delays in making decisions can be both stressful and ineffective. Divination allows a person to make a decision, and this in itself is valuable because in most situations any decision is better than no decision at all. Second, professional diviners are often astute people with wisdom born of experience, and an intimate knowledge of their own people. Frequently, one senses the diviner interpreting the results of a particular ritual to explain and justify a particular course of action. Third, the diviner, like Onyai in the previous example, operates in emotionally charged situations, and the symbolism of his craft strikingly restates the social norms of society. He therefore upholds traditional morality and so brings stability and healing to social tensions. Divination provides a set of rituals, based upon the traditions of the people, to help in the making of decisions. It therefore enables the people to cope with complex situations, and to avoid the nagging guilt when the results would seem to show that a wrong decision was made.

Anyone who has visited the modern city of Hong Kong will have noted the famous Wong Tai Sin temple after which the adjacent Mass Transit Rail terminal is named. Every day the temple is crowded with those seeking guidance from the deity Wong Tai Sin. After first seeking the attention of the god, people then shake a bamboo container holding one hundred numbered sticks. While they are shaking the container, the god causes one of these sticks to rise above the others and fall onto the floor. The fortune associated with each number is graded in a six-step scale, and the number associated to a specific poem. Booklets are available to help interpret the poem to the particular situation, but many people make use of the professional diviners whose huts line the entrance of the temple.

Lang and Ragvald provide an example of the role of the fortune-teller in an urban context.

A female student went to one of the fortune-tellers (a woman) and asked four questions. Her first question was about 'self'. She drew number 47, which the fortune-teller indicated is 'just below average'. The advice: 'Deal carefully, because you are too simple, too honest. Be careful not to be treated badly, because there are many bad people in the world. However, it will be safe to travel abroad.' Regarding 'study', she drew number 85, one of the best. The advice: 'You have a good relation to books, and will graduate from this year of study with excellent results. You will do especially well if instructed by a male professor. You have to study hard. You will have a chance to travel abroad.' Next, she asked about 'love', and drew number 98, characterised as above average. The advice: 'Love will just happen naturally: you don't have to do anything in particular to achieve it. You will find true love next March. Nothing will happen before then, but be patient and wait.' [At this point, the fortune-teller asked her if she was already in a love relationship.] Finally, in regards to 'future', she drew number 99, which is 'average'. The advice: 'You will meet some difficulties and stumbling blocks. Be patient, you will meet someone who can help you. In regards to your future work, it is best to be professional, and best to study arts rather than sciences. In general, your future will be good, and you will overcome the difficulties.[13]

Review the advice given by the fortune-teller: it is evident that she was guided by the content of the associated poem. The last prediction that the student will ultimately overcome difficulties comes from the final line of poem number 99, which says, 'In youth, set yourself goals; [then] nothing will deter you.' However, the fortune-teller also went beyond the poems and gave additional advice. Most of the predictions were general and had a high probability of coming true – most Chinese professors are male. The fortune-teller did make some striking predictions especially about finding love in March. Here, the fortune-teller departed completely from the poem, and took the risk of being proved wrong in the near future. One possible reason was that with a new client, the fortune-teller may be aware of the need to capture the client's attention with a bold prediction and make the fee more worth paying. However, the fortune-teller is also aware that even such bold predictions have a chance of success, and if that occurs the fortune-teller may win a regular client. Among sceptical students the fortune-teller realises that vague prediction alone will not be sufficient.

The coming of Christianity and Western education has had some important effects on the perception of divination. In general, Western education has been a secularising influence on most people, which Max Weber has described as the 'demystification' of society.[14,15] The role of divination has therefore, to some extent been replaced by science, but it has not entirely been rejected and it often continues in a folk tradition. Divination and fortune-telling are often resorted to in times of personal crises.

This raises some significant questions for Christians who can often have the same emotional needs for guidance. The accepted Christian answer is the use of the Bible, prayer, and the prompting of the Holy Spirit. These three aspects are important and the young convert needs to become aware of how to use his Bible, pray and sense the prompting of the Spirit. However, these often appear very abstract and intellectual, and he, or she, may be confused as to exactly what is the will of God. In addition they lack the ritual with which they are more familiar and which gave a definite answer. Christians reading the Old Testament may also be perplexed by some of the provisions made by God for the people of Israel: 'The nations you will dispossess listen to those who practice sorcery or divination. But as for you, the Lord your God has not permitted you to do so. The Lord your God will raise up for you a prophet like me from among your own brothers' (Deut. 18:14,15). The gift of prophecy is very common amongst the people of Israel. During the time of Samuel the prophets were known as 'seers' (I Sam. 9:9), and played an important role in the life of the society. Later, during the time of the classical prophets, the revelations of God were often received through visions (Is. 6:1; Jer. 1:11–13), dreams and even audible voices. In the book of Acts it is reported in numerous places that the members of the church had visions: Ananias (9:10ff.); Cornelius (10:3ff.); Paul (16:9ff.). How do Christians relate what they read to the needs of their own situation?

Abbink's analysis of divination shows how much the methods allow communal discussion in non-threatening ways. Western Christianity may have presented a God who is unable to communicate with human beings except through a book accessible only to the literate, and then with little communal involvement. On the other hand, the Bible also speaks of spiritual gifts that have often been neglected. Perhaps this is why these gifts have become so meaningful in the global expansion of the Pentecostal and Charismatic movements.

Notes

1 Turner, V. W., *The Drums of Affliction* (London: Hutchinson & Co. Ltd, 1981) p. 29.
2 Rose, H. J., 'Divination (Introduction)', *Encyclopaedia of Religion and Ethics,* Hastings (ed.), vol. 4, (Edinburgh, 1911).
3 Beattie, J., 'Divination in Bunyoro, Uganda', in Middleton, J. (ed.), *Magic, Witchcraft and Curing* (Austin: University of Texas Press, 1967), pp. 211–31.
4 McClelland, E., *The Cult of Ifa among the Yoruba* (London: Ethnographica, 1982).
5 *Ibid.* pp. 223–4.
6 Turner, *op. cit.* p. 51.
7 Beattie, *op. cit.* p. 231.
8 Park, G. K., 'Divination and its Social Context', in Middleton, J. (ed.), *Magic, Witchcraft and Curing* (Austin: University of Texas Press, 1967), pp. 233–54.
9 Abbink, J., 'Reading the entrails: analysis of an African divination discourse', *Man* 28 (1993), pp. 705–26.
10 *Ibid.* pp. 712–3.

11 *Ibid.* p. 714.
12 *Ibid.* p. 723.
13 Lang, G. & Ragvald, L., *The Rise of a Refugee God* (Oxford: OUP, 1993), pp. 118–9.
14 Weber, M., *The Protestant Ethic and the Spirit of Capitalism* (London: Allen and Unwin, 1930).
15 Miller, E. S., 'The Christian Missionary: agent of secularisation', *Missiology*, 1 (1973) pp. 99–107.

Chapter Eight

WITCHCRAFT

For most Western people witchcraft is associated with black cats, evil sabbaths, Halloween and blood pacts with the devil. The mere mention of the word 'witch' causes a strong emotive reaction with most people, and yet this very response can cloud our appreciation of what is truth and what is fiction. It is probably the strength of this belief and the fear that it generates that has made the topic of witchcraft fascinating and the focus of much academic study.

The phenomenon designated by the term witchcraft has similar characteristics in many parts of the world, even though it is expressed in different ways. A common starting point for the discussion of this subject is with the observations of Evans-Pritchard among the Azande of southern Sudan. He noted a distinction between witchcraft and sorcery. He wrote: 'There is much loose discussion about witchcraft. We must distinguish between bad magic (or sorcery) and witchcraft. Many African people distinguish clearly between the two and for ethnological purposes we must do the same.'[1] Although this distinction is useful, it is necessary to recognise that in many societies no such simple distinction can be made; however, it does provide a vocabulary to start discussing this complex subject.

Evans-Pritchard defined sorcery, which will be investigated in the next chapter, as a deliberate, conscious act of an individual to harm another by use of non-empirical forces. This usually requires the manipulation of symbolic objects in a ritual performance which is believed to result in malevolent effects. In contrast, witchcraft is essentially the result of an unconscious response of a person towards another that causes harm. In both cases an individual causes harm to another person without recourse to any direct physical assault, and the injured party would have no hesitation in believing that it results from the manipulation of unseen powers. In the past, Colonial Governments in Africa legislated against witchcraft, and missionaries condemned it as evil. Today, most Western-educated Africans are reluctant to speak about this subject to Westerners because they know that they will be misunderstood, and even ridiculed, for what will be called 'primitive ideas'. Even so, throughout the world many people are today still fearful of witchcraft.

The Azande of Sudan

The Azande live in the south of Sudan and across the River Ubangi into Zaire, which even today is one of the least developed areas of Africa. The study by Evans-Pritchard in the 1930s has made them one of the most well-known groups in Africa as far as the subject of witchcraft and oracles is concerned.

Amongst the Azande, witchcraft is seen as the cause of most misfortunes that can affect an individual. Witchcraft can be the cause of sickness, accident, failure of the crops, failure in hunting and general lack of success. For example, if a man is careful to take all the normal precautions, but still wounds himself with his cutlass whilst clearing a field, he assumes that this must be the result of witchcraft. The notion of coincidence, or probability, is not a sufficient answer. There must be an answer as to why it has happened to this individual, and for the Azande, witchcraft is the 'obvious' answer. However, this does not mean that the people are unaware of a technological element to the whole incident. Imagine two people sat under a small food granary, which suddenly collapses killing them. A Western perspective may say that the termites had eaten the supports, which unfortunately gave way while the two men were seated under it. The Azande would say that witchcraft is not necessary for the collapse, but is responsible for the conjunction of the collapse and the people sat underneath. As Evans-Pritchard says, 'The attribution of misfortune to witchcraft does not exclude what we call its real causes, but is superimposed on them and gives to social events their moral value.'[2]

The Azande believe that witchcraft is inherited from one's parents. If a man is a witch, the substance will be passed on to his sons, and likewise a mother to her daughters. The witchcraft substance, called *mangu*, is considered to be a definite physical part of the body which resides near the liver or gall bladder of the person. This substance can be discovered by autopsy, and a crude post-mortem may be performed on the corpse of a person previously accused of witchcraft. With the relatives in attendance, a blood relative of the dead person cuts opens the abdominal cavity to expose the intestines. If no witchcraft substance is found the family rejoices, and put the intestines back into the corpse which is then buried. If, however, the substance is found, the intestines with the witchcraft substance are hung on a tree for all to see. To the question as to what would happen if a father was known not to be a witch, and yet his son is proven to be one?: this can be answered in a logical way; the son was illegitimate.

Although the Azande believe that witchcraft is inherited, other people in Africa have alternative views. The Igbo of Nigeria, for example, believe that witches can infect innocent people by putting a spiritual substance in their food. The person is then open to the influence of the witch, and often develops a craving for human flesh.[3] In Ghana, I have heard a self-confessed witch say that her grandmother gave her a python that now resides in her belly. In most cases a person is reluctant to become a witch, but among the Eggon of Nigeria it can be purchased with cash. The person is then initiated by eating human flesh.[4]

Returning to the Azande, witchcraft can only be dealt with by confession, which is another common aspect of the overall phenomenon. It is therefore necessary to identify the witch, which is why divination is important. The Azande have several means of divination, some of which require an expert while others are more do-it-yourself methods. A common means is the rubbing board in which a smooth wooden block is rubbed over the surface of another board. Whether or not the block slides easily over the surface of the board provides a 'yes' or 'no' answer to particular questions. A more respected means is the use of the Bengi oracle, which consists of administering poison to chicken. As with the rubbing board, Bengi answers in the positive or negative depending on whether the bird lives or dies. When the witch has been identified, a confession is sought. This is never willingly given, but under social pressure the accused usually relents, and offers to 'spit water' in order to cool the witchcraft essence believed to be within her. Only by doing this will the person be free from the accusation of being an active witch, so people usually reluctantly confess.

This ambiguity concerning the nature of witchcraft has lead some Western writers to speak of it as being unreal. Evans-Pritchard himself writes: 'Witchcraft . . . is an imaginary offence because it is impossible. A witch cannot do what he is supposed to do and has in fact no real existence.'[5] However, in talking to the people themselves, one is impressed by the fact that they stress that such things do happen. In some way, they would assert that the soul or witchcraft essence leaves the body, flies in the night and causes harm to others. One must here again recognise the difference between the secular Western and African worldview in the intrinsic nature of human nature. As mentioned in chapter 3, the traditional worldview sees the human body as more permeable with the possibility of the immaterial aspect of human nature leaving the body, and conversely, other elements entering the body. In these terms it is therefore quite logical for the witchcraft essence to both enter the body initially, and later to leave the body at will.

When asking the question, 'Are witches conscious agents when performing these activities?' the answer is almost always given in the affirmative. Most African peoples would believe that these activities are taking place in the spiritual realm, but this does not mean that the activities are illusory. It was to address this criticism of witchcraft being irrational that Evans-Pritchard wrote his famous study. He wanted to demonstrate rationality among Africans. He did this by showing the Azande were asking the question, 'Why did this misfortune happen to me?' The issue is not one of how the misfortune occurred, but why. 'Why did this misfortune have to happen to this particular person?' These are fundamental questions which all religions try to answer in their own ways, and yet for the individual in the midst of a particular crisis the usual answers provided seem remote from his own situation. He is concerned with the immediate situation. 'Why was it that *my* crops failed?' 'Why was it that *my* child died?' Often the answer given is that the event was caused by the activation of evil powers by a person with whom the individual has had bad social relations. Jealousy, spite, and envy within individuals are seen to be the root causes of the suffering and hurt that have been experienced. Evans-Pritchard was therefore able to show that the Azande thinking is no different from that of Westerners, but their underlying assumptions are different.

Witchfinding

Among the Azande a number of measures can be taken to deal with the power of witches. So-called 'medicines' or charms may be prescribed by a diviner, and are worn by the individual, or placed at the door of his house to give protection from witches. A common feature is the activity of the witchdoctor and other witchfinders. Most Western people tend to associate the witch-doctor as being the chief of the witches, and even Colonial Governments used to legislate against him whilst leaving worse people unmolested. The witchdoctor is in fact the specialist to whom one goes when one is suffering harm from witches. He, as it is usually a man, is considered the chief enemy of witches, and is both a respected and feared member of the community. By his supernatural powers he seeks to identify and defeat the powers of witches. Parrinder has described him in the follow-ing way: 'The witch-doctor is not a practising witch, but it is true that he may well have certain affinities with witches. He has something of the same spirit. He has to be like witches so that he may overcome them by his more powerful spirit.'[6]

The witchdoctor would seek to identify the witch in the com-munity who is causing the particular sickness or harm. Often wearing clothes of bark-cloth, or leaves, he will dance to the beat of drums and rattles, until his spirit identifies the witch to him. Almost always those who are identified as witches are women, in contrast to the fact that witchdoctors are almost always men. The accused is often a close relative of the afflicted person, such as the co-wives of a polygamous marriage, or wives of different men living in the same compound. Jealousy is often at the heart of the matter, and in a small community the witch-doctor is usually aware of the sentiment towards the victim.

Although witches are believed to be 'conscious agents', most people accused of such activities are surprised. However, the line between wishing ill of a person or dreaming that one is hurting a person, and that of consciously being aware of witch-craft activities can be very blurred. For example, a wife becomes very angry with her co-wife, and soon she becomes ill. If the first wife is identified as a witch, does it not seem possible that the first wife may even herself believe the accusation to be true?

For the afflicted to be cured the witch must often confess her sins. Some of the confessions can be very explicit, as seen from these gathered from the Ga people: 'I have killed 50 people including my own brother.' 'I have taken the womb of another woman.'[7]

Why do people make such confessions? First, because once a person has been accused of witchcraft they are considered to remain a danger to society until they have confessed. However, once a confession has been made and the appropriate actions taken, the person will be accepted back into society, and the sick person believed to get well. Thus, it is frequently easier to accept the diagnosis than remain under suspicion. Secondly, in all communities there are those people who live on the margin of the society, such as old widows and those with mental illnesses. Often such marginalised people become the scapegoat in a society when problems occur, and they may confess out of fear. Thirdly, there are also those people obsessed with the fear of becoming witches, and so they readily confess when diagnosed as such by the witchdoctor. A comparable attitude is found in most societies in which certain people, out of a neurotic fear of becoming sick, cling to the healer.

The causes of witchcraft

The deep-seated belief in witchcraft has been the topic of much discussion by social anthropologists, who have proposed several theories about why witchcraft exists in some societies. During the 1940s and 1950s the functionalist explanation was common. This analysis was based upon the idea that a social institution exists to fulfil some essential needs of a society if it is to survive. Max Gluckman proposed such an explanation by viewing society as a dynamic balance of forces.[8]

> Some societies are prone to witchcraft beliefs, others are not . . .
> Where social interaction is intense and ill defined there we may
> expect to find witchcraft beliefs. Where human relations are sparse

and diffuse, or where roles are very fully ascribed, we would not expect to find witchcraft beliefs.[9]

In order to examine this theory, Nadel compared two pairs of African societies.[10] Each pair showed a wide range of cultural similarities, but some marked differences especially relating to witchcraft. The two pairs were the Nupe and Gwari of Northern Nigeria, and the Korongo and Mesakin of the Nubian mountains in Central Sudan. For brevity, reference will only be made to the second pair in order to illustrate the nature of the argument.

The Korongo and the Mesakin are neighbours living in the same environment, and although they speak different languages they are often bilingual. They have a similar economy, political organisation, and religious beliefs and practices. However, the Korongo have no witchcraft beliefs at all, while the Mesakin are obsessed by fears of witchcraft and witchcraft accusations. Nadel writes:

Mesakin witchcraft is believed to operate only between maternal kin, especially between a mother's brother and sister's son, the older relative assailing the younger. Mesakin witchcraft further operates only if there is a reason, some legitimate cause for resentment or anger; and the latter is almost invariably a quarrel over the 'anticipated inheritance'. . . In both tribes the mother's brother must see in this insistent demand a reminder that he has definitely grown old; not only has he by then probably begotten children (which fact would merely announce his declining youth), but he has now a ward sufficiently old to claim his 'inheritance', that is, a gift explicitly anticipating the donor's impending death. Now, among the Korongo the older man is prepared for the gradual decline of age and accepts its onset, which coincides with sex life, with good grace or at least without struggle; furthermore, since among the Korongo the anticipated inheritance can be postponed, the mother's brother may by then be an older or old man also in the physical sense.[11]

In this case witchcraft beliefs relate to specific anxieties and stresses arising in social life. Nadel concludes:

> In brief, the witchcraft beliefs enable a society to go on functioning in a given manner, fraught with conflicts and contradictions which the society is helpless to resolve; the witchcraft beliefs thus absolve the society from a task apparently too difficult for it, namely, some radical readjustment. But from the observer's point of view it is doubtful if this is more than a poor and intellectual palliative or can be called a solution 'less harmful' than open hostility or even the break-up of the existing institutions and relations.[12]

The equilibrium model does give many insights into the operation of certain kinds of relationships, but it tends to play down the negative consequences. This view suggests that witchcraft beliefs exist because a society requires stable social relations, and not because people are trying to explain misfortune.

A more recent analysis sees witchcraft as operating within the context of social instability. Rapid social change disrupts the balance within society, with some becoming more wealthy and others feeling marginalised. Famine or economic distress can lead to a resurgence of witchcraft accusations. One example is the emergence of anti-witchcraft shrines in the Gold Coast in the 1920s and 1950s. Both were periods that knew economic crisis after previous periods of wealth through the cocoa production in the region.[13] Fear of witchcraft increased and many resorted for protection to many anti-witchcraft shrines that suddenly sprang up in many parts of the country. Margaret Field, who studied the anti-witchcraft cults in the Gold Coast in the 1950s, examined the personality disorders of those who confessed to witchcraft. She found that depression was the commonest mental illness of Asante rural women, and nearly all such patients came to the shrines to confess witchcraft. She is taken at her word that she has done harm. Field proposed that depressed women take on guilt for the entire community and feel that they are responsible for all the misfortune that occurs.

Stephen Hayes more recently writes: 'Over 200 people who were accused of being witches were burnt to death in South Africa between the beginning of 1994 and mid-1995. These killings were not legal executions, but took place at the hands of lynch mobs, mostly from the communities in which the accused lived.'[14] He concludes that this increased fear of witchcraft is as a result of the social tensions that have been experienced in South Africa in recent years. Bawa Yamba made a similar observation in a recent study on witchfinding in Zambia in the face of HIV transmitted disease and AIDS.[15]

A recent analysis of African witchcraft treats the resurgence of witchcraft as a movement against the post-colonial state and protest against the influence of modernity and market economics. Comaroff and Comaroff write: 'Witchcraft is a finely calibrated gauge of the impact of global culture and economic forces on local relations, on perceptions of money and markets, on abstraction and alienation of "indigenous" values and meanings. Witches are modernity's "typical malcontents".'[16] Despite the prominence given to the world economy, the underlying thesis is that a rise in belief in supernatural causation occurs in times of misfortune and uncertainty.

Conflict theory provides another approach to the existence of witchcraft. Certain categories of persons are particularly open to accusations of witchcraft because of their social position and their relationship with other persons. In small-scale societies accusations of witchcraft are often treated as a personal matter involving individuals or small groups, and require the reconciliation between parties through confession. However, in situations where there is a marked degree of power, as with a king, witchcraft is treated as a very serious offence that is condemned by the whole community. The emphasis is then on the punishment of the guilty, and witches are likely to be killed. Sanders argues:

In early Modern Europe political regimes persecuted witches in order to demonstrate their legitimacy and their control of the legal process. When small-scale societies are undergoing drastic, unpopular change, religious movements may arise whose leaders may blame the new social problems on witches. In contemporary industrial societies particular groups have more secular ideologies, and the 'witch', while endowed with mystical attributes, is not portrayed as overtly magical.[17]

It is obvious that these theories are not mutually exclusive. Societies that are facing social stress for whatever reason may often look for scapegoats to blame, and a witch is a common figure. Those societies that are already dysfunctional will be more open to such accusations. Within these societies individuals who are facing the greatest pressure may become depressed and accept the responsibility for the communal misfortune. This is not limited to traditional societies, but similar expressions can be seen in most societies. As Sanders writes:

In my examination I have taken the view that the witch, as an individual effectively propagating misfortune by mystical means, does not exist. And yet clearly there is a sense in which he or she does exist. Our cases involved real people who were identified with this mystical offence . . . Consequently, in most societies some individuals accuse other individuals of witchcraft, in a continuously recurring process. Whether or not other persons believe their accusations is influenced by cultural beliefs and social factors. And sometimes we have witch-hunts, where the leaders or representatives of social groups seek out witches in their name. This is a process that can explode again and again in human society.[18]

Christian attitudes to witchcraft

Even in Europe the concept of witchcraft has been known from earliest times. The Germanic peoples who spread throughout Europe during the decline and fall of the Roman Empire were known to believe in witches and sorcery. With the coming of Christianity to the Germanic peoples from the fourth century onwards, all other religions together with every class of magic were condemned. In 690 AD, Theodore of Canterbury legislated against those who sacrificed to demons or used divination. Witches, diviners, and adulteresses were to be driven out of the land by the laws of Edward (901 AD). Charlemagne condemned witchcraft as evil and passed the death penalty for those who practice such. The position of the Church was stated at the little known Council of Ancyra in the ninth century.

> Some wicked women, reverting to Satan, and seduced by the illusions and phantasms of demons, believe and profess that they ride at night with Diana on certain beasts, and with an innumerable company of women, passing over immense distances, obeying her commands, as their mistress, and evoked by her on certain nights . . . Therefore, priests everywhere should preach that they know this to be false, and that the Evil Spirit, who deludes them in dreams, sends such phantasms. Who is there who is not led out of himself in dreams, seeing much in sleeping that he never saw waking? And who is such a fool that he believes that to happen in the body which is done only in the spirit?[19]

The parallels between the notion of night-flying to cause harm in African witchcraft and in the European tradition are apparent. However, this statement of the Church that night-flying is illusory did not stop the belief in such events. Folk belief in witchcraft, nocturnal gatherings and werewolves persisted, and even grew stronger in the minds of the ordinary people. Contact with Arabic culture as a result of the Crusades introduced studies such as alchemy, and astrology produced a new interest in what has been called 'natural magic'. This also resulted in many positive new ideas that led to the Renaissance. However, it was also to lead to a reaction against heretics and it was this that was eventually to cause the Church to change her views against witchcraft. This is carefully analysed by Keith

Thomas in his important work, *Religion and the Decline of Magic*. He concludes: 'It was only in the late Middle Ages that a new element was added to the European concept of witch-craft which was to distinguish it from the witch-beliefs of other primitive peoples. This was the notion that the witch owed her powers to having made a deliberate pact with the Devil.'[20]

It was a decree of Pope Innocent VIII in 1484 which opened the door to the change of position, and was to lead to witch-crazes throughout Europe. This decree allowed two Dominican friars, Heinrich Kraemer and Johann Sprenger, to expiate witchcraft in Germany, and two years later these men produced the text *Malleus Maleficarum* (The Witches' Hammer).[21] This was an encyclopaedia of demonology in which witches were condemned not for the harm they may cause to others, but because they were devil worshippers – the greatest of all here-sies. It is difficult to chart the developments of the beliefs through the next four centuries. However, the pact with the Devil came to be a central issue, and this has led to the definition of a witch that is still held by English law today. It originates from Sir Edward Coke who defined a witch as 'a person that hath conference with the Devil to consult with him or to do some act'.[22]

Witch-crazes had arisen in various parts of Europe prior to the decree, especially when people were faced with some notable disaster. The Black Death which spread across Europe from 1346 to 1351, and which killed at least a quarter of the population, led many to look for scapegoats. Jews were com-monly blamed, along with those branded as witches. Following the decree of 1484 the Inquisition spread through many parts of Europe, and it is estimated that some nine million people died in Europe accused of witchcraft. The Reformation saved Britain from the worst of the persecution, but one of the great-est English witch-finders was Matthew Hopkins who was most influential between 1642 and 1649. His method of ascertaining guilt was by 'pricking' which meant that a person was pricked with a needle all over their body to find the insensitive spot produced by being touched by the Devil. Accusations of night-flying, practice of the 'Black Mass' at nocturnal gatherings, and sexual perversions were common. Animal familiars were another common feature of this period.

Confessions were an essential part of witch-finding, in the same way as was noticed in Africa. Torture was common during the witch-crazes, and people were subject to the rack, thumb-screws, and branding. Trial by ordeal was also known, as with the ducking-stool. Trickery was also used: people were promised a light pilgrimage if they confessed, and they died burnt at the stake still confessing their innocence. At the height of such panics people were executed at the testimony of a single person who claimed that they had bewitched him. The last execution for witchcraft in England was at Exeter in 1648, but in Scotland and in other parts of Europe the executions continued into the following century. The famous Salem witch trials of 1692 are usually regarded as the end of the period of witch-craze in Europe. The discovery of trade routes to the New World and to Asia opened up new opportunities. Technological developments began to occur which were to result in the modern secular worldview. Witchcraft was rejected as mere superstition, and the notion of the witch became a figure of fun – an old woman with a black pointed hat riding on a broomstick with her black cat.

Comaroff and Comaroff have shown that most of the missionaries who came to sub-Saharan Africa from Europe in the nineteenth century were imbued with a secular perspective especially with regards to witchcraft.[23] According to Western missionaries, sickness and disease were caused not by witchcraft, but by bacteria, parasites and viruses. A cure was effected by Western medicine and education. Witchcraft was considered not to exist, so Christians should ignore it. Where Christianity became the dominant force in a region, this view was outwardly accepted, but often belief in witchcraft was merely driven underground. The Azande in Sudan, for example, are today mainly Roman Catholic, but they still have a great fear of witchcraft. The previous accounts from Zambia and South Africa, both countries that have significant Christian communities, further illustrate the point.

One of the reasons that witchcraft beliefs continue is that they not only have negative effects in a society in causing fear and accusation, but they also have a positive element. Fear of accusation of witchcraft controls certain anti-social behaviour, and encourages social responsibility. No one person wants to stand out as wealthier than the others in the village in case they are accused of being a witch. However, if the person becomes a Christian and totally rejects witchcraft beliefs, he or she might acquire greater individual wealth whilst neglecting social responsibilities. Looked at in this way witchcraft has been seen as a sort of safety valve that releases social pressure. Christian conversion does not mean that witchcraft can be totally ignored in a society that traditionally has a strong belief in witchcraft.

A second position that has been adopted by Christian missionaries, mainly from Pentecostal churches, is that witchcraft is demonic and the accused needs to be delivered. This direct engagement of witchcraft in the form of a power encounter is also often seen in the African Independent Churches (as will be described in chapter 15). Today, among the Charismatic churches in Africa, and many other areas of the world, witchcraft is dealt with by vigorous prayer leading to the exorcism of the spirit. Witchcraft is perceived as one of the manifestations of the work of Satan in the community, and it is part of the spiritual warfare that the Christian is obliged to fulfil. This is considered as a direct encounter between the power of God and that of evil. Public confession of sin is required after which the person is encouraged to receive the cleansing blood of Christ and the enduing power of the Holy Spirit.

More recently, Harriet Hill – a missionary who worked for

many years in Ivory Coast – has proposed a third option.[24] She argues that witchcraft concepts correspond to what in the West are regarded as psychic powers that may be dealt with by living a pure life. 'It can therefore be considered neutral in the same way that intellectual power, physical power, and emotional power are accepted as neutral. We do not automatically assign them to God or to the devil . . . If this is an accurate assessment of witchcraft, then we need to speak out against the evil use of witchcraft rather than against witchcraft itself. The key message, then, is, love thy neighbour, live a pure life, and renounce evil in all its forms. Do not give Satan a foothold . . . In the end, then, we find we are no different from our African brothers and sisters after all. Do we not all struggle with jealousy, envy, and hatred?'[25]

The sadness of the whole situation is well illustrated in the following story reported from Mwanza in the north of Tanzania:

It was only two days later that we came across Carolina, who lives in a ramshackle hut on the fringe of the village. She told her story with tears in her eyes. She had lived in the family homestead surrounded by sons, daughters-in-law and grandchildren. Her workload had become lighter in accordance with her age, and she was loved and respected by her grandchildren. One day tragedy struck – the latest addition to the family, a baby boy, died suddenly. The distraught parents, desperately seeking a reason for the death, felt increasingly that 'another hand' had been involved. The mother started muttering darkly about her mother-in-law, Carolina.

The next step was routine: they went to consult the local *mpiga ramli* (diviner, or 'witch doctor'). Having listened to their story, he uttered a series of incantations and shook his rattles, then made a decisive cut into the chicken that the bereaved couple had brought.

'Look! You see the furrow here? And this spot here?' he said peering into the innards. 'It's your road, and your house. I see someone dark, not tall, perhaps an older woman . . . Who lives in this house just here?' he demanded, indicating another blob. 'Why

. . . it's my mother's house,' stammered the father. 'There you are, I told you so!' shrieked his wife.

Within hours it was common knowledge that Carolina had been accused of killing the child. The old woman felt she could no longer live with her family, particularly her daughter-in-law, who could hardly bear to look at her any more; so she fled to a hut on the edge of the village.

Carolina's life is now one of hardship and misery. She has no contact with her family and beloved grandchildren, no one helps her cultivate her fields, or fetches water for her from the distant well. And if she ventures into another village, many people she has known since they were children melt away or turn their backs on her.

'It would be better to be dead,' she sobs quietly. This is no idle comment, however, since her all-too-probable fate will be to become another of the victims of witchcraft murders. One night a gang of youths armed with machetes will creep up to her house. Then she will be another statistic that the local radio station can no longer be bothered to report.[26]

Notes

1 Evans-Pritchard, E. E., *Witchcraft, Oracles and Magic among the Azande* (Oxford: Clarendon Press, 1976).

2 *Ibid.* p. 70.

3 Parrinder, G., *Witchcraft: European and African* (London: Faber & Faber, 1970), p. 141.

4 Danfulani, U. H. D., 'Exorcising witchcraft: the return of the gods in new religious movements on the Jos Plateau and the Benue regions of Nigeria', *African Affairs* 98 (1999), 167–93.

5 Evans-Pritchard, *op. cit.*

6 Parrinder, *op. cit.* p. 182.

7 Field, M. J., *Religion and Magic of the Ga People* (London: Oxford University Press, 1961).

8 Gluckman, M., *Customs and Conflict in Africa* (Oxford: Blackwell, 1959).

9 Douglas, M., *Witchcraft: Confessions and Accusations* (London: Tavistock Pub., 1970), p. xxxv.

10 Nadel, S. F., 'Witchcraft in four African societies: an essay in comparison', *American Anthropologist* 54 (1952), pp. 18–29.

11 *Ibid.* p. 23.

12 *Ibid.* p. 29.

13 Field, M. J., *Search for Security* (London: Faber and Faber, 1960).

14 Hayes, S., 'Christian responses to witchcraft and sorcery', *Missionalia* 23 (1995), p. 339.

15 Bawa Yamba, C., 'Cosmologies in turmoil: witchfinding and AIDS in Chiawa, Zambia', *Africa* 67 (1997), pp. 200–23.

16 Comaroff, J. & J., *Modernity and malcontents: ritual and power in postcolonial Africa* (Chicago: University of Chicago Press, 1993), pp. xxvi-xxix.

17 Sanders, A., *A Deed Without a Name* (Washington D.C.: Berg, 1995), p. 7.

18 *Ibid. pp.* 211–2.

19 Parrinder, *op. cit.* p. 19.

20 Thomas, K., *Religion and the Decline of Magic* (London: Penguin Books, 1971), p. 521.

21 Kramer, H. & Sprenger J., *Malleus Maleficarum* (London: Arrow Books, 1986).

22 Thomas, *op. cit.* p. 524.

23 Comaroff, J. & J., *Of Revelation and Revolution: Christianity, Colonialism and Consciousness in South Africa* (Chicago: Chicago University Press, 1991).

24 Hill, H., 'Witchcraft and the Gospel: insights from Africa', *Missiology* 24 (1996), pp. 232–344.

25 *Ibid.* p. 337.

26 Kibuga, K., 'Letter from Tanzania', *Guardian Weekly*, 28 October–3 November 1999, p. 17.

Chapter Nine

SORCERY AND MAGIC

The word 'magic' appears to have its origins in ancient Persia where the Magi were a class of priests. The word was adopted into Latin as *magia* from which it became part of many European languages with both positive and negative connotations. Magic was often associated with healing, but it also was considered to have evil and antisocial dimensions where it was labelled as 'Black Magic'. It was with the Protestant Reformation and the growth of modern science that all magic came to imply a hotch potch of superstitions, charms and spells. However, in many parts of the world it still is a major concern as the following newspaper report shows.

Football fans in the central African state of Congo were hurling accusations of witchcraft at each other yesterday after a freak blast of lightning struck dead an entire team on the playing field while their opponents were left completely untouched. The bizarre blow by the weather to all 11 members of the football team was reported in the daily newspaper *L'Avenir* in Kinshasa, the capital of Congo. 'Lightning killed at a stroke 11 young people aged between 20 and 35 years during a football match,' the newspaper reported. It went on to say that 30 other people had received burns at the weekend match, held in the eastern province of Kasai . . . 'The exact nature of the lightning has divided the population in this region which is known for its use of fetishes in football,' the newspaper commented.[1]

Anthropologists have essentially expanded this common view as illustrated by a definition given by John Middleton.

> Most people in the world perform acts by which they intend to bring about certain events or conditions ... If we use Western terms and assumptions, the cause and effect relationship between the act and the consequence is mystical, not scientifically validated. The act typically comprises behaviour such as the manipulation of objects and recitation of verbal formulas and spells. In a given society magic may be performed by a specialist.[2]

All definitions have their limitations, and in this case the use of the word 'mystical' is unhelpful. Mysticism is the direct experience of the divine, and has little to do with magical rituals that occur in the midst of the problems of daily life. Even so, Middleton's definition provides a useful starting point from which to understand magic and sorcery. As was noted in the previous chapter, sorcery is often considered to differ from witchcraft in that it is a deliberate conscious act of an individual, or group of individuals, to harm another by non-empirical means.

There is always a tension in anthropology between the desire to understand cultural phenomena in context (using local words and concepts), and the comparative approach that uses broader terms. The terms 'witchcraft' and 'sorcery' must be considered as broad labels that cover a range of overlapping phenomena that are perceived in various ways. These phenomena are characterised by motives of jealousy and envy, and seek to cause harm by non-empirical means. There is always secrecy about such matters, and a reluctance to talk about the methods. There are, however, many stories about the effects of sorcery, and it is often difficult to distinguish fact from fiction. Either way, in traditional societies the fear of sorcery is very real and evident, which means that the psychological effect upon the people concerned is great. One cannot merely ascribe the consequences of sorcery purely to psychosomatic disorders.

Because magic is a technique, it is possible for anyone with some knowledge to use it to either help or harm. Most people, however, only have a vague idea of the rituals, but everyone is aware of the need to correctly perform such rituals if they are to be effective. For this reason, a person would make use of an individual recognised as being skilled in the arts of magic when they are in need. For a price, the practitioner will perform the necessary rituals. Success will enhance his reputation within the community, whilst failure will be explained away or go unnoticed.

A man once had a cow on whose milk he relied for his food and livelihood. One day the cow stopped giving milk, and the man knew that a witch had cast a spell on it, either by means of some mantra or with his evil eye. So he went to a Tantric guru and asked for help. The guru said, 'I can help you with your problem, but you must answer this: What do you want more, to catch and punish the witch or make the cow give milk again?' The cow owner considered his words carefully because he knew he had to be truthful.

'Both, Swamiji. I want the milk, and I also want to punish the witch.'

The guru was unhappy with the answer and insisted that only one choice was possible, so the man chose milk.

The Tantric guru gave him some herbs over which he has cast a mantra and told him to burn these under the cow's nose. Then he added, 'The cow will give you milk, but the first milking will produce yellowish and poisonous milk, so throw it in the river.' The man did as he was told and got his milk back.

One day when the man was sitting with Swamiji, a neighbour came in and complained about severe pains. Swamiji examined him thoroughly and finally said:

'You have been coveting the property of your neighbours instead of being satisfied with what you have. Go home and avoid even looking at your neighbour's things, and your trouble will disappear.' The man nodded gratefully and left.

'You see?' said Swamiji to the milkman. 'There was no need for revenge. His own actions took revenge on him.'[3]

The local people marvelled at the power of the swami to both heal and demonstrate justice with one simple act. The Western observer may consider the swami as cleverly using an opportunity to enhance his reputation. The curing of domestic animals by smoke inhalation is a common practice throughout India.

The complex that is here considered as sorcery may be considered in three aspects: the 'evil eye', the evil word (or curse), and the evil act (magic ritual).

The evil eye

According to Brian Spooner the main regions of the world in which the evil eye is common are North Africa, the Middle East, the Indian sub-continent, and southern Europe.[4] The fact that the concept is found within each of the major religions of the region (Islam, Hinduism, Christianity, Judaism and Zoroastrianism) suggests that it pre-existed them all. Alan Dundes describes the evil eye in his article 'Wet and dry, the evil eye'.

> The evil eye is a fairly consistent and uniform folk belief complex based upon the idea that an individual, male or female, has the power, voluntarily or involuntarily, to cause harm to another individual or his property merely by looking at or praising that person or property.[5]

All over the Muslim world the evil eye (*nazar*) is considered to be a frequent cause of misfortune. According to Arab proverbs, 'The evil eye empties the house and fills the graves'; 'One half of mankind die from the evil eye'; 'The evil eye owns two-thirds of the graveyard'.[6] So firmly is the belief held in North Africa that if a person looks at another's animal and shortly afterwards it dies, he is held responsible for the loss. The eye is regarded not only as an instrument for transmitting evil wishes, but also as an originating source of injurious power. This power need not be a voluntary act, but can work automatically from a person desiring something of another. Thus, a man blind in one eye is assumed to be envious of another man with two good eyes, and a barren woman would be envious of a woman with many children. The danger is considered to be even greater if it is accompanied with speech which expresses admiration or envy. A mother would feel great fear if a European woman was to smile at her baby and compliment the mother on a lovely baby. This may be normal practice in Europe, but in north Africa it could be regarded as the exercise of the evil eye.

In North Africa, not everybody is considered to have the power of the evil eye, and some people may have it in higher degrees than others. For example, persons with deep-set eyes and eyebrows meeting over the nose are regarded as particularly dangerous. Blue eyes are uncommon in the Muslim world, and so often leave an uneasy impression. Women are particularly liable to suspicion, especially if they are behaving in ways outside the cultural norm. Individuals passing through a rite of passage are particularly vulnerable, as would be expected from the earlier discussion of rituals (chapter 6). Amongst the Berbers of North Africa, a person would not eat in the presence of another who did not have food. The envious look of the hungry person may mean that the eater would take poison into his body as he eats. Even a dog present when a person is eating would be given a morsel to prevent it covetously looking at him.

People use many means to protect themselves from the evil eye. One approach is to use some manner of ruse to counteract the influence. A child may be left unwashed, or a child may be dressed in rags, or a baby boy may be dressed in girl's clothing.[7] Amongst the Pukhtun of Pakistan a black spot made of kohl powder is placed upon the child's face.[8] All these things will make the child less attractive, less open to envy, and so divert the evil eye. Another means of protection is the use of charms of which there are a great many in the Muslim world. Charms made of iron, or the claws of a tiger or a bear, are thought to be able to resist the influence of the evil eye by some inherent property of the material itself. Other objects, such as bones or cowrie shells are of no value in themselves but serve to catch the eye and avert the covetous look. One of the quickest methods of protection is the hand itself which when the fingers are stretched is considered an effective means of protection. The number five, as signified with the spread fingers, is also a common symbol of protection. Muslim women often wear a charm that has the hand of Fatima: an open hand with an image of an eye on the palm. The symbol of the eye itself is regarded as having great power in throwing back evil, and it is often used in patterns and designs.

The Qur'an is another important means of protection in the Muslim world. A charm may be made by writing words from the Qur'an on some material which is then kept in a locket or leather bag. The Qur'an recognises the effects of the evil eye as seen in sura 113.

> In the name of God, the Merciful, the Compassionate
> Say: 'I seek refuge in the Lord of Daybreak
> from the evil of that which He created;
> from the evil of the darkness when it gathers,
> from the evil of women who blow on knots,
> from the evil of the envier when he envieth.'[9]

Knotting pieces of thread and blowing on objects are common in black and white magic rituals throughout the Middle East.

The belief in the evil eye was most likely the heritage of pre-Islamic folk belief which the Arabs had in common with other Semitic peoples. However, the belief in the evil eye has been found outside the Middle East and North Africa. For example, amongst the Mexican migrants into Texas one finds the belief in *mal ojo* – evil eye. Children are believed to be especially susceptible to this misfortune for they lack the spiritual strength of an adult. If a child's illness is diagnosed as being due to the evil eye, the parents will review those who have admired the child during the day and decide which one sent the affliction. That person is then sought out and asked to touch the child on the head. This action is believed to remove the power that the admiring look sent into the child and returns the patient's body to its normal state.[10]

The curse

The concept of uttering curses or blessings appears universal amongst human societies. To appreciate the concept behind these oral expressions it is necessary to realise that, in the traditional worldview, words are not merely viewed as vibrations in the air. Words, which are said deliberately with intention take upon themselves a reality of their own which can bring about the desires of the speaker. India especially has developed an elaborate cosmology of sound in the use of mantras that are considered as effective words that establish a relationship between the cosmos and the magician.

The effectiveness of the curse is dependent upon several factors: the intensity of the desire for the wish, the manner of its expression, and the personality of the curser. Behind the spoken word stands the personality of the one who expresses the words. The greater the personality of the speaker, the greater will be the effectiveness of the spell. Thus, if a god, or his devotee in his name, utters a curse the effect will be very great indeed. This is reflected in the Old Testament passages in which God says to Adam, 'Cursed is the ground because of you' (Gen. 3:17). The curse here is God's judgement against sin. The potency of the word is seen in many of the healing miracles of Jesus, and also in the cursing of the barren fig-tree (Mark 11:14,20,21).

For this reason, calling upon the name of a deity often strengthens a curse or blessing. These may consist of pleas, commands, and threats designed to persuade or coerce the spirit to do the speaker's bidding. They may also make use of certain traditional secret words and phrases considered to be of great power. The following spell has been recorded amongst the Muslims of Malaysia and was recited when a person buried a wax image of an enemy:

'Peace be to you! Ho, Prophet 'Tap, in whose charge the earth is,
Lo, I am burying the corpse of somebody,
I am bidden (to do so) by the Prophet Mohammed,
Because he (the corpse) was a rebel to God.
Do you assist in killing him or making him sick:
If you do not make him sick, if you do not kill him,
You shall be a rebel against God,
A rebel against Mohammed.
It is not I who am burying him,
It is Gabriel who is burying him.
Do you too grant my prayer and petitions, this very day that
     has appeared,
Grant it by the grace of my petition within the fold of the
     Creed La ilaha.'[11]

Some people believe that a curse may also be increased in its effectiveness by using some simple ritual. A common practice in West Africa, for example, is the licking of certain medicines prior to the utterance. These are often contained in an animal horn, and most sorcerers would have such a horn. Amongst the Yoruba of Nigeria the curse (called *epe*) is believed to be one of the commonest causes of psychiatric disorder. The results may be immediate or may not appear for several days, depending upon the power of the medicine used and the defences of the victim.

With *epe*, the man does what he is told to do. He may hang himself or run about the market showing his penis (or her vagina), or he may lay hold of a machete, and run about attacking people. He doesn't talk rationally or see spirits; he does what he is told to do. *Epe* may take nine days to work . . . *epe* is like a slow poison.[12]

The relationship of the curser to the cursed is also an important factor in the effectiveness of the curse. In many societies the curse of a parent upon a child is considered the worst form of curse. Amongst the Karimojong of Uganda, the curse of an elder upon a young warrior is considered to be of greatest force. In both these cases, the possibility of cursing strengthens the authority structures within the society and stabilises the social structure and values.

The effectiveness of a curse may be removed in many ways. Charms may offer protection, but if the curse is stronger they will be overcome and the person will need to go to a healer who himself may be a sorcerer. Raymond Prince described such a Yoruba healer. 'One healer showed me his pair of horns, both filled with a solid black medicine that protruded from the top of the horn; one was a cow's horn and showed evidence of constant use, for the black medicine was worn away in the shape of his mouth; the other was a twisted antelope horn, and thrust into the medicine were a cobra fang and a pin made he said of copper and lead. To use it, he pulls out the pin and rubs it over the tip of his tongue, then whatever he says will come to pass. I have reason to believe that the former horn is the one he uses for patients, and that the latter is for *epe* (curse), but the healer vehemently denied it.'[13]

The efficacy of a curse is also commonly believed to be influenced by the guilt or innocence of the person on whom it is pronounced. A North Africa proverb illustrates this: 'A curse without a cause does not pass through the door.' Many societies even believe that if a curse is undeserved it may recoil onto the curser himself. A blameless life is the greatest protection against the power of the curse. 'Like a fluttering sparrow or a darting swallow, an undeserved curse does not come to rest' (Prov. 26:2).

Another style of curse is that which is conditional. In other words, the person calls down some form of evil upon himself or another if they fail to fulfil a particular promise. A plea for innocence may be of this form: 'May God strike me dead if I did this act.' A person may also make a vow before a particular deity or person promising to offer a sacrifice if the request is granted, and accepting punishment if they fail to fulfil their promise.

Magic rites

In most traditional societies, an unusual death, sickness or misfortune is believed to be the result of black magic or sorcery. This frequently makes use of curses, but some ritual often accompanies this. There are several elements that are common to this form of sorcery in most societies.

The first is the need of 'labelling' the victim. The sorcerer will often use a substance that has been in contact with the victim, e.g. hair, excreta, clothing. He may also name the person so that there is no error in identity. This is considered to be a way of opening a passage through his defences. Janice Reid describes the importance of this aspect amongst the Yolngu, an Australian Aboriginal people. 'When the victim goes to the toilet someone may take his excrement and put it in the fire. His stomach will blow up like a football. Occasionally a person may take another's soiled clothes or underpants – particularly those soiled by his sweat or urine – make a fire inside a hollow log, put these inside and seal it. The victim's body will swell until the flesh inside is soft. When the skin is touched it leaves an impression. The victim is hot. He can't bear clothes. He will soon die.'[14]

This illustrates a second principle, which is that the sorcerer will carry out a ritual which tends to demonstrate that which he wants to occur. These rituals are usually models or pictures of the desired effects. The voodoo doll is one of the most commonly known examples of this form of magic. In this case a wax image of the victim is made by the sorcerer. Then with the recitation of certain curses pins are pushed into the image. As the pins are pressed into the image it is believed that a similar hurt will affect the victim himself.

Finally, the power is believed to be derived either from certain spirits who are summoned or from certain powerful medicinal substances. An example described by Raymond Prince from the Yoruba illustrates this. 'You take the hair of a man's head. You prepare medicine and put it with the hair and put them both in an ant hill. As the ants are circulating about the medicine, so the victim will feel it inside his head or you may put the medicine and the man's hair under an anvil, and every time the blacksmith strikes the anvil so he will feel it inside his head.'[15]

A healer will use similar methods to those used by the sorcerer to cause the victim's sickness. The healer only succeeds in obtaining a cure by the use of his powers and knowledge because it is greater than that of the sorcerer. Writing of the Yolngu people, Webb expresses this dichotomy. 'In East Arnhem Land there are two classes of magicians or medicine-men. Members of the one, whose operations arc wholly of an evil character, are known as "ragalk", while members of the other, whose operations are always of a benign character are known as "marrngit".'[16] A kind of warfare exists between the forces which do good and those which do harm to man.

Why does the belief in magic persist?

When confronted by magic, most Western people question whether it really works. In a technically sophisticated society it seems difficult to believe in magic – as illustrated by Janice Reid who, after her years of studying Yolngu sorcery, wrote: 'An axiom of the ethnographic enterprise is that sorcery is not "real" in any empirical sense, or, if it is, performed . . . it does not actually harm the intended victim.'[17] However, even she is not free from the perplexity raised from the study of this phenomenon. She realises that she was brought up with one set of assumptions about the nature of reality, and the Yolngu with another. She writes, 'My short answer to the question, "Do you believe in sorcery?" is usually, "Not when I'm in Sydney".'

Marwick, in his pioneering study of sorcery among the Cewa of East Africa, states that there is a widespread belief that sorcerers injure and kill people by putting magical substances (*majkhwala*) into the food or drink of their victims. His observations showed that Colonial Administration had an influence upon Cewa views. 'It is doubtful whether Cewa originally distinguished between poisoning and sorcery. They have to now, however; for, though it is a public duty to report a case of murder-by-poisoning, it is an offence in terms of the Witchcraft Ordinance to accuse anyone of sorcery. In effect, Cewa have come to recognise that the Administration believes in one type of sorcery, viz. poisoning. They therefore now distinguish between "visible magical substances", which they hope will impress the Administration, and others that will probably not. Despite this emphasis on poisoning, enquiries I made of the Health Department revealed that very few cases of it are brought in to hospitals or dispensaries.'[18]

Marwick's study confirms the insights of Evans-Pritchard on the Azande mentioned in the previous chapter: '. . . beliefs in mystical evil-doers explain the course of events by relating the occurrence of misfortune to disturbances in the moral relationships between persons'.[19] He argues that accusations of sorcery amongst kin can increase during times of social change. In the 101 cases he studied, about one quarter focused on modern objects of competition such as cattle, money and other property. The norms defining new relationships, such as those between unrelated fellow employees, produce conflicts that are sometimes expressed in accusations of sorcery.

Christian approaches

Christian missionaries have generally applied similar approaches as those discussed for witchcraft in the previous chapter. Sorcery and magic were either seen as issues which will decline with education, or were accepted as genuine phenomena. In the latter case, various principles were drawn from the Bible.

Firstly, Christians are adamant that the use of sorcery is explicitly forbidden amongst the people of Israel. 'Let no-one be found among you who sacrifices his son, or daughter in the fire, who practices divination or sorcery, interpretation of omens, engages in witchcraft, or casts spells . . .' (Deut. 18:10,11). 'You shall not allow a sorceress to live' (Ex. 22:18). The Old Testament uses a variety of words to describe various magical practices. Today it is not possible to exactly know what were the original forms of magic employed, but the use of so many terms demonstrates the fact that all forms of magic were forbidden. The Hebrew word translated sorcerer is *ksp* which comes from the root meaning 'to cut', so probably refers to herbs cut for the making of charms and spells. The Hebrew term translated 'casts spells' has the idea of binding in the sense of making amulets. The most striking reference to this form of sorcery in the Old Testament is found in Ezekiel 13:18,20,21: 'Woe to the women who sew magic charms on all their wrists and make veils of various lengths for their heads in order to ensnare people . . . I am against your magic charms with which you ensnare people like birds and I will tear them from your arms; I will set free the people that you ensnare like birds.' This would suggest that a form of ritual magic was being employed in which the sorceress was symbolically binding the victim in a knot with the result that he would become sick and die.

Secondly, although the Bible recognises the power of magic, it is not something which should cause the Christian fear. The power of God is continually seen to be greater than that of the sorcerer. This is seen in the case of Moses and the Egyptian magicians (Heb. *hrtm* meaning 'chief priest', the title borne by the greatest magicians). The Exodus record says that the magicians copied Moses in turning their rods into serpents, in turning water into blood, and in producing frogs (Ex. 7:11–8:20). They failed, however, to perform any of the other acts. Numbers chapters 22 and 23 record the incident in which Balak commissions Balaam to curse the People of Israel: 'Now come and put a curse on these people, because they are too powerful for me' (Num. 22:6). This is a typical form of malevolent magic. Balaam however was not able to effectively curse those whom God had blessed. 'How can I curse those whom God has not cursed?' (Num. 23:8,20). Balaam was only able to bless or curse according to the will of God.

Thirdly, many Christians are convinced that the New Testament shows that converts who have been involved in magic should destroy the paraphernalia they have used. A frequently quoted example is that of Paul on his visit to Ephesus where the sorcerers were famous for a particular form of charms known as 'Ephesian letters'. These were scrolls on which certain magic phrases were written, and were believed to provide the owner with safety in his travels, children to barren women, and success in love. Of the Ephesians, it is written: 'Many of those who believed now came and openly confessed their evil deeds. A number who had practised sorcery brought their scrolls together and burned them publicly' (Acts 19:18,19).

Fourthly, Christians should be aware of the social context of witchcraft and sorcery. It has already been mentioned that frequently those accused of being witches were people at the fringes of society, such as an old widow living on her own, or minority groups. The accused were usually from minority groups who become 'scapegoats' for the social tensions. The Christian message should result in the restoration of social harmony through reconciliation and mutual acceptance.

Mary Douglas tells a sad story of the Roman Catholic mission working among the Lele of the Republic of Congo.[20] The mission had associated the god of the Lele with Satan of Christian traditions. Whereas before they had believed in one god, the universe now seemed to be controlled by two deities, one good and one bad. The priests of the old religion, including the herbalists, were classed as sorcerers and all seen as

Satan's servants. As most of the younger people had been baptised in the church and educated in the mission schools, the youth increasingly derided the traditions of their parents and grandparents. This resulted in a tension between younger and older generations. Newly ordained Catholic priests began persecuting the practitioners of the traditional religion. Eventually the mission began to run its own anti-sorcery cult to detect and expose all sorcerers. The practice of the movement resulted in physical abuse and accusation of the old, the handicapped and mentally defective. When the anti-sorcery activities came to the attention of the Bishop he promptly suspended the young priests from their duties and sent them overseas for two years. Douglas concludes with a significant warning.

> Contemporary Western theology is not attuned to answering the questions that plague Africans about the causes of evil in the world, the causes of sickness and death, questions which their pagan traditions answer all too plausibly in terms of sorcery. On this there is a block, or a gap, a pregnant silence.[21]

Fifth, for a person who believes that a curse or witchcraft has been done to them it is insufficient to dismiss the matter as being either imaginary or without consequence. The person needs to be reassured that their God has the resources to overcome the powers of evil. Does this however mean that some Christians are advocating the reality of spiritual power as embodied in an object or phrase? This has been the subject of many debates among some Christians, under the rubric of spiritual warfare. Charles Kraft identifies the heart of the matter when he distinguishes between spiritual power being seen as *conveyed* in cultural forms, and power that is thought to be *contained* in cultural forms. He writes,

> Words, anointing oil and other items that might be used only *convey* . . . the power with which the spirit being (whether God or Satan)

that stood behind them invests them. They do not, contrary to the perception of animists themselves, *contain* that power. Our critics need to learn the difference between the empowerment of words and objects that God and, unfortunately, Satan gives their followers the authority to convey and the magical concepts that things may possess power in and of themselves.[22]

Notes

1 Tanner, M., *The Independent*, Thursday 29 October 1998.
2 Eliade, M., (ed.), *The Encyclopedia of Religion* (New York: Macmillan, 1987), vol. 9 p. 82.
3 Glucklich, A., *The End of Magic* (New York: OUP, 1997), pp. 39–41.
4 Spooner, B., 'The evil eye in the Middle East' in Maloney, C. (ed.), *Evil Eye* (New York: Columbia University Press, 1976), pp. 76–86.
5 Dundes, A. 'Wet and dry, the evil eye', in Dundes, A. (ed.), *The Evil Eye: A Casebook* (London: Garland, 1981), pp. 258.
6 Westermarck, *Pagan Survivals in Mohammedan Civilizations* (London: McMillan, 1933), p. 24.
7 Bevan Jones, V., *Women in Islam* (Lucknow: Lucknow Publishing House, 1941), pp. 359–60.
8 Ahmed, A. S., & Hart, D., *Islam in Tribal Societies* (London: Routledge & Kegan Paul, 1984).
9 Arberry, *Koran*, vol. 2, p. 362.
10 Madsen, W., 'Value conflicts and folk psychotherapy in South Texas' Kiev, A. (ed.), *Magic Faith & Healing* (New York: Free Press, 1974), p. 426.
11 Endicott, K. M., *An Analysis of Malay Magic* (Oxford: Clarendon Press, 1970), p. 91.
12 Prince, R., 'Indigenous Yoruba psychiatry', in Kiev, A. (ed.), *Magic, Faith & Healing* (New York: Free Press, 1974).
13 *Ibid.* pp. 99–100.
14 Reid, J., *Sorcerers & Healing Spirits* (Canberra: Australian National University Press, 1983), p. 43.
15 Prince, *op. cit.* p. 90.
16 Reid, *op. cit.* p. 57.

17 Reid, *op. cit.* pp. xix.
18 Marwick, M. G., *Sorcery in its Social Setting* (Manchester: Manchester University Press, 1965), p. 75.
19 *Ibid.* p. 281.
20 Douglas, M., 'Sorcery accusations unleashed: the Lele revisited, 1987', *Africa* 69 (1999), pp. 177–93.
21 *Ibid.* p. 189.
22 Kraft, C. H., 'Christian animism or God-given authority?' in Rommen, E. (ed.), *Spiritual Power and Mission: Raising the Issues* (Pasadena: William Carey Library, 1995).

Chapter Ten

SPIRIT POSSESSION

It was past midnight, and the Saharan sky was devoid of moon or stars. The desert winds scattered sand and dust in eyes, nose, ear, and mouth. Shadowy figures arose from mats, clutching at voluminous robes, sleepily weaving their way across the village among rocks and goats to the compound where there was to be a possession performance. Asalama, the woman in trance, sat silently in a shimmering white blouse as kerosene lamps flickered in the background. Slowly she arose from beneath a blanket and began swaying from side to side to the sounds of singing and drumming. Her motions became more rapid, and the audience praised her dancing. She then danced wildly, throwing herself from one side to the other, remaining seated all the while, until she flung herself to the ground, exhausted.[1]

The first question that most Westerners ask when they are first confronted with possession is whether spirit possession is a reality or merely some psychological problem. In practice, the phenomenon is common among most societies, and especially so in traditional societies. The former illustration comes from the Tuareg of the Sahara, and illustrates many of the issues common to the experience of possession. One study in the 1970s showed that in a sample of 488 societies in all parts of the world, 437, or 90 per cent, had some form of possession-phenomenon. Many popular books have focused upon the descriptive elements, so frequently the dramatic details of the practice obscured the major issues involved. This is especially true in a cross-cultural situation where the outsider can easily misinterpret behaviour as exotic and bizarre.

In recent years most anthropologists have taken a relativist position, so that possession is seen as a culturally normative experience. Thus, possession must be accepted when the people concerned consider they are possessed and their community endorses this claim or even initiates it. Thus, Stewart writes:

> It matters little whether manifestations of possession are in reality due to physical or psychological abnormalities or whether they are artificially induced by auto-suggestion. The essential factor in possession is the belief that a person has been invaded by a supernatural being and is thus temporarily beyond self-control, his ego being subordinated to that of the intruder.[2]

Although the anthropologist may be willing to accept this position, many in the medical profession and Christian missionaries find such a position insufficient. Unlike the anthropologist, the medical practitioner may be called upon to heal a person, and this requires him, or her, to try and understand the situation in terms of his own profession. However, in a cross-cultural situation the position of the anthropologist provides the most useful starting point. Within the complexity of possession phenomena, the only way to gain an understanding is by accepting the local perception of what is happening. Later, the medic may try and explain the situation in his own terms, but the distinction between what the people believe and what he may interpret it as being must be clearly held.

Spirit possession can be regarded as a variety of complex phenomena with various expressions. In the following two chapters, possession will be considered from two perspectives. The first perspective will consider possession as an affliction. Possession by an intrusive spirit is rarely welcomed in the initial stages, especially as it often results in sickness or loss of control in which the individual is shaken and convulsed. Societies often consider that the spirit has to be appeased and exorcised. A second dimension is when the individual gains control over the spirit and uses the ability to heal. The term 'shaman' has often been used to identify this role.

Turning first to examine the role of possession as an affliction on an individual, it is necessary to explore the wider social context.

Possession in social context

Possession has been widely researched in north-east Africa, and the writings of Lewis on the Somali have provided the basis of considerable discussion. Lewis has argued for the so-called 'deprivation theory', which regards possession rituals as a disguised attempt at self-assertion on the part of marginalised sections of the community and especially women. These possession phenomena that develop within the marginalised community Lewis called 'peripheral cults' as opposed to 'central cults'.

The Somali are pastoral nomads who would call themselves Muslims. This public cult is almost exclusively dominated by men, who hold the main positions of religious authority and prestige, and women are considered merely passive agents. In this male-dominated society spirit-possession is regarded as one cause of a wide range of illnesses ranging from slight debility to acute organic illnesses. Lewis identifies four fairly well-defined contexts.

The first context is illustrated by a girl who has been jilted by a boy she loved and who promised privately to marry her. The symptoms are extreme lassitude, withdrawal, or even physical symptoms, which are attributed to possession by the object of her affection. Similarly, a young man who is forced by the over-riding control of his elder kinsman to renounce the girl he loves and marry another may evidence similar symptoms. Lewis provides the following explanation:

> My own interpretation is virtually the same as that offered by young educated Somalis themselves. In the case of the jilted girl, no other institutionalised means is available to express her outraged feelings ... Her private emotions and feelings are of little concern in a jural world dominated by men. Illness and the associated care and attention offer her some comfort.[3]

The second context is that which is attributed to bouts of hysteria to which young camel herdsmen are sometimes prone. The camels are usually herded by unmarried youths, and in the dry season are required to take their camels many miles away from their homesteads and the women. In the dry season the herdsmen move monotonously looking for pasture and water, constantly in fear of attack from enemies and wild animals. In the wet season, the herding communities can draw closer to the homestead with its comforts and the possibility of meeting girls of marriageable age. At this time, the young herdsmen sometimes develop symptoms of hysteria attributed to possession by *zar* spirits. This is regarded as a temporary form of madness and is not taken very seriously.

The remedy is provided by arranging a dance called 'beating the *zar*', in which it is essential that girls should attend if the youth is to recover. The songs that are sung often have implicit sexual connotations, but the virginity of the girls is carefully guarded. Today, it is said that young men often feign such symptoms to indicate the girl of their choice who is especially invited to the dance. In modern slang 'beating the *zar*' is a synonym for sexual intercourse.

A third context of possession among the Somali is perhaps the most significant, and that is the case where a married woman is the victim of the *zar's* malevolent attention. The situation here is that of a hard-pressed wife struggling to survive and feed her children in a harsh environment, and often subject to prolonged absences from her husband, and sometimes the subject of jealousy as her husband plans to marry a second wife. The *zar* is considered to cause a whole variety of ailments whether accompanied by physical symptoms or not. The *zar* usually demands luxurious cloths, perfumes and delicate foods from the husband. It is only when these demands are met, as directed by the female shaman, that the symptoms are expected to disappear.

> What the wives call *zar* possession, their husbands call malingering, and they interpret this affliction as yet another of the deceitful tricks employed by women against men. Men support this charge by alleging that the incidence of the disease is much higher among the wives of the wealthy than among the poor. This insinuation women in their turn counter with the sophistry that there are some *zar* sprites that attack the wealthy and others that molest the poor.[4]

Depending upon the marital circumstances, the husband usually reluctantly accepts one or two such bouts. If this situation becomes chronic and the wife becomes a regular member of a *zar* cult he may beat her and finally divorce her.

The final context of Somali possession primarily concerns adult men who are struggling to bear the pressures of society. The *zar* are not only considered as especially deadly, but also particularly religious. As a result of describing the social context of these various forms of possession Lewis concludes:

> These four contexts of Somali spirit-possession are connected by the common themes of confinement and frustration, which occurs in different ways in all of them. This is perhaps most evident in the case of the aggrieved wives, where, to adopt current phraseology spirits enter the 'sex-war'.[5]

Not all have agreed with the theory of Lewis. Boddy, in a study of possession in the Sudan, agrees that this possession is mainly in the province of women. About 40 per cent of women in the town in which she worked claimed a *zar* affliction, and most of them were between the ages of thirty-five and fifty-five.[6] By contrast, only a handful of men publicly acknowledged to be possessed. However, Boddy argues that the villagers do not understand the sexes as being engaged in any war, but as a dialectic relationship of disparate parts.[7]

Another example of deprivation is illustrated from a totally different area of the world. Chuuk is the most populous state of the Federated States of Micronesia. Francis X. Hezel SJ recounts the following story of a young women who is possessed by an ancestor:[8]

An incident involving Fermina, the 15-year old daughter of devout Christian parents, is rather typical. One evening a few years ago she went to bed complaining of a pain in her stomach. By the next morning her body was twitching uncontrollably and she was seized with convulsions. As the family gathered around her mat to comfort her, they heard her suddenly reprimand a much older male relative, angrily telling him 'Leave the house, because I don't like what you are doing.' The words came from Fermina's mouth, but the voice was that of her mother who had died a year or two earlier. Fermina recovered within two or three days of the incident, but she has had similar experiences a few times since this one.

The Chuukese people believed in three classes of spirits: gods, nature spirits and ancestors. Before converting to Christianity they used to believe that each individual had a good spirit and a bad spirit. At death the bad spirit would remain around the grave, frightening those who live nearby. The good spirit however had the power to roam more widely, but would eventually go to its abode in the sky. This spirit is usually well disposed to the family, but if the family caused offence it could cause problems. This is what happened in the case of Fermina, and many similar cases reported by Hezel.

In each of these cases the victim was thought to be possessed by the spirit of the dead relative. A change in voice often signals that the woman is 'possessed'. As Hezel notes, this does not mean that everyone in their family accepts their possession as genuine. He mentions one case in which the father of the victim slapped her and accused her of faking the possession. Whether all of the family accepted the authenticity of the possession or not, everyone immediately recognised the role that the woman was assuming, and she was defined as a 'possessed person'. For the Chuukese, one of the most dramatic and telling signs of possession is the change in voice that occurs when the spirit begins to speak. Although the change in persona is usually quite brief, lasting only a few minutes at a time, the entire seizure may range from days to weeks.

Possession among the Chuuk is an ancient cultural practice, but in recent years it has been mainly women who have exhibited the phenomenon. Hezel argues that with the contraction of the extended family some important female roles in family affairs have been lost. The opportunities for women to share in corporate decision-making within the family have diminished, and possession allows one means by which a young woman may forcibly express her views. Possession draws attention to the plight of the afflicted woman and the family comes together in her sickness. 'If spirit possession is therapeutic for the person possessed, it is often just as much so for the family. The voice of the spirit does what few members of the family would dare to do; it brings out into the open family tensions that may have been festering for weeks or months and, in drawing explicit attention to these, often hasten their resolution.'[9]

Healing and exorcism

If a particular society believes that a sickness is caused by spirit intrusion then the only cure is the expulsion of the spirit by exorcism. Therefore, in these societies there are often exorcists who both know the appropriate rituals, and claim to be endowed by a more powerful spirit. Among the Shona, for example, a common means of exorcism is by transferring the spirit from the patient to an animal such as a sheep or a fowl. The animal is then driven into the woods, taking with it the spirit which has caused the sickness. This 'scapegoat' approach is one which is common in many forms of exorcism. Another method used by the Shona is that in which the patient is taken to a crossroads where pronouncing a spell exorcises the spirit. The spirit leaves the person and remains at the crossroads to afflict some other passer-by.[10]

Among the Ngbak-Mandja of the Central African Republic, the healer becomes possessed by his gods whilst singing appropriate songs, shaking his rattles and directing his musicians. He calls to his gods, 'Come and help me cure the sickness!' and threatens the spirits in the person, 'If you try to come back into her and poison her again, you shall all die!' Here is an example of what Rouget has termed peaceful coexistence: let both sides stay in their own place.[11]

These stories show some similarities with the account of the Gerasene demoniac recorded in Mark chapter 5. Jesus recognises, as did the local people, that this man's sickness is due to spirit possession. The spirits clearly recognise the greater power present in the person of Christ, but it is notable that the spirits are not merely dismissed from the man. A process of artful bargaining then ensues. As Duncan Derrett, an anthropologist, remarks, 'Without the bargaining we should not have known whether the man was a lunatic, fanatic, etc., as opposed to a subject of possession.'[12] He goes on to stress the fact that many similar events have occurred in exorcisms recorded by anthropologists throughout the world. The spirits are finally transferred to the herd of pigs, and the death of the pigs confirms the complete deliverance of the man from the power of the spirits. What is notable is that no blood is shed, so this cannot be regarded as being in any way a sacrifice to appease the spirits. Neither does Jesus make any capital out of the successful exorcism.

Possession cults

In the forms of possession that have been described above the affliction is identified and dealt with appropriately. Exorcism may provide relief from the affliction for a period, but it may be that the bouts become chronic and the person needs to be treated in another way. An alternative treatment is that the person is initiated into a possession cult.

In the region of Sudan in which Boddy was living, the people had their own reasons why women were more vulnerable to spirit attack. One reason was that spirits were attracted to women, and especially married women because they are the ones who use henna, perfume, soaps, and wear fine jewelry. A second explanation was that the potentially weakest point is the vaginal meatus, so women need to take great ritual precautions. A third reason is that women have greater contact with the impurities of daily life such as blood and faeces, dust and sweat. Another characterisation of women often mentioned is that they lack sufficient moral strength to uphold the ideals of Islam.

Men are reputed to hold to the orthodox view that spirits can and must be dislodged from the body by force. By contrast, women maintain that *zar* cannot be rid of at all, and no Islamic or Western medicine can effect a cure. Symptom remission alone can be achieved, and only if the person agrees to hold a propitiatory ceremony on behalf of the *zar*. During the ceremony the possessed enters into a contractual relationship with the spirits responsible for her sickness. As a result of drumming and singing the person goes into a trance state and the *zar* enters the body of its host, where its identity can be affirmed and the demands revealed. In return for certain offerings and observances, the spirit agrees to restore its host to health. From then onward, the host and *zar* are joined in continuous but unequal partnership. The spirit remains above her, able to exert its influence or infiltrate her body at will.

In possession cults the individual therefore comes into a working relationship with the afflicting spirit. The individual remains free from the recurring sickness so long as the person takes part in the periodic cult festivals. During these festivals the person becomes possessed by the spirit, which acts out its particular character. The person needs to be initiated into the cult. In the course of time the person may graduate to a position in which she is in full control of her own spirit, and is capable of controlling and healing others with similar afflictions.

Another example of this type of cult is that of *Sopono*. *Sopono* is a Yoruba name for a family of smallpox spirits which include a range of sicknesses far wider than that implied by the word smallpox: fevers, boils, rashes, and psychoses. The initiation, which is secret, is reported to take twenty-one days. The initiate is taken to the shrine dressed in a white cloth. She enters the shrine backwards, and after calling the Sopono spirits the woman would finally become possessed by the spirit that had 'born her'. For the next three weeks the girl remains at the shrine, and every morning she is washed, and sacrifices made on the third, seventh, fourteenth, and twenty-first days.

It is during the annual festival that the members of the cult become possessed by the particular spirits that 'chose' them on the first days of their initiation. These rituals have a festive mood with most of the village in attendance. Raymond Price vividly described the actual possession.

> They placed one of the sacrificial bowls upon the girl's head, and the (cult) women began to sing louder, calling upon the spirits of the particular Sopono that habitually possessed this girl. The girl's face became vacant, and her eyes focused upon a distant place. Suddenly she fell forward in a kind of swoon; the 'mother' supported her; someone else seized the calabash so that it wouldn't fall; others threw water on her feet. In a few seconds she revived a little; they guided her fingers up over the rim of the calabash, and she was drawn to one side, where she stood, somewhat dazed, the 'wife' of the god.[13]

The roots of Voodooism, as will be discussed in chapter 15, initially derive from the people of West Africa who were taken as slaves to the West Indies. For this reason one finds a number of characteristics common to the cults of Africa, and the marital theme is even more developed in the cults of Haiti. The person who wishes to secure the permanent protection of one of the *loa* (spirits) may make a formal proposal of marriage. Once the marriage has been agreed the *loa*'s duty is to watch over his wife, but he must be given presents in return. Some human spouses make up a separate bed for their spirit and sleep on it on the allotted night.[14]

Possession cults are generally associated with music and dance especially, it seems, in producing the initial trance state. Music has often been thought of as endowed with a mysterious power of triggering possession, and the musicians know the secret. It is true that music and rhythm have a complex and important role in possession cults. Rouget, after a detailed study of such possession cults, suggests that music has the following three roles.[15] First, at the level of ceremony music creates a certain emotional climate for the adepts. Second, music leads the adepts to a heightened state of imagination in which the identification with the spirit becomes more manifest. Third, it provides the adept with the means of manifesting this identification through movement and so exteriorising the trance. 'It is at the last stage that music is indispensable. Why? Because it is the only language that speaks simultaneously, if I may so put it, to the head and the legs; because it is through music that the group provides the entranced person with a mirror in which he can read the image of his borrowed identity; and because it is music that enables him to reflect this identity back again to the group in the form of dance.' For Rouget, there is no mystery in the power of music, it merely allows the socialisation of the ritual.

It has already been shown that many of these cults relate to the religious beliefs of the people before the coming of the world religion to which they would now acknowledge allegiance. The Hausa of Nigeria, for example, are Muslim, and yet the 'bori' cult is an important one amongst the women. The traditional religion of the Hausa was displaced from the public realm of society which is dominated by men. 'Women became possessed by the old gods which their men had discarded.'[16]

Although it is true that in such rituals there is always some degree of acting on the part of the participants, these rituals cannot just be regarded as merely interesting cultural ceremonies. For the Christian, possession contradicts the very dignity of humanity as created by God, and robs the people concerned of their integrity and self-respect.

Christian responses to possession

The attitude of Christians has changed during the period of the missionary impact on traditional societies. Birgit Meyer has made a study of the concept of Satan among the Ewe Christians of the Evangelical Presbyterian (EP) Church of Ghana.[17] She argues that the missionaries arriving in the nineteenth century brought the concept of Satan and identified it with Ewe traditional religion with the attendant notions of witches and spirits. Thus although the missionaries intended to abolish the old religion, they actually made it an element of their Christian faith. Although witchcraft was denied and dismissed as superstition by the educated church leaders, as it was by the Western missionaries, it remained the basic belief of the ordinary church members. Thus, although spirits and witchcraft has never been part of the curriculum of denominational theological colleges in Ghana, it was still a major issue of concern for the majority of members.

The African Independent Churches that arose in the 1920s and 1930s accepted spirit possession and witchcraft as a real phenomenon that needed to be dealt with by the power of prayer. The prophets cast out spirits by means of prayer, holy water and the Bible. This was undoubtedly one of the major reasons that these new churches attracted many illiterate people. In the 1950s and 1960s, the Pentecostal missionaries found a similar response as they ministered to people they considered to be possessed.

Within the Roman Catholic Church Emmanuel Milingo, the Archbishop of Lusaka, Zambia from 1969 to 1983 had a remarkable healing ministry. It was in 1973 that he gained the reputation as a spiritual healer. According to Milingo this occurred when a woman consulted him about her baby who, although physically healthy, she persistently regarded as non-human. After trying every pastoral means to help her with no success, he suddenly became aware of God speaking to him.

> I contemplated various ways of helping the woman when suddenly an idea glowed in my mind: look three times intently into her eyes and ask her to look three times intently into yours. Tell her to close her eyes the third time and order her to sleep. Then speak to her soul after signing her with the sign of the cross.[18]

The woman was subsequently made well, and Archbishop Milingo became convinced that God had given him the gift of healing through the power of the Holy Spirit. 'From then on I discovered that I could help thousands and thousands of people under obsession or bondage of evil spirits.' He began to hold frequent public healing sessions, and people possessed by evil spirits sought his help. However, his healing ministry attracted much controversy, and in April 1982 he was summoned to the Vatican after a papal investigation. Gerrie Ter Haar argues that Milingo accepted the views of the common people of Zambia, and in so doing undermined the central authority of Rome.[19] This is analogous to Lewis' model of Central and Peripheral cults.

Gerrie Ter Haar and Stephen Ellis have made a study of the many letters received by Milingo, and these give evidence that a large number of Zambians, including town-dwellers, believe in the reality of spirit possession, and attribute their misfortune to it. They argue that both Church and state have failed to address the issue.

> The Milingo affair indicates that the Church itself, which enjoys good relations with the government for the most part, is not perfectly equipped to deal with popular spiritual needs. The case of Milingo shows that the Church does have the potential to deal with these, but is unwilling to do so because of the problems it poses in both the theological and political spheres.[20]

In the 1980s, the so-called 'deliverance phenomenon' spread around many parts of the world with the Charismatic movement. The basic concept is that Christians may be hindered from entering into the entire blessing that God has for them because they are somehow blocked by demons. The Christians themselves may have no idea of the cause of the hindrance or the particular demon who blinds them to the truth. However, a Christian gifted by God can discern such spirits, and through prayer can deliver the individuals so that they may enjoy health and prosperity. A favourite text used to illustrate this teaching is John 11:1–44, in which Lazarus is called forth to life, but is still bound and must be delivered. Demons are believed to be able to enter human beings through various 'doorways' such as traditional gods, curses, divination, clan and family covenants, and a wide variety of sins. A person may be delivered from such demons when the spirit is first identified, and then cast out usually after some simple ritual. Yawning, coughing, vomiting or convulsions usually accompany the exorcism of the spirit.

A popular and influential book on this subject in West Africa is that of Emmanuel Eni, *Delivered from the Powers of Darkness*.[21] Eni tells his personal story which commenced after he dropped out of school and began living with a young woman who worked as an accountant at a bank. During the night she could change into a boa constrictor. One day, after she had gone to work, he looked around her flat and found refrigerators full of skulls and body parts. She soon had him involved in slaughtering and eating people. He was then taken spiritually to India for further initiation, after which he could travel instantly to any part of the world. On one occasion a beautiful woman took him to a city beneath the sea, and revealed herself as the Queen of the Coast. She gave him powers to change into all kinds of animals including crocodiles and hippopotamuses. In the city under the sea scientists were working in laboratories developing all sorts of inventions like television and cars to distract people from God. When they returned to Lagos, the Queen of the Coast gave him power to kill people by causing natural disasters. Eni also tells of a conference that he once had with Satan (Lucifer) where he was given more powers such that he could change into a woman or an animal. He describes in detail the difficulties he had in attacking born-again Christians as long as they don't get 'entangled in the affairs of this life'. In 1985 Jesus wonderfully appeared to Eni and saved him and has kept him faithful to God despite Satan's temptations.

The account is a fascinating mixture of elements from both West African traditional religions and Western Charismatic Christianity. The writings of American Charismatics such as Derek Prince, Frank Peretti and Rebecca Brown have helped form new local interpretations of the spiritual realm in many parts of the world.[22] The writings of Peter Wagner on territorial spirits have been accepted by many Pentecostal and Charismatic Christians in Africa who have applied them to their specific local contexts. Here global and local dimensions interact and reinforce each other to produce a new local understanding of spiritual deliverance.

Notes

1 Rasmussen, S. J., *Spirit Possession and Personhood Among the Kel Ewey Tuareg* (Cambridge: CUP, 1995), p. 1.

2 Stewart, K., 'Spirit-possession in native America', *Southwestern Journal of Anthropology* 2 (1946), p. 325.

3 Lewis, I. M., *Religion in Context: Cults and Charisma* (Cambridge: CUP, 1986), p. 30.

4 *Ibid.* p. 33.

5 *Ibid.* p. 34.

6 Boddy, J., *Wombs and Alien Spirits: Women, Men and the Zar Cult in Northern Sudan* (Madison: University of Wisconsin Press, 1989), p. 138.

7 *Ibid.* p. 139.

8 Hezel, F. X., 'Spirit possession in Chuuk: a socio-cultural interpretation', *The Micronesian Counsellor*, Occasional Papers, No. 11 July 1993.

9 *Ibid.* p. 12

10 Gelfand, M., 'Psychiatric disorders as recognised by the Shona', Kiev, A. (ed.), *Magic Faith and Healing* (New York: Free Press, 1964), p. 163.

11 Rouget, G., *Music and Trance* (Chicago: University of Chicago Press, 1985), p. 150.

12 Derrett, J. D. M., 'Spirit-possession and the Gerasene Demonic', *Man* 14 (1979), p. 288.

13 Prince, R., 'Indigenous Yoruba psychiatry' in Kiev, A. (ed.), *Magic, Faith, and Healing* (New York: Free Press, 1964), pp. 107–8.

14 Lewis, I. M., *Ecstatic Religion* (London: Penguin Books, 1971), p. 63.

15 Rouget, G., *Music and Trance: A Theory of the Relations between Music and Possession* (Chicago: University of Chicago, 1985), p. 325.

16 Lewis, *op. cit.* p. 96.

17 Meyer, B., 'If you are a devil, you are a witch, and if you are a witch, you are a devil': the Integration of 'Pagan' Ideas into the conceptual universe of Ewe Christians in Southeast Ghana', *Journal of Religion in Africa* 22 (1992), pp. 98–132.

18 Milingo, E., *Healing: 'If I tell you, you will not believe me!'* (Lusaka, 1976), p. 1.

19 Ter Haar, G., *Spirit of Africa: The Healing Ministry of Archbishop Milingo of Zambia* (London: Hurst & Company, 1992), p. 130.

20 Ter Haar, G. & Ellis, S., 'Spirit possession and healing in modern Zambia: an analysis of letters to Archbishop Milingo', *African Affairs* 87 (1988), pp. 185–206.
21 Eni, E., *Delivered from the Powers of Darkness* (Ibadan: Scripture Union, 1987).
22 Prince, D., *Blessing or Curse: You Can Choose* (Milton Keynes: Word, 1990).

Chapter Eleven

SHAMANISM: WARRIOR HEALERS

When my brother was sick, my grandmother who was a shamaness tried her best to get him well. She did all her part, acting as though a dog, singing some songs at night, but he died. While she was singing, she fell down so hard on the floor, making a big noise. After about fifteen minutes later we heard the tapping of her fingers and her toes on the floor. Slowly she got up, already she had become like a dog. She looks so awful. My grandfather told me that he used to hide his face with his drum just because she looks different, changed and awful like a dog, very scary. She used to crawl back and forth on the floor, making big noises. Even though my brother was afraid of her, he tried not to hide his face, he looked at her so that he would become well. Then my grandmother licked his mouth to try to pull up the cough and to blow it away. Then after half hour, she fell down so hard on the floor again.[1]

A second category of possession-like phenomena, like this example from St Lawrence Island, Alaska, is generally known as 'shamanism'. This is an exotic institution, which has fascinated explorers and anthropologists for many years. The word 'shaman' comes from the language of the Tungus people of Siberia, and in the strict sense is pre-eminently a religious phenomenon of Siberia and Central Asia. In other languages of the region the corresponding terms are: Yakut *ojuna*, Mongolian *bugu*, Buryat *udagan*, and Turko-Tarta *kam*. The term shaman has however been applied to a broad category of related observations. Eliade wrote one of the first major texts on this subject in 1951, and his ideas have been widely followed.[2] He writes:

> Throughout the immense area comprising Central and North Asia, the magico-religious life of society centers on the shaman. This, of course, does not mean that he is the one and only manipulator of the sacred, nor that religious activity is completely usurped by him. In many tribes the sacrificing priest coexists with the shaman, not to mention the fact that the head of a family is also the head of the domestic cult. Nevertheless, the shaman remains the dominating figure; for through this whole region in which ecstatic experience is considered the religious experience par excellence, the shaman, and he alone, is the great master of ecstasy. A first definition of this complex phenomenon, and perhaps the least hazardous, will be: shamanism = *techniques of ecstasy.*[3]

By using this more restricted definition, Eliade differentiates the shaman from other magicians and medicine men of other traditional societies around the world. Holmberg tries to avoid the practice of universalising the Arctic definition of shaman by speaking of a plurality of 'shamanisms'.[4] Kendall similarly writes of 'common themes in the experiences of a contemporary Korean shaman seated in front of her television set and a Chuckchce shaman on the Siberian steppe at the turn of the century'.[5] These common themes appear among widely dispersed populations, some attributable to historical connections and others not. Hultkrantz identifies five main roles of a shaman: doctor, diviner, psychopomp, hunting magician and sacrificial priest.[6] The complexity of the shaman's role may be attributed to the fact that the shaman is found mainly in small band societies and as a result must play many parts.

Shamanism may be distinguished from other forms of possession phenomena by three particular features. First, the role of the shaman in society is that of a healer and protector of the people from spiritual powers. Second he, or she, is considered to be working in co-operation with the spirits rather than be controlled by them. Raymond Firth has called the shaman a 'master of spirits', with the implication that the shaman incarnates the spirits.[7] Finally, the ecstatic experience is usually expressed in the form of a flight or journey in the spirit realm.

Acquiring shamanistic powers

The powers of the shaman are often the result of some initiatory experience, which radically affected the person's life. In central and north-eastern Asia there are three means by which a person becomes a shaman: 1) by a 'calling' or 'election' by a spirit; 2) by the hereditary transmission of the shamanistic profession; or 3) by personal decision. The cases of individuals who of their free will choose to become shaman are rare, and are considered less powerful than those who are called or inherit the profession.

An Inuit (Eskimo), for example, would say that a person would never choose to become a shaman of his own free will, but would be called by the spirits – usually through some physical or mental sickness. The procedure of becoming a shaman is intended both to cure the initiate and to produce a valuable healer in the society. These people are often described as being 'out of their minds', but this is distinguished from being 'crazy'.[8] For five days the person may be disturbed, unable to eat or drink, yet they become increasingly strong so that several men are unable to restrain them.

Among the Tungus the child is chosen and brought up with a view of becoming a shaman, but the first ecstasy is decisive in confirming the candidate.

Thus it may happen that candidates run away to the mountains and remain there seven days or longer, feeding on animals 'caught . . . directly with their teeth', and returning to the village dirty, bleeding, with torn clothes and hair dishevelled, 'like wild people'. It is only some ten days later that the candidate begins babbling incoherent words. Then an old shaman cautiously asks him questions; the candidate (more precisely, the 'spirit' possessing him) becomes angry, and finally designates the shaman who is to offer the sacrifices to the gods and prepare the ceremony of initiation and consecration.[9]

Although not all potential shaman go through such a marked period of crises, the general process of becoming a shaman is remarkably similar throughout the world. Initially there is a period of suffering which is interpreted as an assault by a spirit. Whilst this is considered an experience which may occur to any person, in the case of the shaman it is merely the first indication of his future vocation. By overcoming this spirit assault a new relationship is established between the shaman and the spirit. With the support of his friends the person manages to establish a new identity, that of a shaman. Even when the ministry is hereditary, the election of the future shaman is preceded by a change of behaviour. The Akawayo of South America have the saying, 'a man must die before he becomes a shaman'.[10]

Often a novice will join himself to an experienced shaman, and begin what may be a long and arduous apprenticeship. Some may even apprentice themselves directly to a spirit. In this way the novice learns how to perform the shamanistic rites, and so call the spirits. During this time he may abstain from food, sex, or sleep. Through this arduous process he learns how to control and even master the spirits. Fantastic stories are recounted by the shaman of journeys to the underworld in which he has had to do battle with all kinds of strange and horrific spiritual opponents. 'According to the Yakuts, the spirits carry the future shaman to Hell and imprison him there for three years in a house. It is there that he undergoes initiation: the spirits cut off his head, which they put aside (because a novice must look on with his own eyes as he is torn apart), and they cut him into little pieces, which they then distribute to the spirits of diverse illnesses. It is only by experiencing this condition that the future shaman will obtain the power of healing. His bones are then covered over again with new flesh, and in certain cases he is also supplied with new blood.'[11]

To aid him in this task the shaman must have the aid of particular spirits. The Inuit word for these spirits is *tornaq*, often translated into English as 'familiar spirits'. The shaman is not considered as being dominated by these spirits, but to be at least on an equal footing with his spirit helpers. Many South American shaman refer to their spirit-helpers as their 'pets'. A Malay shaman gets possession of a spirit-familiar by inheritance from another shaman, usually a father, uncle or grandfather. He may wait beside the grave of the ancestor in a trance-like state waiting for the gift of the spirit. He may alternatively wait in the dark forest for the coming of a tiger spirit. Endicott thinks that the ghost of a shaman is believed to take the form of a tiger spirit.[12] This spirit gives the shaman *ilmu*, power in the form of knowledge.

Lewis sees the making of a shaman as a second phase in the process of possession. The first phase is usually involuntary and uncontrolled, and the spirit may either be exorcised or if the affliction persists, the person is initiated into a possession cult. In the second phase, the person voluntarily enters into a trance and learns to control the spirits.

The psychological states of the shaman

The shaman has been described as a person who goes into trances, 'sees' strange visions and shows many of the behaviour patterns that a Western doctor may diagnose as schizoid. In the West, such a person may be regarded as in need of psychiatric help, and it is therefore not surprising that the mental health of the shaman has dominated the literature on shamanism. Most anthropologists have finally concluded that shamanism is not a function of mental illness, but must be understood as an individual functioning according to the worldview of his or her society. The things that the shaman does and says may seem to be totally strange to another society, but to his own society they seem reasonable within the context of how the people perceive the universe. As Lewis colourfully expressed it: 'In the society of the mad, the normal mentally healthy person will be condemned as a lunatic.'[13]

This shift in the way of thinking about shamanistic behaviour occurred in the 1960s, when shamanistic behaviour moved from the category of abnormal psychology to that of universal psychobiological capacities. This mainly resulted from the study of the South American shamanistic tradition where shamanistic states were within the capacity of ordinary people. Drugs are found to 'jumpstart' the possibility of experiencing firsthand the visions and sensations of shamanistic seances.[14] For example, the shamans from the Akawayo Indians of the Amazon consume greater and greater quantities of herbal preparations containing enormous amounts of tobacco juice. Scholars have therefore spoken of shamanism in terms of 'altered states of consciousness'. Harner characterises a single 'shamanistic state of consciousness',[15] while Winkelman argues for a single kind of trance state that is characteristic not only of shaman but all magico-religious practitioners.[16] Encouraged by the discovery of endorphins, opiate-like compounds the brain releases in response to certain stimuli, shamanistic states of consciousness and the therapeutic responses of patients have been considered as functions of chemically induced euphoria.[17]

Porterfield, however, has criticised the way that some scholars have glossed over shamanistic practices of manipulation and deception.[18] Shamans often demonstrate their powers through practices that impress their clients with a sense of awe. For example, W. F. Doty, a missionary on St Lawrence Island in 1898, was present during a rite when the shaman sank slowly into the ground until only the hair of his head remained visible. In his diary, Doty describes putting his hand on the shaman's head and feeling it sink lower.[19] Although many shaman are known to be experts at conjuring tricks and ventriloquism, in ecstasy shaman can do more than they themselves understand through contact with their particular spiritual powers.

Because of the shaman's supposed ability to move between the natural and supernatural worlds there are some aspects of his behaviour that are different from that of the local culture. His ambiguous role means that he does not conform to some of the expected modes of behaviour. One of the most surprising aspects of this is that the shamans of many Polar societies are homosexual or transvestite. According to Bogoras, 'amongst the shamans of the Chukchi, various degrees of transformation are recognised. In the first, the shaman changes only the manner of braiding and arranging his hair; in the second, he adopts female dress; in the third, he leaves off all the pursuits and manners of his own sex and takes up those of a woman. Even his pronunciation changes from the male to the female mode. At the same time his body alters, if not in its outward appearance, at least in its faculties and forces . . . He seeks to win the good graces of men, and succeeds easily with the aid of his "spirits" . . . From these he chooses his lover and after a time takes a husband.'[20] The ambiguity of the role is further confounded by the fact that he may also have a 'spirit' husband or wife!

Although some anthropologists have questioned the sanity of the shaman, many others have recognised that most are mentally healthy. The Soviet ethnographer Anisimov reports of Evenk shamans that 'although some revealed hysterical neurotic characteristics, there were also many who were extremely sober individuals'.[21] To disregard the shaman as being neurotic is to miss an important aspect of the society. They may be far-sighted and ambitious members of society pursuing the only avenue of specialisation available. In a more technological society their talents may have made them inventors or artists, but in the limits of their own society they seek for new horizons through shamanizing the spirits.

The warrior healer

The striking imagery of the spiritual adventures of the shaman highlights their role as the champions of the people who combat the forces of evil. They must fight not only against evil spirits, but illnesses and even black magic. Amongst the Polar shaman the imagery of the warrior is even more distinct with the use of bows, lances, and swords in their rites. They are seen as the champions, who through their ability to travel into supernatural worlds and to 'see' spiritual beings, can defend the community. In order to appreciate how he can operate it is necessary to consider the ways in which his society thinks of sickness. Five general causes of sickness are common in shamanistic societies.

The first is the belief that an individual's soul may leave their body on certain occasions such as during sleep or when startled. This concept of the 'external soul' was discussed in chapter 3. Whilst the soul, or one of the multiple souls, is away from the body it may be captured by one of the many evil and predatory spirits that exist in the world. Until the soul is returned to the patient's body the person continues to be ill.

During the curing rite the shaman goes into a trance usually assisted by drumming, rattles, smoke or hallucinogenic drugs. His 'soul' is said to leave his body, and then with the aid of his spirit-familiars he searches the supernatural worlds for the lost soul of the patient. 'The son of one of St Lawrence Island's famous shamans said that his father's spirit-familiar would undertake such an errand and could travel the eighty miles to and from Indian Point or Savoonga in less than five minutes – "just like electricity," he said – and would come back with information important to the search for the lost soul.'[22] The recounting of such stories plays an important part of the Polar shamanistic rites, and the shaman may have even to fight with the evil spirit who does not want to return the patient's soul. Because of these accounts a shaman has often been defined in terms of a healer who effects cures through the flight of the soul and contact with spirits.

A second perception of sickness is that a spirit may intrude into a person's body. Intrusion is believed to cause illness and can be detected by divination, while possession does not imply illness. Amongst the circum-polar peoples, spirit intrusion is believed to account for insanity or hysteria, and exorcism is required. Among the Inuit of St Lawrence Island there is believed to be a difference between ghost and spirit intrusion. It is believed that ghosts of a recently dead person may hover about and attack a living relative with sickness, especially if they were in some way to blame for their death – through a broken taboo, for example. With time the power of the ghost is considered gradually to wane. The main role of the shaman in this case is to identify the cause of the sickness and prescribe what appropriate behaviour should be followed.

A third perception of the cause of sickness is object intrusion. Not only is it believed that spirits can intrude into a person's body, but so can various foreign objects that may be shot into the patient's body by a spirit or sorcerer. The object must be removed if a cure is to be achieved, and the shaman first does this by entering into a trance state. Among the Polar peoples a common practice is for the shaman to suck the afflicted part of the patient's body. The spirit-familiar of the shaman in this way draws the object until it is finally sucked out. The shaman will often take from his mouth a small stone, a worm or piece of bone, which he shows to those who have gathered for the healing ritual.

Jane Murphy has described such a ritual from amongst the Inuit on St Lawrence Island.

During the singing and drumming of the seance, he (the shaman) would appear to thrust his own drum-stick into the stomach of the patient. When the stick was removed, there would be a writhing black thing – 'something like a worm' – attached to the end of it. In the dimly lit room, the shaman would show the stick about and then eat the worm-like thing, demonstrating by this final act that the disease had been consumed by the spirit-familiar and was no longer noxious to the human patient.[23]

A fourth perception of sickness is the breaking of a religious sanction – a taboo. Incest, sexual perversions, or offending a god are often regarded as disease provoking transgressions. This may not only affect the individual, but the family and the community. The shaman in these cases uses his powers of divination to find out what transgression had been committed, and to discover what atonement is necessary in order to expiate the sin. In many cases public confession of the transgression plays an important part of the healing ritual.

Finally, as I have shown previously, misfortune can be caused by sorcery. Polar societies make a clear distinction between the healing magic of the shaman and the black magic of the sorcerer. Only the most powerful sorcerer would deal with those sicknesses requiring counter-sorcery. David Hicks described such a ritual amongst the Tutum of Indonesia:

After the advance payment has been made, the shaman escorts the invalid into the womb of his house. Here a sleeping mat lies spread near the fire blazing in the hearth. Both sit on it. The shaman takes a betel leaf, a few pieces of areca and lime, places them in his mouth and chews. A couple of seconds later he spits a gob of the areca blood onto the floor. He must throw this bridge across to make connection with the spiritual powers causing the trouble. The shape of the glob of spittle and its shade of red tell the shaman what sort of spiritual attacker he is up against. If he decides an ancestral ghost is the invader, the shaman can only suggest what gift must be sacrificed by the victim to persuade the ghost to leave him in peace.

But if the culprit is a witch, he can grapple with him mentally on the spot . . . If the shaman's willpower proves stronger than that of the witch, he will sooner or later thrust the alien soul out. So the shaman sits night after night on the same mat as the victim, to protect him and prevent the evil soul from re-entering his body. When the witch realises the hopelessness of its evil ambition, the shaman's nightly visits end and the sick person recovers . . . Should the shaman prove weaker than the witch, however, the victim's health deteriorates until death claims his body.[24]

The shaman's role is not limited to curing the sick. He may often use his powers to obtain information about which is the best direction to go on a hunting party, or if a fight with an enemy group will be successful. He may even have a legal role, and deal with social disputes.

Shamanism in the modern world

Although shamanism is, as Eliade says 'an archaic technique of ecstasy' it should not be considered as a static phenomenon. Asiatic shamanism was constantly transposed by a series of contributions culminating in the coming of Buddhism. The Tungus term 'shaman' itself appears to have its origins from the Indian Pali *samana* through the Chinese transliteration *sha-men*. This would suggest that shamanism among the Tungus was influenced by Tibetan Buddhism which spread through the region when it was adopted by Kublai Khan in the thirteenth century.[25]

Classical forms of shamanism appear to have been common among most ancient nomadic communities. As a more central-ised political control emerged within a society, a universal relig-ion tended to become dominant and shamanistic authority was displaced. As the central cult was dominated by men, women tended to take on the role of the shaman. In Korea, for example, over 95 per cent of shamans are women, and the remainder are men who perform in women's dress.[26] In such societies, women have often been labelled as 'spirit mediums' even though they perform similar roles to shaman in non-state societies. As was mentioned in the previous chapter, Lewis has attributed this pattern to the peripheralisation of women within society.[27] Men control the centre of religious practice within society, and women are only allowed to express their practice within the so-called 'folk' tradition.

In the twentieth century two powerful states sought to erad-icate shamanism in the interests of scientific atheism – the former USSR and China. Balzer has given an extensive account of Soviet efforts to eradicate shamanism and their pernicious effects on Central Asian peoples.[28] Soviet scholars have regarded shamanism as a form of religious practice in pre-class societies. As specialists who demanded payment from their clients, shaman promoted growing economic inequality and the rise of the feudal society. With the emergence of the state and monarchies, shaman were pushed 'into the dark corners of daily life'.[29] The resurgence of shamanism has been regarded as the final throes of a dying practice that must be eradicated.

The strong stance towards shamanism has invited indige-nous political response. Korean students and intellectuals have even adopted shamanism as a weapon for anti-government protest. Shamanistic performances have become a form of mass demonstration in Korea.[30]

Now, in post-Soviet the Buryat, shamans who used to live dispersed in remote steppes and valleys live and practice in the cities of Siberia.[31] They now practice in the confines of the anonymous blocks of flats that characterise the Soviet period. From the kitchen window is flung libations of vodka and milk given to the spirits. The gas stove is used for offerings of meat and fat to the fire god. The client sits head bowed on a chair in the kitchen whilst the shaman calls out to the spirits. The client who is suffering with pains in her legs and back is purified with sacred smoke. Then kneeling down the shamaness goes over the body sucking out the harmful 'something'. Suddenly, she leaps to her feet and rushes to the toilet where after loud retching the harmful substance is flushed away.

The most significant developments in shamanism have, however, emerged in North America and Europe as part of the New Age Movement. Michael Harner, an established authority on shamanism, left his academic position to teach shamanistic techniques and establish *The Foundation for Shamanistic Studies*. So-called 'neo-shamanism' or 'urban shamanism' encourages clients to heal themselves through shamanistic experiences. It is claimed that shamanism allows people to quickly achieve altered states of consciousness. His favourite technique is that of the 'spirit canoe'. In this case, some ten to fifteen people sit on the floor in a canoe configuration facing the same direction. The person needing healing lies in the centre of the canoe, and one of the members begins to beat the drum. The shaman then enters the canoe and lies beside the sick person. The shaman and his helpers then visualise the vessel passing down into an opening in the earth. As drumming continues, the shaman moves into an altered state of consciousness where he calls on his spirit animals. Once the animal has appeared the shaman returns to the ordinary state of consciousness, and places the animal on the patient's chest and breathes the animal into the patient. The patient then rises to dance the newly received power-animal to the continuing beat of the drum.[32]

Generally, anthropologists have been critical of these 'invented traditions' as a romanticism of shamanism by Euroamericans. Clifton has written an amusing critique entitled 'Armchair shamanism: a Yankee way of knowledge'.[33] Nevertheless, as gatekeepers to the knowledge and experience of shamanism, anthropologists are concerned about the adoption of shamanism within Western society based upon a romantic idealism of traditional societies.

Jesus and Beelzebub

The role of the Shaman as an exorcist raises for Christians questions concerning the difference between what he does and what is seen in the ministry of Jesus. Within the Synoptic Gospels the accounts of the many exorcisms of Jesus are not only of importance in their own right, but because they show that these were questioned by the people of his own day. In the so-called Beelzebub controversy, Jesus is accused of being spirit possessed, and by this spirit he is able to cast out spirits in a similar way to that of a shaman. The story is recounted in Mark 3:23–27, and with some additions in Matthew 12:22–37 and Luke 11:17–22. The accusation comes as the watershed in Jesus' ministry for it is here that his rejection begins. In the Matthew and Luke accounts, the controversy commences not with an accusation of insanity as in Mark, but with a specific exorcism. On the one hand, the people wondered if Jesus was indeed the Son of David, whilst on the other the Pharisees charged him of performing the exorcism by Beelzebub, 'the prince of demons'.

Jesus answers the charge in two parts. First, he shows the absurdity of the charge by asking a rhetorical question. 'If Satan drives out Satan, he is divided against himself. How then can his kingdom stand?' (Matt. 12:26). If Satan's kingdom is divided then it will soon fall, and so God's purposes will be achieved anyway. In the second part of his reply, Jesus once again poses a question. If exorcism means that one is in league with Beelzebub, by what means do the Pharisees perform their exorcisms? This is the only reference in the Gospels to the fact that the Pharisees performed exorcisms. By logic there can only be one of two answers, either by Satan or by God. If it is the latter then the conclusion must be that in Jesus, the Kingdom of God has come. Jesus once again poses a question. 'Or again, how can anyone enter a strong man's house and carry off his possessions unless he first ties up the strong man? Then he can rob his house' (Matt. 12:29). This merely reinforces the point that the many remarkable exorcisms of Jesus are a sign of the presence of the Kingdom of God.

Fear is a major factor for many people as illustrated in the following quotation from an Inuit man:

> We fear the Spirit of earth that we must fight against to wrest our food from land and sea. We fear *Sila* (the Weather Spirit). We fear death and hunger in the cold snow huts. We fear Takankapsaluk, the Great Woman down at the bottom of the sea that rules over all the beasts of the sea. We fear the sickness that we meet with daily around us; those of the air, of the sea, and of the earth that can help wicked shaman to harm their fellow men. We fear the souls of dead human beings and of the animals we have killed.[34]

The first missionary to the Yahgans of Tierra del Fuego, who were a shamanistic people, had been a young clergyman who arrived on the Beagle with Charles Darwin. He was threatened and stoned, so that he was immediately withdrawn. The second mission occurred in the winter of 1850–1, and consisted of a mission of seven, who had to flee for their lives into the wilderness, where they died. A third attempt, in 1859 got as far as building a chapel; but one Sunday morning, 6 November, in the middle of the first verse of the first hymn of their opening service, the little group of four was set upon, clubbed, speared, and stoned to death. Finally, in 1871, when the Rev. Thomas Bridge disembarked with his wife and infant daughter, there was a change of attitude amongst the people. They realised that the missionaries had come to tell them of the Supreme creator who they had always thought of as distant and unknown. The Yahgans realised that the creator God must be more powerful than the familiar spirits of the shaman, and so they turned to the new religion.[35]

Mark Ritchie recounts the remarkable story of Shoefoot, a shaman of the Yanomamo Indians of the Amazon Forest. Shoefoot had many spirits that came to him when he took a drug called *ebene*. These spirits continued to warn him of a dangerous spirit Yai Pada of whom the missionaries spoke. Finally Shoefoot prays to Yai Pada, but he knows he does not have the power to throw away his old spirits. Eventually, Omawa, the greatest of the spirits of the forest comes to carry him away in death.

> He had been lying in his hammock almost asleep when Omawa himself, the leader of all our spirits, had come to him from deep in the jungle. As he came he swooped his hand down into the jungle and gathered from it all the sweetest smells in the world. His beauty, his power, and his sweet smell were so wonderful that Shoefoot knew right away that he could never resist him. Shoefoot's body was filled with excitement. He was important enough to be visited by Omawa himself. Omawa had scooped Shoefoot up from his hammock and they began to dance across the jungle . . . Just as they had been about to dance forever out of the jungle, they were suddenly hit with a white light as bright as many suns, more dazzling than anything Shoefoot had ever seen. It was like the sharpest flame of lightning but it didn't stop. The bright light stayed there, and the warmth from it filled Shoefoot with a new feeling he had never felt, a feeling of safety. It felt so good.
>
> Just when the light appeared a huge voice had said, 'You can't have him. He's mine.' And Omawa ran in terror! Across the top of the jungle he ran until he was out of sight. It's him, Shoefoot thought, when he heard the voice. *It's Yai Pada, the great spirit – and he's not the enemy! He heard me when I asked him to chase my spirits away! He must be friendly to me after all!*[36]

Notes

1 JMM, August 22, 1955, p. 21 quoted in 'Psychotherapeutic Aspects of Shamanism on St Lawrence Island, Alaska', Kiev, A. (ed.), *Magic, Faith, and Healing* (New York: Free Press, 1964) p. 59.

2 Eliade, M., *Shamanism: Archaic Techniques of Ecstasy* (London: Routledge & Kegan Paul, 1964).

3 *Ibid.* p. 4.
4 Holmberg, D. H., *Order in Paradox: Myth, Ritual, and Exchange Among Nepal's Tamang* (Ithaca: Cornell University Press, 1989).
5 Kendall, L., 'Healing thyself: a Korean shaman's afflictions', *Society of Scientific Medicine* 27 (1988), p. 446.
6 Hultkrantz, A., 'Shamanism: a religious phenomenon?' in Doore, G. (ed.), *The Shaman's Path* (Boston: Shambhala, 1988), pp. 35–7.
7 Lewis, I. M., *Ecstatic Religion* (London: Pelican Books, 1971), p. 49.
8 Murphy, J. M., 'Psychotherapeutic aspects of shamanism on St Lawrence Island, Alaska' in Kiev, A. (ed.), *Magic, Faith, and Healing* (New York: Free Press, 1974). p. 58.
9 Shirokogoroff quoted in Eliade, *op. cit.* p. 18.
10 Lewis, *op. cit.* p. 70.
11 Eliade, M., *A History of Religious Ideas*, vol. 3 (Chicago: University of Chicago Press, 1985), p. 13.
12 Endicott, K. M., *An Analysis of Malay Magic* (Oxford: Clarendon Press, 1970), p. 17.
13 Lewis, *op. cit.* p. 180.
14 Harner, M., *Hallucinogens and Shamanism* (London: OUP, 1973).
15 Harner, M., *The Way of the Shaman* (New York: Bantam, 1982).
16 Winkelman, M. J., 'Trance states: a theoretical model and cross-cultural analysis', *Ethos* 14 (1986), pp. 174–204.
17 Prince, R., 'Shamans and endorphins', *Ethos* 10 (1982): Special edition.
18 Porterfield, A., 'Shamanism: a psychosocial definition', *Journal of the American Academy of Religion* 55 (1987), pp. 721–39.
19 Murphy, *op. cit.* p. 59.
20 Campbell, J., *The Way of Animal Powers* (London: Time Books, 1984), p. 174.
21 Lewis, *op. cit.* p. 182.
22 Murphy, *op. cit.* p. 62.
23 *Ibid.* p. 67.
24 Hicks, D., *Tetum Ghosts and Kin* (Palo Alto: Mayfield Publishing Company, 1976), p. 112.
25 Eliade (1964) *op. cit.* p. 499.
26 Covell, A., *Ecstasy: Shamanism in Korea* (NJ: Hollym International Corporation, 1983).

27 Lewis, I. M., 'What is a shaman?' *Folk* 23 (1981), pp. 25–35.
28 Balzer, M. M., *Shamanism: Soviet Studies of Traditional Religion in Siberia and Central Asia* (London: M. E. Sharp, 1990).
29 *Ibid.* p. 34.
30 Kim, K., 'Rituals of resistance: the manipulation of shamanism in contemporary Korea', in Keynes, C. *et al.* (eds.), *Religion and the Modern States of East and Southeast Asia* (Honolulu: Univeristy of Hawaii Press, 1992).
31 Humphrey, C., 'Shamans in the city' *Anthropology Today* 15 (1999), pp. 3–10.
32 Burnett, D., *Dawning of the Pagan Moon* (Eastbourne: Monarch, 1991), pp. 179–93.
33 Clifton, C., 'Armchair shamanism: a Yankee way of knowledge', in Schultz, T. (ed.), *The Fringes of Reason* (New York : Harmony Books, 1989), pp. 43–9.
34 Lewis, (1971) *op. cit.* p. 163.
35 Campbell, *op. cit.* pp. 159–60.
36 Ritche, M. A., *Spirit of the Rainforest* (Chicago: Island Lake Press, 1996).

Chapter Twelve

THINGS FALL APART

Turning and turning in the widening gyre
　The falcon cannot bear the falconer;
Things fall apart; the centre cannot hold;
Mere anarchy is loosed upon the world.
W. B. Yeats: The Second Coming

Chinua Achebe entitled his reflective book on changing life in Nigeria *Things Fall Apart.*[1] The impact of the European expansion upon traditional societies has been immense, and many elements of daily life have indeed fallen apart. This chapter seeks to explore the nature of that impact on traditional societies, and especially to examine the role of the missionaries as agents of change and destruction.

First contacts with the Europeans

When Columbus first sailed the Atlantic Ocean in 1492 he not only discovered the Americas, but also opened new trade routes for the aspiring European peoples. It was a technological achievement that was to bring about an immense change to the world scene. By the end of the fifteenth century the Spanish had finally managed to establish their domination of the peninsular and pushed the Muslims out of Europe. Unfortunately, the crusading mentality of this long period of struggle against the Muslims continued as the Europeans looked across the Atlantic and along the sea routes to India and China.

Conquest

Many traditional societies were decimated by early contact with Europeans. There were cases of massacres of whole communities, which destroyed substantial proportions of the indigenous population. This occurred in both North and South America where 'the only good Indian is a dead Indian' was the view of many European settlers. The Spanish conquest of Central America similarly had a devastating effect on the local population where tens of thousands were hunted down or massacred. Many more died enslaved working in the Spanish gold and silver mines. Alongside the *conquistadors* in the Americas rode the missionary priests, baptising the natives in the name of Jesus Christ.

Traditional societies were not always passive to the coming of the Europeans. Even though the Europeans had a superior military technology sometimes the local people continued a long and effective resistance. The most effective resistance came from the highly centralised societies with large armies. Notable examples were the Zulus and the Asantes, who held back the European advance for many years. In the Pacific, the Maoris with their hill forts were able to hold the British infantry at bay in the face of superior military weapons.

Even in advance of the actual colonisation by the European powers there were major cultural changes. One of the most dramatic examples was the emergence of the nomadic horse culture on the American plains. The Spanish first brought the horse to the Americas, and from a few animals that escaped from the conquistadors horses became an important part of American Indian culture. The Cheyenne, for example, were transformed from settled maize-cultivating villagers into buffalo-hunting nomadic warriors on horseback.

Disease

It was probably disease that was the more destructive force upon traditional societies. Traditional people had no immunity to many European diseases such as smallpox, influenza, measles, whooping cough, venereal disease and, more recently, polio.[2] In most cases few statistics are available, but some are available for the Mandan Indians of North America.[3] In 1750, at the beginning of the fur trade, some nine thousand Mandan lived in large permanent settlements. The first smallpox epidemics occurred in 1764 and 1782 and they halved the population. The community was then vulnerable to the attacks of the nomadic Teton Sioux, so that by about 1800 the population had declined to about fifteen hundred. Another devastating smallpox epidemic spread through the two villages into which surviving Mandan had regrouped. The survivors numbered less than 63 adults.

The Indian populations on the Caribbean islands disappeared entirely. New Spain (Mexico) had a dramatic fall in population from approximately eleven million in 1519 to about one and a half million in 1650.[4] Many of the peoples of the Amazon forest have suffered huge decline in numbers through sickness. The Nambiquara Indians, for example, were known to have a population of about twenty thousand in 1911. In 1946 they were affected by an epidemic that killed 98 per cent of the total population. It is not certain what the illness was, but it could have been measles or the common cold. The effect was to leave the people totally discouraged, and their social structure shattered. Women stopped wanting to have children because they would only die. Today there are only 250 people who are left and each has painful memories of the past.[5]

The depopulation did not go without notice amongst the Europeans and in 1922 W. H. R. Rivers reported his study of the population dynamics of Melanesia.[6] The population of Tahitians declined from forty thousand in 1780 to six thousand in 1980. Similarly the New Zealand Moaris declined from approximately 100,000 in 1799 to 37,000 in 1979. Bishop Wilson of the Melanesian Mission wrote in 1914:

> Ten years ago we had 8,929 baptised people, and now we have not quite 13,000, and yet there have never been less than 1,000 persons baptised in each of these years, and in 1900 the number baptised was 1,800. There had probably been at least 13,000 people baptised in the last 10 years, which would give us, if none had died at all, 22,000 Christians now.[7]

This was a loss of 40 per cent of baptised Christians in ten years.

The introduction of disease was certainly a cause of depopulation, but another popular view at the beginning of the twentieth century was that Melanesians were dying from *tedium vitae*, a loss of interest of life. The main exponent of this view was Rivers, who advocated a vigorous Christianity as a functional substitute that would restore the Melanesian's zeal for life.

Slavery

Slavery has been common in most parts of the world since earliest times, but it was with the emergence of the Atlantic Sea routes that slavery took on new dimensions. Even in the sixteenth century Portuguese and Spanish ships were kidnapping Africans from the West Coast and selling them in the Americas where they were set to work like animals. African slaves were stronger and replaced the many Indians who were dying in the mines and plantations. In the seventeenth and eighteenth centuries the Dutch and the British companies developed the trade into an efficient economic system known as the 'Triangular Run'. African slaves were taken to the Americas where they were sold and sugar cane and other produce loaded. These items were then sold in Europe from where machine-made fabrics and goods were exported back to West Africa.

As the Europeans were confessing Christians they faced many dilemmas. The Bible clearly teaches that all humans are equal, and care should be given to the weaker members. The Roman Church saw itself as the protector of the native Americans in the face of the activities of Spanish soldiers and settlers. The Church argued that both Blacks and Indians could be taught and baptised for their eternal salvation. Some Roman orders established Christian villages of refuge to try and protect the Indians from abuse by the growing number of European settlers in Latin America. The popular film *The Mission* illustrated some of the issues that occurred during the period.

In Protestant Europe, the social conscience found difficulty gaining a hearing in the light of the wealth generated by the increasing Atlantic trade. Many of the merchants and sailors were Christian, and only slowly were they to realise the full impact of their trade. A notable example was John Newton, who was baptised as a child and brought up as a churchgoer. He worked for some years on a ship that was ordered to pick up a cargo of slaves from West Africa and take them as 'cargo' to the Americas. He was suddenly converted to a personal loyalty to Jesus Christ during the great Evangelical Revival in Britain. He then became aware of the incredible suffering that some of these African slaves endured, and he spent the rest of his life trying to end this trade. Leading British Christians such as Lord Shaftesbury finally brought about the abolition of slavery in 1807, and began to institute a sea blockade of West Africa to stop the trade.

Colonisation

Although throughout history larger nations have impacted and conquered small communities, what happened with the European expansion was essentially new in its extent and nature. The Colonial powers divided the geographical territory amongst themselves. This was most notable when at the end of the nineteenth century the European powers met to divide up

'the great Africa cake'. Little notice was taken of the indigenous people who occupied the continent. Out of these divisions
was to emerge the boundaries of the nation states that distinguish the continent of Africa today.

What actually happened to traditional societies in the path of
European expansion depended upon a number of factors. The
first factor was the relative size, political organisation, and technology of the societies concerned. The second was the period of
the initial subjugation, and consequently the goals, which the
Europeans were pursuing. Third was the location of the society,
in terms of remoteness to Europeans and the territory they
occupied. Fourth was the colonial policy of the Europeans,
which varied between colonial powers at different times. The
British, for example, tended to follow the policy of indirect rule
in their Colonies, whilst the French did not.

Language, translation and ethnicity

The Colonial powers not only marked out much of the territory
into geographically defined areas, but their presence was to
have other effects. One that has been unnoticed until recently
relates to the formation of ethnicity. Europeans tended to have
the notion that traditional societies were tribal, characterised
by a chief, a distinct area in which they traditionally lived, and
their own language. Even though they found peoples without
rulers who migrated over large areas, the general model of a
tribe was still assumed. Recent historical studies have shown
there was much greater fluidity within the social scene, and the
European presence actually formed a new sense of ethnicity.

An example can be seen in the way that Bible translation was
to have repercussions in the creation of social identity. The
process may be summarised as follows. First, the missionaries
would identify the centre of what they regarded as a distinct
language group. The Bible was then translated based upon the
dominant dialect, but with some contributions from other

dialects. Through its use in the schools and the churches, the Bible dialect eventually became the accepted standard language of the region. It therefore came to be one of the prime identity markers for the ethnic group. The following two examples illustrate this process in more detail.

The first example is the Luba in the former Belgian Congo. Jewsiewicki has described how an aggregate of migrants from various regions acquired their own language and identity through the work of the missionaries.[8] These missionaries assumed that the different languages spoken were actually different dialects of one language. They therefore took what they considered to be the dominant dialect and created a written standard Luba, which they went on to teach in the schools that they founded.

The second study is of the Igbo of Nigeria, where the development of a written dialect on the basis of a vernacular was not without its problems as shown by Van den Bersselaar.[9] There is no reason to assume that the formulation of a written language is automatically accepted and will consequently define an ethnic group. As Peel warns from his study, 'the Yoruba, of course, did not present a cultural *tabula rasa* to the missions; the cultural map was not to be redrawn as arbitrarily as the political map of colonial Africa'.[10]

After the British abolition of slavery in 1807 the British government stationed a Royal naval squadron on the coast of West Africa. Illegal slave ships were then stopped and the slaves released in Sierra Leone. This resulted in the formation of one of the most cosmopolitan areas in Africa, and as such made an ideal centre for the study of many of the West African languages. In preparation for the proposed Niger expedition of 1841, J. F. Schon, one of the team linguists, studied Igbo. When the expedition was to reach Igboland Schon was disappointed to realise 'that the dialect of the Ibo language on which I had bestowed so much labour in Sierra Leone differs widely from that spoken and understood in this part of the country. It never escapes my observation, that a great diversity of dialectics existed: but I must blame myself much for not making stricter inquires about that which would be most useful for the present occasion.'[11]

Every Igbo town seemed to have its own dialect often very distinct from the others. Some groups had similarities resulting in a cluster of languages. This caused a major debate among linguists as to whether there was one or more language in an area. Back in England Schon published the first Igbo grammar, and Samuel Crowther later used this to study Igbo. Crowther based his translation on the 'Isuama dialect', which he also called 'proper Igbo'. This version of Igbo was probably not spoken anywhere in the Igbo area, but was a mixture used in Sierra Leone. Although missionaries kept looking for the region in which pure Igbo was spoken, it was twenty years later in 1876 before the linguistic complexity, and the fact that each region contended the superiority of its own dialect, were finally recognised.

Eventually two isolated centres of missionary work produced two sets of Igbo translations: one centred in Onitsha on the river Niger, and the other at Bonny, on the coast. Between 1870 and 1905 two different sets of Igbo translations were produced, each in a different local dialect, and both of use only in the region of the towns in which they were made. In 1904, T. J. Dennis proposed the production of a new translation for the whole of the Igbo region, to be used by all Protestant missions. By 1909 the New Testament was produced, and the whole Bible completed by 1913. Protests occurred from the main regions each saying that the translation sounded strange. Union Igbo was never accepted as the lingua franca of the Igbo area, and one reason for this was that the people preferred to learn English in school. An interesting element was that African non-Igbo speakers willingly learnt Union Igbo.

The missionaries failed to create a widely-accepted written standard, but as a result they stimulated a continuing debate on the Igbo language. 'Their standard failed, but their notion that there should be a standard has remained.'[12] Thus, whatever the problems in the emergence of written Igbo, the Igbo language became an important identity marker for the people. 'The notion of the one shared Igbo language was later taken up by others who began to promote the appreciation and use of Igbo language and culture.'[13]

Missionaries as agents of change

In the popular form of anthropology commonly shown on television, the missionary has often been accused as being an agent of destructive change, and the anthropologist the enlightened defender to traditional culture. As Keesing has written:

> Anthropologists and missionaries have, at least in stereotype, been at odds with one another for many decades. The caricatured missionary is a strait-laced, repressed, and narrow-minded Bible thumper trying to get the native women to cover their bosoms decently; the anthropologist is a bearded degenerate given to taking his clothes off and sampling wild rites. Things are more complicated that that.[14]

The issue of greatest debate in recent years has been the role of Christian missionaries in 'domesticating' small-scale societies. A well-known case reported by Lauriston Sharp has been that of the Yir Yoront aborigines of the Australian Outback, which provides a useful introduction to the nature of the impact.[15]

Yir Yoront of Australia

The Yir Yoront were a stone age society before the missionaries arrived. The missionaries adopted a policy of giving steel axes to these members of the community who assisted them in getting water and similar domestic chores. The aim was to provide simple technology which the local people would understand and so slowly raise their standard of living. However, as these helpers tended to be the younger women, sceptics have suggested that this was to target the more potentially malleable members of society.[16] The steel axes, however, had a detrimental effect which resulted in the total demoralisation of the tribe. Sharp argued that this resulted because the role of stone axes was far more complex than being simple technological devices.

Stone axes symbolised a variety of inter-personal relationships. External to the tribe, stone axes were important in the extensive trade network throughout the region. Internally, only men were allowed to own stone axes, so that a woman was always dependent on a man, usually her father or husband, to have the use of an axe. The missionaries therefore not only introduced new technology, but also introduced that technology according to their own criteria. Steel axes were given to those persons who helped the missionaries irrespective of whether they were male or female, young or old.

Second, women moved from being unable to possess axes to being able to possess the most efficient axes. They were therefore, according to Sharp, no longer so dependent upon men, which resulted in a confusion of gender and leadership roles. Old men were no longer respected and independent, and suddenly found themselves dependent upon women and younger men for the use of steel axes. The old men were therefore distrustful of the whites, and excluded themselves from receiving the axes directly.

Third, the external trading patterns were also confused as the demand for stone axes declined. Associated with this was the ending of the annual tribal gatherings, and a sense of demoralisation filled the people.

Some of the excitement surrounding the great ceremonies evaporated and they lost their previous gaiety and interest. Indeed, life itself became less interesting, although this did not lead the Yir Yoront to discover suicide, a concept foreign to them.[17]

The predictions of Sharp concerning the Yir Yoront have been proved to be over-pessimistic. Veronica Strang has argued that however often the missionaries gave axes to the women the axe continued to remain a male object, embodying masculine gender and all its associations. 'This was partly because the Aboriginal community, in a classic response to colonialism, led a double life; externally, it engaged superficially with the missionaries and settlers, but, on the whole, Aboriginal culture, like the ancestral beings, simply shifted to a slightly different dimension, just out of sight. As soon as the successive regimes of church and state were lifted and the community regained some self-determination, it was pulled back into the foreground, like the ancestral forces, through the performance of customary practices.'[18]

Amazonian Indians

From the mid-1960s the criticism has mainly been levelled against missionaries working among the more isolated and smaller communities. These people have been the main focus of activity for the New Tribes Mission (NTM) and Wycliffe Bible Translators (WBT/SIL) who have therefore taken the brunt of such criticism. Early criticisms came from the World Council of Churches (WCC) who co-sponsored the Declaration of Barbados in 1971, which warned against paternalism and patronage.[19]

The German anthropologist Mark Munzel in 1974 published a report claiming that the Ache Indians in Paraguay were being hunted and killed, or sold into slavery by local ranchers.[20] Although the Paraguayan government maintained a 'reservation' for the Ache in the area, Munzel reported that the Indians were being subject to appalling abuse. He claimed that this was all done with the full knowledge of the senior Paraguayan government officials. The government responded to the criticism by asking the NTM to take over the running of the camp. Munzel soon wrote a second report in which he claimed that there was little change at the camp, and Indians were hunting 'wild' Indians. The same story was reported by the journalist, Norman Lewis, in the *Sunday Times Magazine* of 26 January 1975 with an illustrated article entitled 'Manhunt'.[21]

NTM responded with the following explanation and denial:

> Indians from the camp go out to bring in other Indians only when they hear that such other Indians are in need and want to come into the camps. The other Indians are always given a free choice of coming into the camps or staying in the jungle. It is not true to suggest that they are brought in by force or coerced in any way. The Indians going out from the camps usually carry shotguns but these are only for the purpose of hunting and are not in any way used against other Indians.[22]

The accusation continued, and in September 1980 Survival International launched a photographic exhibition in London entitled 'Hunting the Pig People: Indians, Missionaries and the Promised Land'.[23] In 1981, Survival International co-published a book that claimed to be an anthropological perspective on the work of SIL.[24] In 1988, Norman Lewis published his controversial book *The Missionaries*, which gained much media attention.[25] NTM and SIL have both responded to the accusations, pointing out the many inaccuracies in these articles and the evident bias of the writers. Today, most anthropologists realise that accusations are biased and inaccurate, but it is worthwhile examining the charges that have been made.

Missionaries to these small-scale societies have been accused of two crimes. The first is genocide, which is the act of actually accomplishing or being responsible for the death of an entire tribe. The argument is as follows. The Indians are living in natural isolation until white missionaries contact them. These first contacts usually consist of the exchange of gifts, as with the Yir Yoront example mentioned previously. After gaining the friendship of the Indians the missionaries then seek to live in the area and learn their language. The presence of the missionaries brings the people into contact with the wider population, and some of the forest people may even be taken by plane to the city where they are exposed to civilisation. It is during this period that epidemics can occur amongst the people resulting in a great loss of life. Christian teaching encourages the people not to fight, and this allows traders and farmers to move into the territory without fear of attack. The gradual loss of their lands leads to economic problems, and finally social demoralisation. The missionary is considered guilty of genocide because he, or she, established the initial contact.

It is true that Indians often die as a result of contact with Westerners. The Indians are susceptible to Western diseases, but often the presence of the missionary with modern medical treatment saved lives. Often the Indians are mocked by the townspeople and regarded as second-class citizens. It has been the missionaries who have helped the Indians retain their land and some of their personal dignity. To accuse missionaries of genocide is clearly a distortion of the actual events.

The second accusation is ethnocide, which is the act of causing the death, or destruction of a culture by imposing a foreign culture. The argument here is that the missionaries convert the Indians from their traditional religion to that of a foreign religion. As a result the traditions are lost, and the people adapt to the national way of life. Some of the Indians may migrate to the city where they become the lowest class of society.

Do missionaries destroy cultures? All cultures are in the process of change and the contact of Indian culture with that of a vigorous national culture has a great impact upon a small-scale society. As will be described in the following chapter, the sudden exposure of a society to a wider community causes major questions about the traditional cosmology. Conversion to a major world religion is therefore likely, but as will be shown in the following chapter this is never a simple shift from the traditional religion to that of the missionary religion. Societies make the new religion their own. A culture may have gone through a radical transformation, but it cannot be simply considered as having died.

Yanomamo of Northern Amazonia

There are approximately 22,500 Yanomamo in the Amazon basin, making them the largest indigenous group in the area. They are spread among some two hundred villages in Venezuela and Brazil north of the Amazon River. Each Yanomamo village is autonomous, but each actively forms alliances with some villages whilst carrying out warfare with others. For this reason, Napoleon Chagnon entitled his book *Yanomamo: The Fierce People.*[26] This book quickly became a standard textbook for all undergraduates studying anthropology and brought the Yanomamo to the attention of the world. As such the Yanomamo have become a symbol of all marginal and endangered people.

A bitter dispute erupted between Chagnon and the Salesian Roman Catholic missionaries working among the Yanomamo, which illustrates many of the issues relating to indigenous people in a changing world. The event that triggered the dispute was the slaughter of 16 or 17 Yanomamo in August 1993 by illegal Brazilian miners who had journeyed into Yanomamo territory in search of gold. Chagnon and his friend Charles Carias had gone to the area to investigate the event when their presidential appointment was superseded and another presidential commission named. The Roman Catholic Bishop of Amazonia who was a member of the commission ordered Chagnon from the region. The missionaries argued that Chagnon was himself engaged in illegal mining, and wanted to keep the Yanomamo in a kind of human zoo and retard their technological development. Although only about 5 per cent of the Yanomamo were Christian and related to the mission stations, these Yanomamo expressed a desire for technological development. Chagnon responded that it was only 'mission

Yanomamo' and those controlled by miners who wanted technological development.

Without going into the bitter feelings of the dispute, it is important to identify the hub of the debate – 'Who speaks for the Yanomamo?'[27] Because the Yanomamo have a diffuse political structure there are no real tribal spokespersons. Only a handful of Yanomamo associated with the mission speak Spanish, and so are able to speak to the government. Is Chagnon correct in saying that only those Yanomamo who live in the forest are authentic Yanomamo? It has already been pointed out that it is inadequate to describe whole societies as a homogenous unit. If the Yanomamo are to survive, they must be able to make their own case to the Venezuelan officials, and they must also be aware of the dangers of certain changes. For example, they may want outboard motors for their boats, but they need to realise that to pay for the fuel they will have to work more and this will change their way of life. If people want to change, then outsiders telling them they cannot change are as guilty of cultural imperialism as those who want them to change.

In 1998, major fires raged through many of the tropical forests in the Amazon destroying the habitat of many traditional societies and the rich animal life. The Yanomamo were badly affected by these forest fires which were started by farmers and miners who had encroached on their land. As Frank Salamone shows, Yanomamo evaluations are sharp but fair.

We are content with the missionaries. The missionaries have done good things for us but the new missionaries are cheap. They are not generous like father Coco (one of the early Catholic missionaries in the area). They don't give us things like he did. They always tell us to work, to plan. We think it is better to be generous and to give things. But they are good men. They have built schools and they tell us not to fight and to settle our problems in peace. To protect ourselves from outsiders who bring sickness and who come to kill us.[28]

Both anthropologists and missionaries are concerned for the Yanomamo and similar peoples around the world. Many societies have been completely destroyed because of sickness and killing. These people cannot be penned into a human zoo, but must be allowed a voice to express their own views. The Christian Gospel invites change with the opportunity of a new lifestyle. Missionaries have been at the forefront of preserving indigenous languages, providing medical care and education. The danger is that the missionaries can impose their own lifestyle rather than allow the Indian Christians to develop a Christian culture that is meaningful to them with their unique history.

Notes

1 Achebe, C., *Things Fall Apart* (Nairobi: Heinemann, 1958).

2 Kunitz, S. J., 'Disease and the destruction of indigenous populations' in Ingold, T. (ed.), *Companion Encyclopedia of Anthropology* (London: Routledge, 1998), pp. 297–325.

3 Bruner, E. M., 'Mandan' in Spice, E. H. (ed.), *Perspectives in American Indian Cultural Change* (Chicago: Chicago University Press, 1961).

4 Wallensteen, P. 'Scarce goods as political weapons: the case of food', in Harle, V. (ed.), *The Political Economy of Food* (Westmead: Saxon House, 1978), p. 89.

5 Personal comments from Ivan Lowe, an SIL missionary who has worked among the Nambiquara.

6 Rivers, W. H. R. (ed.), *Essays on the Depopulation of Melanesia* (Cambridge: CUP, 1922).

7 Quoted in Whiteman, D., *Melanesians and Missionaries* (Pasadena: William Carey Library, 1983), p. 202.

8 Jewsiewicki, B., 'The formation of the political culture of ethnicity in the Belgian Congo', in Vail, L. (ed.), *The Creation of Tribalism in Southern Africa* (London: Currey, 1988), 324–49.

9 Van den Bersselaar, D., 'Creating "Union Ibo": missionaries and the Igbo language', *Africa* 67 (1997), 273–95.

10 Peel, J. D. Y., 'The cultural work of Yoruba ethnogenesis', in Tonkin, E., Chapman, M., McDonald M. (ed.), *History and Ethnicity* (London: Routledge, 1989), p. 201.

11 Schon, J. F., quoted in van den Bersselaar, *op. cit.* p. 276.

12 Van den Bersselaar, *op. cit.* p. 289.

13 *Ibid.*

14 Keesing, R. M., *Cultural Anthropology* (New York: Holt, Rinehart and Winson, 1981), p. 402.

15 Sharp, L., 'Steel axes for stone-age Australians', *Human Organisation* 2 (1952), pp. 17–22.

16 Strang, V., 'Familiar forms: homologues, culture and gender in Northern Australia', *Journal of the Royal Anthropological Institute* 5 (1999), p. 91.

17 *Ibid.* p. 20.

18 Strang, *op. cit.*

19 Bartolome, M. A., *et al.*, *Declaration of Barbados: For the Liberation of the Indians* Copenhagen: International Work Group for Indigenous Affairs, 30 January 1971.

20 Munzel, M., 'The Ache: Genocide in Paraguay', IWGIA document 1974.

21 Lewis, N., 'Manhunt' in *Sunday Times Magazine*, 26 January 1975.

22 NTM, 11 September 1977, quoted in *Survival International Review* 6 (1981), p. 6.

23 'Why missionaries and not multinationals? An introduction to the Paraguay exhibition', *Survival International Review* 6 (1981).

24 Hvalkof, S. & Aaby, P., *Is God an American? An Anthropological Perspective on the Missionary Work of the Summer Institute of Linguistics* (Copenhagen: IWGIA & SI, 1981).

25 Lewis, N., *The Missionaries* (Sekker & Warburg, 1988).

26 Chagnon, N. A., *Yanomamo: The Fierce People* (New York: Holt, Rinehart and Winston, 1983).

27 Salamone, F. A., *The Yanomamo and Their Interpreters* (Lanham: University Press of America, 1997).

28 *Ibid.* p. 77.

Chapter Thirteen

RELIGIOUS CONVERSION

Harold Turner's definition of 'Primal Religions' as those religions that anteceded the major world religions implies that many
have changed their allegiance to the new religion. History has
in fact shown that traditional societies have more readily converted to major religions than people from one major religion
to another. In other words, if a traditional society converts to
one of the world religions they are unlikely at a later date to
turn to another major religion.

The growth of Christianity, for example, in the main
occurred through the conversion of traditional societies.
Christianity emerged initially as one of many Jewish sects, but
it quickly became a distinct religion in its own right mainly
through the acceptance of Gentile converts. These Gentiles of
the Roman Empire had formerly practised the many religions
in the Empire that could be defined as a 'primal' or 'traditional'.
With the conversion of Constantine in the fourth century,
Christianity was made the state religion of the Roman Empire.
The fifth century saw the eventual fall of the Western Roman
Empire, and the invasion of the northern peoples. However,
many of these northern people who had previously worshipped
nature gods converted to Christianity. The sudden expansion of
Islam in the seventh century resulted in a halt in the expansion
of Christianity for several hundred years, because Christianity

was essentially locked into the continent of Europe by the sea to the north and west, and the countries of Islam to the south and east. Then, in the sixteenth century, with the development of the sea routes to Asia, Africa and the Americas, a new expansion of Christianity occurred as many indigenous people from these regions were converted.

In this chapter I want to explore the question of why traditional societies have been so responsive to the major missionary religions such as Christianity, Islam and Buddhism. The issue is therefore one of the history of interplay between the culture and religion of the traditional societies on the one hand and missionary culture and religion on the other.

Theories of conversion

In the nineteenth and early twentieth century Western scholars had straightforward answers to the question of conversion. In their view, world religions could be distinguished by at least three characteristics. First, they had a greater intellectual coherence than traditional religions, and monotheism was 'obviously' more logical and sensible than polytheism. Second, the rationality of the major world religions allows scientific advance by avoiding the delusion of magic and taboo. Third, traditional religions were regarded as having no real scheme of ethics, so people were naturally attracted to the morality of world religions. Thus, as a society's intellectual and technical knowledge developed there was a need for a more systematic and rational cosmology, which encouraged people to adopt the 'higher' world religions. According to this view all the religions of the world were part of the upward evolution of humanity. For all societies, the history of religion is one of evolution towards greater reason and deeper ethical awareness. Thus, it was only natural that conversion would occur, and missionaries were only assisting the general process of religious evolution.

During the period of the 1940s and 1950s anthropologists came to a better understanding of traditional societies. They rejected the idea that all traditional religions were the same, and also questioned the model of unilinear religious evolution. One of the most elegant theories for religious change was put forward by Robert Horton, and is generally known as the 'Intellectual Theory'. Horton first went to Nigeria in the 1960s to teach at the University, and has continued to live among the Kalabari people ever since.[1] Although some of his ideas have been criticised, his continued presence in Nigeria has given him a practical relevance that has been much respected.

Horton argued that African Traditional Religions essentially relate to people's needs at two levels. The first is that of communion with God, which is also common with Western Christians. The second relates to the practical aspect of controlling the environment by means of magic in the sense of failed science. Horton stated that this second level sought to 'explain, predict and control' (EPC) events in the world. Anthropologists, Horton continues, have mainly come from Christian backgrounds where the element of communion has been stressed more than EPC. The result has been that Western scholars in their study of African religions have neglected the importance of the nature spirits, ancestors and local gods. Thus, the importance of EPC does not mean that traditional societies are less rational, only that they are more relevant to the restricted local situation.

Although Horton recognises that African cosmologies vary greatly he argues that there are common elements. Horton writes:

In the first tier we find the lesser spirits, which are in the main concerned with the affairs of the local community and its environment – i.e. with the microcosm. In the second tier we find a Supreme Being concerned with the world as a whole – i.e. with the macrocosm. Just as the microcosm is part of the macrocosm, so the

> Supreme Being is defined as the ultimate controller and existential ground of the lesser spirits ... The essence of the pre-modern situation is that most events affecting the life of the individual occur within the microcosm of the local community, and that this microcosm is to a considerable extent insulated from the macrocosm of the wider world.[2]

As the macrocosm is beyond the perception of the local communities there are no defined cults of the Supreme Being. As societies become more aware of the wider social structure, through trade, exchange of ideas, bigger states, the boundaries of the microcosm are dissolved and people are propelled to the major religions. The world religions such as Islam and Christianity also give important answers as to how the Supreme Being may be worshipped. He concludes:

> The crucial variables [in conversion] are not the external influences (Islam, Christianity), but the pre-existing thought-patterns and values, and the pre-existing socio-economic matrix.[3]

The theory has many strengths. First, conversion is set in the local context, and not that of the mission of the world religions. Second, it emphasises the similarity between Islam and Christianity rather than the differences. This is significant because initially African traditional societies see little difference between the teaching of these two monotheistic religions. Whether a village chooses to accept Islam or Christianity often has more to do with which of these religions arrives first than the actual teaching. Third, it does not try to explain all the complex aspects of culture change only that of religion. Finally, it provides a theory that can to some degree be tested.

Islamisation of West Africa

Although the model was appreciated, there were many who considered it to be too simplistic. Fisher, for example, in a vigorous debate with Horton pointed to the complexity of the process of Islamisation of West Africa. Conversion to Islam did not come about as a single stage as Africans became aware of the expanding Islamic world. The history of Islam in Africa covered a period of almost a millennium, and displays a pattern that can be roughly characterised as three-stages: quarantine, mixing, and reform.[4] In the quarantine stage, newcomers migrated into the region and came to represent Islam. These were often traders from North Africa, refugees, or clerics employed in providing religious services such as prayers and divination to their non-Muslim patrons. 'Orthodoxy is relatively secure as there are no converts, and thus no one to bring into the Muslim community heterodox beliefs and observances drawn from his or her non-Muslim past.'[5] For example, among the Asante of Ghana, non-Akan were required to live in separate areas of the towns known as *zongos*. It is through the presence of foreigners within the local community that Horton would argue that the macrocosm begins to impact on the microcosm.

Quarantine was not maintained indefinitely, and soon an increasing number of people began to accept Islam – bringing with them their traditional beliefs and practices. These converts then combined the profession of Islam mixed with their previous religious traditions. The outward signs of Islam are manifest, such as the manner of dress and the prayers that suggest a specific religious identity. During this period Fisher describes Islam as a 'juggernaut' moving forward, sometimes at an almost imperceptible pace, but with a momentum resulting in the cumulative impact of Islam.[6]

Finally, after a lapse of decades, or even centuries, a wave of reform sweeps away the mixed Islam and establishes orthodox Islam. This often resulted from the devotion of some cleric who after pilgrimage to Mecca initiated a holy war, and the establishment of a fundamentalist state. Here the juggernaut is at full speed resulting in militant reform. The nineteenth century was the high point of Islamic reform in West Africa with many important jihads. An example was the ministry of Uthman dan Fodio who initiated a holy war among the Hausa and Fulani peoples, and established the Sokoto caliphate in what is now Northern Nigeria.[7]

The heart of the discussion between Horton and Fisher is that while Horton considers Islam more as a catalyst for change, Fisher considers that this fails to take seriously how world religions impose their own terms on society. 'One fundamental novelty introduced, in the long run, by Islam [and Christianity] has been the idea of an exclusive religious allegiance.'[8] Fisher therefore draws out a useful distinction between 'conversion' and 'adhesion'. Conversion implies a 'deliberate turning from indifference or from an early piety to another', while adhesion allows a believer to adopt new forms of worship as useful supplements to his former beliefs. The relative ease with which Islam can be adopted in Africa encourages conversion as well as mixing, so one can speak about a first and second conversion. Alternatively, one can look at the term 'conversion' as being used to denote three different types of change, as pointed out by Emefie Ikenga-Metuh:[9]

i)   Change of affiliation without change of conviction – Adhesion, e.g. a 'mixed' Islam or Christianity.
ii) Change of affiliation with change of conviction – Conversion I, e.g. from traditional religion to fervent Islam or Christianity.
iii) Change of conviction without change of affiliation – Conversion II, e.g. from 'mixed' Islam or Christianity to fervency.

Comparison of two African societies

The discussion of the subject of conversion in West Africa has raised many questions. One puzzle has been why the Asante of southern Ghana were much slower to adopt a world religion than the Yoruba of southwestern Nigeria. The Asante and Yoruba both straddle the savannah and forest, and have had a long contact with Muslim traders from north of the Sahara. Both Asante and Yoruba had well-organised city-states with a king. Why then did they have such different response to Islam? Today about 50 per cent of Yoruba are Muslim, while less than 5 per cent of Asante are Muslim. John Peel has considered this question.[10]

The Asante had a strong well-organised state that retained a strong sense of mutual integrity dependent upon the sanction of the traditional society. This is illustrated at the annual yam festival when chiefs from various parts of the Asante State journeyed to the capital Kumase to make sacrifices to the ancestors of the Asante. An important symbol of this religious act was the Gold Stool mentioned in chapter 4, which was the focus of the ancestral cult of the nation. The powerful status of the king (*asantehene*) meant that he was also able to exercise foreign policy, and so was able to control strangers coming into the state. The Asante effectively quarantined Islam and prevented its spread outside the designated areas for traders (*zongos*).

In contrast, the Yoruba perception of themselves was very different. The Yoruba were a less organised society, and allowed more religious tolerance. The Yoruba were never a single political unit until the twentieth century, but were organised in groupings of local kingdoms of various sizes. They recognised a common affinity through the claim of all their kings to descent from Oduduwa, a god who has reigned as Ile-Ifa. Ifa had been the first great kingdom in the West African forest, and even after its decline in political importance it was still considered the supreme cultic site and centre for the creation of the human race. Ifa was therefore an image of a past great civilisation and an important cosmological site, but it was not an active centre of political control like Kumase, the capital of Asante. Even after the British dismantled Asante State control, the people remained loyal to the *asantehene*. As late as 1944, the

Christian clergy, both missionary and Asante, petitioned the king affirming their loyalty to their chiefs, even though their religious scruples prevented them from treating Thursdays, sacred to the earth goddess, as rest days. The same attitude of respect to the *asantehene* was seen in the enduring sense that the roles of chieftancy and church membership were incompatible.

This comparison tends to undermine Horton's argument that the new experiences of a people renders their old explanations inadequate. Peel reminds his readers that religion also serves to define the membership of a social group and to underpin authority in them. Thus, if a traditional society has a strong central authority it is less likely to convert than one without a defined state. Writing of the Asante, Peel comments: 'Religion had its power because it was already the shared idiom in which both chiefs and people confronted the pains and anxieties of the human situation.'[11] Peel also suggests that historians, like Fisher, have tended to focus on the outside forces that trigger African conversion to Islam or Christianity, while anthropologists, like Horton, have tended to focus on local social institutions that provide the foundations for the acceptance of Islam or Christianity.[12] In practice both perspectives are important.

Another expression of Horton's model is the difference in the conversion of men and women from the same community. Women tend to be more localised looking after the children, whilst the men have to migrate in order to trade, find work and pay taxes. This means that men move into the 'macrocosm' earlier than the women, and this agrees with the general observation that it is usually the young men who first accept Christianity and Islam. In many West African societies it is the men only who are educated in Islam, and the women retain much of the traditional beliefs. In Christianity it is often the young men who join the Church first, and the women follow and eventually outnumber the men.

Horton's model is helpful with regards to the phenomenology of conversion by stressing as it does the local perspective.

However, it fails to address the way in which religious change relates to power structures within society – as with the Asante-Yoruba example. As Hefner concludes: 'Even if politically imbalanced, conversion encounters are always two-sided, and the social and intellectual dynamics of each example affect the outcome. Rather than overemphasise intrinsic and extrinsic variables in conversion, then, we should explore the way in which the two interact and expect that the relative importance of each may vary in different settings.'[13] This will clarify why some traditional peoples eagerly embrace Christianity, while others tend to appropriate selectively, and some make an outright rejection.

The Pitjantjatjara of Australia

Most of the previous discussion has related to Africa, but in recent years the conversion debate has been applied to other areas of the world. The general notion that has been assumed is a shift from the traditional to a rational world religion or, as Horton argued, from 'microcosm' to 'macrocosm'. Yet in many cases the religious changes have been unexpected or have not occurred at all. For example, the Pitjantjatjara of the desert region of central Australia have not converted to Christianity.[14]

The Pitjantjatjara are one of the largest groups in the western desert with a population of about one thousand living in an area of several thousand square miles. They were hunter-gatherers, but since the 1960s they have moved to a mixed cash economy with dependence upon social welfare funds. In spite of these changes the social and religious structure of the Pitjantjatjara have remained intact. Initiation rituals have been precisely followed, and supported by the virtual prohibition of marriage to non-initiates, and the practice of the 'Red Ochre' ceremonies by individuals from different regions. Ritual and religious totemism remain an essential basis for all human activity.

Missionary work among the Pitjantjatjara began in the late 1930s with the establishment of a Presbyterian mission at Ernabella, in the Musgrave Ranges. In addition to evangelism the mission was charged with buffeting the people from the gradual encroachment of European settlers. From that time the mission has successfully cared for the people, providing employment, medical aid, and selling commodities and provisions. Initially the Pitjantjatjara were hired to work as shepherds to provide meat, and the wool that was spun to make rugs for tourists shops in Alice Springs. By the mid-1970s the sheep industry was phased out because of the high costs.

The most important element of Pitjantjatjara religion is myths expressed in the Dreamtime. These myths explain not only how the world came into being, but how the Pitjantjatjara fit within that universal scheme. Two vehicles reproduce these myths: physical markers and language. Most of the environment is marked by the tracks of mythic heroes and ancestral beings who travelled across the ancient landscape. The myths tell the unfolding of the Dreamtime from the ancient past to the present world. Myths do not stand apart from human intervention, but exist as moral imperatives revealed for the present. Any individual who has been fully initiated has equal access to spiritual and economic knowledge, such that within a group all individuals have the same knowledge with the possible exception of the medicine man.

From the commencement of missionary work until the mid-1980s, the missionaries counted only about eight or ten 'true' converts. These are those who have not undergone the initiation rites. Yengoyan in his article suggests three reasons why the Pitjantjatjara have not accepted Christianity. First, Christianity has a futuristic orientation with life hereafter being a central belief. 'For the Pitjantjatjara, salvation, damnation, and the future of each person are non-issues. It is not the future which is important but the message of the ancient past that lives in the present to determine what will happen.'[15] The second point is that in Pitjantjatjara religion there is no belief in a single omnipotent force. Third, the importance of collective action among the Pitjantjatjara means that they are negative of any individual claiming particular knowledge, such as the prophetic figures of the Bible. They are also suspicious of individuals who either have left the local area or are trying to gain influence through the manipulation of other people. Yengoyan writes: 'When the Pitjantjatjara hear prophetic accounts from the Bible, and when they understand that they are the words of one individual, their first reactions are distrust and caution; eventually they express denial through lack of involvement. They cannot accept that this edifice of religiosity emerged and evolved from biblical characters like Moses, Abraham, Christ, and the disciples.'[16]

As an epilogue to the issue of Christian conversion of traditional societies, one might ask whether Westerners have been converted to traditional religions. Among the Aborigines at least eight whites have undergone initiation rites, and have adopted local traditions to a limited extent.

The Maisin of Papua New Guinea

John Barker has examined the conversion of the Maisin of Papua New Guinea to Christianity.[17] Uiaku consists of two beach villages, separated by a broad shallow river, on the southwest shores of Collingwood Bay in northeastern Papua New Guinea. The local economy was based on subsistence farming, fishing and hunting, and the local people make extensive use of the local trees and plants. The New Guinea mission of the Australian Anglican Church sent teachers to the village of Uiaku in 1901 and by 1911 large numbers of the villagers began to accept baptism. The first missionaries expressed admiration for village life and were reluctant to interfere directly with native customs. The Rev. Henry Newton, for example, wrote in 1914 that the church 'is not to be a body distinct from the native life, but rather one that permeates the whole by its influence . . . The Mission have not come . . . to change native life into a parody of European or Australian civilisation.'[18] However, the missionaries believed that they could not but make an impact on the community through the way they set up their mission station, and ordered their schools, religious programmes, and work schedule.

Barker argues that in Maisin society there are two conversion processes, one he calls 'external' and another 'internal'. The external is characteristic of the station domain. The church is the largest building in the village and the centre of its largest celebrations. When important visitors came to the village they always stay at the mission station. The church is therefore the outward face of Uiaku, and the link to the wider world. Young people grow up attending the school and church and model their roles on the teachers and their ideas on Europeans. But the picture of rampant Western Christianity is misleading when applied to Uiaku as a whole. As Barker states:

> Indeed, from a number of standpoints the eighty-year attempt to plant Christianity has been an abysmal failure. Only a small minority of Maisins – mostly women and children – regularly attend church services; few individuals have more than the vaguest notion of church doctrine; most villagers are firmly convinced of the reality of local bush spirits and sorcerers; and individuals frequently disregard church strictures on marriage and divorce.[19]

The 'internal' quality of conversion occurs within the village domain, drawing upon received notions and is not easily noticed. This is because both historical resources are unreliable, and the modification has gained an indigenous quality. 'On the one hand, Maisins often insist that their customs are unchanged from the time of creation. On the other, they credit missionaries with making fundamental changes in the very bases of the community.'[20]

The Maisin have tended to assume that Christian figures

exist in the same cosmology as their more familiar entities of
the microcosm. People tell of encounters with Jesus, the Virgin
Mary, and Jacob's ladder in dreams. However, these manifestations are rare compared with those of local spirits, ghosts and
sorcerers. As Horton's theory suggests, the people have tried to
understand Christianity in terms of their existing familiar cosmology of the invisible world.

> Thus all Maisins participate in the macrocosm and the microcosm,
> and all engage in station and village activities and ideas that
> together influence the overall direction of conversion. Understood
> in this way, Maisin conversion cannot be adequately understood in
> unilinear terms as either capitulation of resistance. Instead, we
> must view the Maisin as active participants in a much more com-
> plicated and ambiguous conversion process, participants who draw
> upon a variety of old and introduced tools to refashion themselves
> in a more complex world.[21]

From these various examples one may conclude that although
Horton's intellectual model has a general relevance, the local
religious tradition can hinder and even halt the process altogether. Some people like the Maisins can draw the world religion into their existing cosmology to form an even more complex
religious expression.

Religious diversification

More recent studies have also shown that religious conversion
is not a one-way process from traditional religion to major
world religion. Where there are competing world religions
other factors come into play that can result in a religious
diversification. Mario Aguilar has examined the particular case
of the Waso Boorana in Kenya.[22]

The Waso Boorana live around the river Waso Nyiro in the
North Eastern Province of Kenya and number some several
thousand people. They are one of the Oromo-speaking peoples

of East Africa who number nearly twenty million. The Boorana of this region originally came from Ethiopia and northern Kenya and were forced south by famine and feuding. Many fights then occurred between the Boorana and the Somali until in 1932 the British moved and settled some of the Boorana into the Waso area. The result was a lessening of tension between the Boorana and the Somali through the establishment of a clear boundary. However, it also resulted in the isolation of this group of Boorana from the majority in the north, and the Waso Boorana were no longer able to take part in the initiations at the traditional sacred places.

The Boorana religious system had a Supreme Being, *Waga*, who is considered to have the same attributes as the Supreme Being in Christianity and Islam. There were also *ayyaana* spirits, which were manifestations of good or evil. This Oromo cosmology sounds very much like that assumed by Horton. It could therefore be argued that the Waso Boorana had to change their way of explaining the world because of their isolation from the other Boorana in Ethiopia. From a microcosm that was previously assumed by the Oromo people, the Waso Boorana changed to a macrocosm that was a larger British and Somali construction of the cosmos. The lesser spirits, *ayyaana*, were identified with the *jinn* of the Islamic religious system of the Somali, and were assumed still to be effective. Aguilar explains, 'They became 'somalised' as their cosmological order was taken away through the establishment of political and tribal boundaries in the Northern Frontier District.'[23]

Horton would argue that the Muslim traders and clerics would act only as a catalyst in the process of conversion to Islam. If one applies Fisher's historical periods of conversion to Islam, the Boorana would be considered to have accepted Islam, the mixing had also taken place, but the reform had not occurred. There are few signs that the Waso Boorana are going to move onto the third stage because they still have great respect for their own traditions.

With Kenyan independence in 1963, further changes were forced upon the Waso Boorana. At this time there was concern that this northern region may become part of the Somalia Republic. A state of guerrilla warfare occurred during the period 1963–9 during which the Waso Boorana were concentrated into camps, which resulted in thousands of their animals dying. Somali politicians encouraged the Waso Boorana to join the rebels' fight against the Bantu-speaking people of Kenya. During this period the Muslim religious leaders (Boorana and Somali alike) were moved out of the Waso area, because they were accused of causing agitation. This meant that during this period the people did not have any religious leaders to lead them in prayer and instruct them in Islam.

In 1969 peace was finally restored. The Waso Boorana had lost their animals and were almost destitute as a result of their support for the Somalis. They then realised that when the Kenyan soldiers had moved into the area, the Somalis had moved out and left them. Questions began to be raised about the benefits of practising Islam. In contrast, during the post-war famine, efforts were made by the Roman Catholic and Methodist Churches to establish food aid programmes. The Methodists built a secondary school and orphanage for the people. Some of the young people who attended the school became Christian. New traditional ritual specialists also arrived in the area and sacred enclosures for the *ayyaana* cult were built in the region. Women became prominent in the traditional practices in the home. Later the Islamic Foundation also established primary schools. The Waso Boorana have therefore become very diverse in their religious beliefs and practices. This process of diversification has been a rational communal response to the need to keep peace at a communal level amidst a changing situation.

Aguilar's conclusion sums up the important lessons of this whole chapter:

In summary, I have argued in this article that historical processes of conversion need to be assessed not only from the point of view of one of the world religions but also in terms of the adaptability of a local religious tradition or the committed preaching of a group of missionaries. The discussion of local categories related to social organisation can provide another category for understanding religious change. Conversion from a local tradition to a world religion does not happen once and for all but is constantly taking place through historical processes at different levels of a particular society.[24]

In the following three chapters I shall explore some of the processes that can take place within societies as a result of their impact with a dominant missionary religion and culture. The first process is one of demoralisation, then syncretism, and finally revitalisation.

Notes

1 Horton, R., 'The Kalabari world-view: an outline and interpretation', *Africa*, 32 (1962), pp. 197–220.

2 Horton, R., 'African conversion', *Africa* 41 (1971), p. 101.

3 Horton, R., 'On the rationality of Conversion', *Africa* 41 (1975), p. 221.

4 Fisher, H., 'Conversion reconsidered: some historical aspects of religious conversion in Black Africa', *Africa* 43 (1973), pp. 27–40.

5 *Ibid.*, p. 31.

6 Fisher, H., 'The Juggernaut's Apologia: conversion to Islam in Black Africa', *Africa* 55 (1985), pp. 153–73

7 Last, M., 'Reform in West Africa: Jihad movements in the nineteenth century', Ajayi & Crowder (eds.), *History of West Africa*, vol. 2 (London: Longman, 1987), pp. 1–47.

8 *Ibid.* p. 165.

9 Ikenga-Metuh, E., 'The shattered microcosm: a critical survey of explanations of conversion in Africa' in Petersen, K. H. (ed.), *Religion, Development and African Identity* (Uppsala: Scandinavian Institute of African Studies, 1987), pp. 11–27.

10 Peel, J. D. Y., 'History, culture and the comparative method: a West African puzzle', in Holy, L. (ed.), *Comparative Anthropology* (Oxford: Blackwell, 1987), pp. 88–118.

11 *Ibid.* p. 108.

12 Peel, J. D. Y., 'Religious change in Yorubaland' *Africa* 37 (1967), pp. 292–306.

13 Hefner, R. W., *Conversion to Christianity* (Berkeley: University of California Press, 1993), pp. 23–4.

14 Yengoyan, A. A., 'Religion, morality, and prophetic traditions: conversion among the Pitjantjatjari of Central Australia', in Hefner, R., *Conversion to Christianity* (Berkeley: University of California Press, 1993), pp. 233–57.

15 *Ibid.* p. 248

16 *Ibid.* p. 249.

17 Barker, J., 'We are *Ekelesia*: conversion in Uiaku, Papua New Guinea' in Hefner, R. W., *Conversion to Christianity* (Berkeley: University of California Press, 1993), pp. 199–230.

18 *Ibid.* p. 202.

19 *Ibid.* p. 209.

20 *Ibid.* p. 210.

21 *Ibid.* pp. 216–7.

22 Aguilar, M. I., 'African conversion from world religion: religious diversification by the Waso Boorana in Kenya', *Africa* 65 (1995), pp. 525–43.

23 *Ibid.* p. 532.

24 *Ibid.* p. 536.

Chapter Fourteen

RELIGIOUS SYNCRETISM

The previous chapters have shown that the response of a people to a foreign religion is not a simple process of merely accepting new ideas and rituals. The new religion is usually crafted in various ways to make it more immediately relevant to the specific local needs. Many of the former ideas and rituals may remain, and become incorporated with the symbols of power of the new religion. This process of mixing, or syncretism, is the subject of this chapter, and especially the way a world religion may be expressed in the lives of ordinary people.

Redfield's model

Redfield was particularly concerned to describe the culture of many Latin Americans who were farmers living in small villages, but dependent upon the market town for important aspects of their daily needs. They were different from the Indians whose culture had essentially been self-contained, and yet these farmers were unlike the urban dwellers. These people are often called 'peasants'. In his book *Peasant Society and Culture*, published in 1956, Redfield argued that peasant societies are not autonomous, but an aspect of a wider civilisation of which they are merely a part.[1] Thus, peasant culture must be considered as only a half-society that can only be fully understood in relation to the whole. Shanin proposed the following definition to cover a similar class of people around the globe.

> The peasantry consists of small agricultural producers, which with the help of simple equipment and the labour of their families produce mainly for their own consumption and the fulfilment of obligations to the holders of political and economic power.[2]

Redfield and Shanin were here trying to show that societies could not simply be portrayed as bounded groups, but are 'open' and continually under the influence of the wider civilisation.

The peasants of Latin America generally state their allegiance to the Roman Catholic Church, but even so they manifest many of the beliefs and practices that have similarities to traditional religions. In order to discuss the religious nature of peasant society, Redfield therefore employed a two-tier model with the concepts of the 'great' and 'little' traditions. The great tradition is the culture of the priests, theologians, and literary people who live mainly in the great cities. Although it is the most respected and authoritative, it is usually only followed by the elite educated minority. In contrast, the lesser tradition is the religion of the majority of villagers who were essentially illiterate and had little access to the teaching of the Bible. Redfield never suggested that these traditions were totally discrete, but argued that they were like 'two currents of thought and action, distinguishable, yet ever flowing into and out of each other'.[3] This approach stimulated much academic discussion on what was often known as 'The Little Community' following Redfield's book.[4] The basic question was how the small world of a village may be expressed within the wider context of a greater civilisation. Often the local religious expression is a reworking of long existing beliefs, but within the confession of the major religion. This notion of the great and little tradition has led to the structuralisation of the religious system of a given village in terms of layers, one on top of the other. Frequently, the lowest level has been associated with the ill-defined term 'animism', which was a convenient term for a variety of traditional religious beliefs and practices.

This model has become a popular concept among Christian missionaries because it gives a simple way of explaining the differences they have observed between philosophical and local aspects of religions. Westerners have often noted that Islam, for example, is like a veneer over the traditional religious system of a people. An individual may claim to be a member of a major world religion, but their religious practice is a complex mixture of elements of the world religion and those of the earlier traditions. These local beliefs have often been classed as 'Folk Religion', as, for example, in *The Unseen Face of Islam* by Bill Musk.[5]

Norman Allison proposed the following characterisation of 'high' and 'low' religion. At the 'folk' level there may exist a range of associated ideas, beliefs and rituals.[6]

High Religion	Low Religion
Answers cosmic questions: origin of the universe, meaning to life	Answers everyday issues: sickness, drought, war
Written texts with fixed system of beliefs	No written text. Myths and rituals.
Specialist leadership roles	Informal leadership, no specialists
Central institutions: church, mosque, temple, and formal training of leaders	Few formal institutions
Formalised moral code	Pragmatic

An example would be the British celebration of Christmas. A theologian would explain Christmas as a ritual to celebrate the historical events of the incarnation of the second person of the trinity in human form. However, at a popular level one finds numerous mythical characters such as Father Christmas, flying reindeers, talking snowmen, and the angel at the top of the Christmas tree. A stranger could easily be forgiven for thinking he or she was observing two totally different religious traditions.

Religion in village India

The discussion on 'little communities' was taken further by academics studying village religion in Asia, and notably by Mc Kim.[7] He studied the religious experience of people in a small village in Uttar Pradesh, north India. During his period in the village he saw the people worship ninety gods, goddesses, and godlings at one time or another. Of these deities one third were recognisably gods of the great pantheon including Vishnu, Rama, Krishna, Laksmi, Hanuman, and Siva. The majority, however, were not part of the great tradition, and consisted of widely known regional deities, down to local ghosts and spirits.

For example, the widespread festival of Krishna the Cow Nourisher has taken on many local variants that have no justification in the higher Sanskritic myth. The sacred hill of Krishna is symbolised in each household yard by little piles of dung, and the benefits granted by Krishna to his worshippers upon the sacred hill are represented by cattle and household objects also made of dung. These objects are made to increase the wealth of the household, which is a theme also apparent in the Cowdung Wealth song chanted the next morning before the objects are broken up and used for fuel. However, a portion of the cowdung from this celebration is reshaped into a wafer, which is then contributed to a great annual all-village celebration around a bonfire in which differences between households are set aside.

Adherence to deities of the great and little traditions is dis-
tributed through the hierarchy of castes with the Sanskrit
deities of the great tradition playing a more significant role
among Brahmins than members of the lower castes. Even so,
only 45 per cent of the deities worshipped by the Brahmins were
of the great tradition, and this was in a region that has been
settled by the Aryans for over three thousand years. As one
would expect the Brahmins, as priests of the great tradition,
were the local agents of the great tradition, but even they were
influenced by themes of the lesser tradition. Mc Kim therefore
concluded that one must not consider the higher and lower traditions as two distinct religious traditions. The religion of the
villages of India may be conceived as resulting from a continuous process of communication between a little local tradition
and greater traditions that have their place partly inside and
partly outside the village. 'Only residual fragments of the religion of such a little community can be conceived as distinctive
or separate . . . great and little traditions may remain in equilibrium within the little community, neither tending to exclude the
other: elements of the great tradition may undergo parochial
transformation as they spread, while the great tradition itself,
where it originates as a universalisation of indigenous material,
lacks authority to replace elements of the little tradition.'[8]

Javanese religion

In his now classic study of Javanese religion, Clifford Geertz
also brought out the contrast between peasant religion and that
formulated by the religious specialists.[9] In Java, one can identify three streams of religious expression. The first is *prijaji*. The
word originally referred only to the hereditary aristocracy
which the Dutch pried loose from the kings of the vanquished
native states and turned into salaried civil servants. These
people follow the Hindu traditions that aim at spiritual excellence and aesthetic polish.

The second is the Javanese form of Islam, known as *santri*, which is associated mainly with the merchant stratum of Javanese society, but has also been joined by some of the wealthier peasants. *Santri* emphasises the careful and regular execution of the basic rituals of Islam – the prayers, the fast, the pilgrimage, and the contribution to the poor. Not only do the Javanese Muslims regard themselves as part of a distinct community in Java, but they are also aware of being part of a wider Islamic community of believers – the *Ummah*.

The third pattern is that of the peasant and is known as *abangan,* which includes elements of traditional religion, Hinduism and Islam. Prior to the coming of Hinduism to the island in about 400 AD, it seems likely that the traditional religion comprised the total religious system. The traditional religion proved to be remarkably resilient and over the centuries has absorbed many elements from both Hinduism and Islam. Today, the main focus is around the performance of the *slamestans*, or ritual feasts. A *slamestan* can be given on almost any occasion when one wishes to neutralise spirits that threaten to cause disorder and create disturbances. They may be used to deal with life crises, to cleanse a village of evil spirits, to celebrate dates in the Muslim calendar, to counter such irregular events as illness, change of residence or dangers of going on a journey. The *slamestan* are performed by curers, sorcerers or ceremonial specialists.

Prijaji, the religious variant of the town-dwelling gentry differs at almost every point as described in the previous table of contrast proposed by Allison. Whereas *abangan* is practical, *prijaji* is mystical. *Abangan* deals with polytheism and local spirits, whilst *prijaji* deals with abstract and speculative pantheism. *Abangan* is a curing technique in contrast to the mystical practices of *prijaji*. *Abangan* focuses upon the household, and *prijaji* upon the individual. The *abangan* shadow-plays tell the stories of the legendary heroes, while in *prijaji* these plays have a deeper meaning representing the conflict between crude passion and detached, effortless self-control. Although these two variants are polar opposites of each other, Geertz showed that they complement each other as symbolic statements of a reciprocal social relationship.

In his study of the village in Java, Geertz stressed the fact that the three religious variants did not encapsulate 'pure types' within a plural society. The three groups are all enclosed in the same social structure, and share many common values. The tension between the adherents of the various religious orientations is moderated by several important factors: the sense of a common culture has gained increasing importance following independence, the fact that religions have not become embodied as distinct classes, and the absence of any attempt to convert members of other traditions.

Village Buddhism in South Asia

Obeyesekere made a significant study of Buddhism in the villages of Sri Lanka.[10] He basically agreed with Redfield's model, and believed that in any civilisation there is a 'great tradition' and a 'great community'. In Sri Lanka, the great tradition is that of Theravada Buddhism, embodied in the Pali canon, which is expounded by the Buddhist monks. However, he argued that there is not just one 'lesser tradition', but many expressions within the peasant societies. Neither is there one exponent of the lesser tradition. The beliefs and practices are not explicitly presented, and vary greatly from village to village. Even so, Sinhalese Buddhism is a single religious tradition in which the various 'levels' of belief form an integral part of the whole.

The Sinhalese cosmology may broadly be described as falling into a hierarchy. Exalted at the top of the hierarchy is of course the Buddha, who, having achieved *nibbana*, is no more. Most people would agree that there is no point therefore praying to the Buddha, but in practice many still do in times of crises. The

Buddha is believed by many people to have transported himself to Sri Lanka on at least three separate occasions during his lifetime. He is said to have visited the holy places of Mahiyangana, Nagadipa, Kelaniya, and some say his left footprint remains embedded in the rock on top of Adam's peak (*Sri Pada*). The Buddha never forbade the worship of deities; he merely said they provided no release from human suffering. In times of personal crisis, it is therefore not unusual for a person to seek help from the gods.

According to tradition, the Buddha allocated to Sakra (the Vedic god Indra) the role of protecting the entire Buddhist Sangha, and Sakra in turn, delegated to Vishnu the task of protecting Buddhism in Sri Lanka. Vishnu is head of the pantheon, and according to some he will be Buddha after Maitreya. Vishnu is considered a benevolent moral deity with the capacity to grant favours to his devotees. Below Vishnu are the 'Four Guardian Deities' of the island, which are traditionally considered to be Natha, Saman, Kataragama and goddess Pattini. The identity of these four guardians has changed somewhat over the years, and Saman has often been replaced by Vishnu. This is shown in the names of the four *devales* (shrines for the gods) that surround a major Buddhist temple. For example, the famous temple of the Tooth in Kandy, probably the most sacred centre for Buddhists on the island, has *devales* for Natha, Vishnu and Pattini, and a short distance away the shrine for Kataragama.

Natha was formerly the Mahayana Bodhisattva Avalokitesvara, and appears to have been a very popular deity in the fourteenth and fifteenth centuries. Nathan is an active intercessory god who is sometimes considered to be the next Buddha – Maitreya. Pattini was the most popular deity among the peasants of Sri Lanka, and practically every village or group of villages had its Pattini priest. Her role was associated with curing of infectious diseases like smallpox, plagues and pestilence. She was propitiated in times of drought and consequent famines, and she was also believed to cure children's illnesses. Her popularity was then to be expected, but in fact Obeyesekere has noted a decline in her popularity during recent years.[11] He believes that this is in part due to the free medical treatment that is now available on the island, and compulsory inoculation for smallpox. Below these four guardians' deities are twelve gods who are less powerful and considered less pure. Below them are the demons, and finally at the bottom of the hierarchy are the spirits or *prete*.

The god Kataragama has increased in popularity in Sri Lanka during the twentieth century. He is a popular deity in south India where he is generally known as Murugan or Skanda. In higher tradition of Sanskrit mythology he is the second son of the great god Siva, and is perceived as a powerful, resourceful, god of war. In Sri Lanka, as in India, he is viewed as possessing six faces, twelve arms, and his vehicle is the peacock. Kataragama is considered to have two wives, or rather a wife and a concubine. He is the only major deity of the pantheon who is propitiated once a week with meat offering at the central shrine in the village also named Kataragama.[12]

The first reference to Skanda is recorded in the ancient text of the history of Sri Lanka, the *Mahavamsa*, in relation to a prince in the seventh century. The prince, whilst uttering magical incantations to the god, incurred the god's wrath, and the peacock on which the god was riding plucked out the eye of the prince.[13] This incident shows that Skanda is considered able to give magical powers to his devotees, but any slight will be resented. In the thirteenth century the worship of Vishnu and Saman were very widespread, and there is no reference to Skanda. From the sixteenth century onwards references to Skanda increase, and he is finally regarded as one of the guardian gods of Sri Lanka. He also became known by the name Kataragama, suggesting that the central shrine was prominent. It was during the time of the Kandyan Kingdom (1474–1815) that Kataragama assumed the role of the great god of war, and some of the kings gave patronage to the god especially when conflict emerged with foreign invaders such as the Portuguese, Dutch and British. Attempts were made to link him with Buddhism, for he is said to have made obeisance to the Buddha and obtained permission to help humans. The Buddha ordained that people should respect him but not worship him, which may indicate his inferior status.

The British conquest of Kandy in 1815 was followed by several rebellions, including one launched from Kataragama in 1817. The fact that all these attempts failed showed that Skanda's help was not of much use against the British. There was therefore a marked decline in the popularity of the deity from 1817 to 1920. However, since about 1920 there has been an increase in the numbers who are attending the shrine at Kataragama. The town originally nestled in deep jungle, but now the banks of the Menik Ganga river have been cleared. In 1949, Kataragama was connected by main road, and in 1952 buses were introduced to the route. In 1973, Obeyesekere records that there were 800,000 pilgrims, and most of these were Buddhists.

The central drama of the annual festival is the grand procession that leaves the main shrine for the Valli shrine every night for fifteen days. The area of the main shrine is connected to the shrine of Vallai Amma by a narrow street a few hundred yards long, leading towards the east. It celebrates the god's joyous union with his mistress Valli Amma, and it is significant that he does not visit the shrine of his first wife and legitimate spouse. Her shrine is sacred for Hindus but not for Buddhists. At the back of the main shrine is a street leading west to the white painted dome of the ancient Buddhist stupa Kiri Vehera.

The most remarkable feature of the celebrations is the self-mortification practised by some of the devotees, generally in repayment of vows. These include minor acts, such as rolling half-naked around the precinct on the scorching sand, or carrying on their shoulders the decorated arched frames known as *kavadi* for a hundred miles or more. Others skewer their cheeks and tongues with miniature spears, or are suspended from trestles on hooks that bear the weight of their whole body. One of the most famous spectacles at Kataragama is the fire-walking. Devotees walk over a bed of burning embers without visible sign of discomfort or injury to the soles of their feet. These acts of self-mortification are confined to a minority, and most pilgrims are involved in less flamboyant forms of worship such as giving offerings, or giving alms to the many beggars. They would also worship at the Buddhist *dagoba* known as Kirivehera.

Obeyesekere's central assumption is that cultures are integrated, and peasant cultures are therefore compounded inseparably from both great and little traditions. He argues that the term 'great tradition' is useful in describing the intellectual thought and interests of civilisations, and groups of individuals who promote those interests. This is the teaching of the experts, theologians, or lawyers of the world religion. It is the senior Buddhist monks who teach the profound philosophy of the Dharma in Sri Lanka. Likewise, in the Muslim world it is the Islamic scholars who teach the Shariah Law to the Muslim community. One can add that it is the Christian theologian who will give the authentic Christian teaching about Christmas, to use the illustration mentioned earlier.

The 'little tradition' is the whole culture of the peasant society, which is linked with the great tradition through common idioms. It is therefore not possible to identify discrete elements that belong to folk religion because it is integrated into the whole culture. Common cultural idioms establish channels of communication between the two traditions, and link peasant society with the greater tradition.

Defining orthodoxy

The question that emerges from this discussion is who defines the content of the great tradition? In the previous example of

Buddhism in Sri Lanka the answer is that it is the leading abbots of the Theravada tradition. In contrast, diverse local versions of a notionally standard Theravada Buddhism are often considered as examples of syncretism in a critical sense. The term syncretism has often been used for the mixing of a supposively 'pure' major tradition with a mixture of local elements. However, Buddhism, like all major religious traditions, has changed during its long history. Recently the issue of 'purity' and 'authenticity' in religions has been the centre for academic discussion. Rosalind Shaw and Charles Stewart have expressed the views of many anthropologists when they wrote:

> Simply identifying a ritual or tradition as syncretistic tells us very little and gets us practically nowhere, since all religions have composite origins and are continually restructured through ongoing processes of synthesis and erasure . . . If we recast the study of syncretism as the politics of religious synthesis, one of the first issues which needs to be confronted is what we have termed 'anti-syncretism': the antagonism to religious synthesis shown by agents concerned with the defence of religious boundaries. Anti-syncretism is frequently bound up with the construction of 'authenticity', which in turn often links to notions of 'purity'.[14]

In these terms the discussion of syncretism relates to those who have authority to label others as authentic or syncretistic. In the Sri Lankan example, the abbots are supported by the national government who in turn provide the necessary services on a national level. Similar anti-syncretistic elements can be seen in many other world religions. In Islam, the imans and scholars teach the 'authentic' teaching to villagers who claim allegiance to Islam. Similarly in Christianity, theologians and missionaries teach new converts the essentials of the Christian Faith. In each case the religious authorities are closely associated with the political government of the day that shows a link between orthodoxy and political power.

This link is especially notable in religious movements that are loosely called 'fundamentalist'. Islamic fundamentalists, for example, aim to establish an Islamic State that upholds the Shariah law. The anti-syncretistic process seeks to erase all elements deemed alien from Islam, and restore 'pure' Islam. Selected elements may be identified as foreign and rejected, or alternatively recast and retained through claims that they have always been part of orthodox religion. Similar processes can be seen in Hindu Fundamentalism and Christian Fundamentalism.

Modernity

A final dimension to this discussion relates to the globalising (Westernising) influences of modernity. Terwiel has sought to discuss this issue with regards to monks in modern Thailand.[15] As a result he found it useful to make a distinction between what he called 'syncretistic' and 'compartmentalised' Buddhism. Syncretistic Buddhism is more akin to what has previously been described as 'folk' religion. This is typically found among lower income earners such as farmers, factory workers and servants. Their usual residence is in the rural areas and in the poor quarters of towns and cities. These people have little or no formal education. In contrast, 'compartmentalised' is the way many more educated people make a distinction between their religious practice and their involvement with the contemporary global world. These people are higher ranking government officials and include nobility and even church dignitaries. Although they have a commitment to philosophical religion this is partitioned from the world of computers and international finance.

As the peasants migrate into the urban slums they bring with them their syncretism of religious ideas, beliefs and rituals. This mixes with the folk practices of peasants from other regions, and with the ideas of modernity. The result is a complex mixture that is markedly different from that of the orthodox tradition. In urban communities popular religion must not be considered as a melting pot of religious variants, but more of a stew pot in which various elements retain their integrity whilst gaining some of the more diffuse ingredients.

What characterises 'folk religion' is its practicality in seeking to meet the basic needs of the people themselves. They are more concerned with the question 'Does it work?' than 'Is it correct?' The following two chapters explore the growth of new religious movements that have emerged from the social tensions experienced by traditional societies. Although attempts have been made to classify these there is no simple pattern as such movements try to revitalise societies struggling in the midst of rapid change.

Notes

1 Redfield, R., *Peasant Society and Culture* (Chicago: University of Chicago Press, 1956).
2 Shanin, T., *Peasants and Peasant Societies* (Harmondsworth: Penguin, 1971).
3 Redfield *op. cit.* p. 72.
4 Redfield, R., *The Little Tradition* (Chicago: Chicago University Press, 1955).
5 Musk, B., *The Unseen Face of Islam* (Eastbourne: Monarch 1992).
6 Allison, N., 'Make sure you're getting through', *Evangelical Missions Quarterly,* 20 (1984), pp. 167–8.
7 McKim M., 'Little communities in an Indian civilisation', in Leslie, C. (ed.), *Anthropology of Folk Religion* (New York: Vintage Books, 1960), pp. 169–218.
8 *Ibid.* p. 213.
9 Geertz, C., *The Religion of Java* (Glencoe: The Free Press, 1960).
10 Obeyesekere, G., 'The Great Tradition and the Little in perspective of Sinhalese Buddhism', *Journal of Asian Studies* 22 (1963), pp. 139–53.
11 Obeyesekere, G., 'Social change and the deities: rise of Kataragama cult in modern Sri Lanka', *Man* 12 (1977), pp. 377–96.

12 Wirz, P., *Kataragama: The Holiest Place in Ceylon* (Colombo: Lake House, 1972).

13 *Mahavamsa* 1953, p. 193.

14 Stewart C. & Shaw, R., *Syncretism/Anti-syncretism: The Politics of Religious Synthesis* (London: Routledge, 1994), p. 7.

15 Terwiel, B. J., *Monks and Magic: An Analysis of Religious Ceremonies in Central Thailand* (White Lotus: Bangkok, 1994).

Chapter Fifteen

SLAVE RELIGION: AFRO-AMERICAN RELIGIOUS MOVEMENTS

'Mountains cannot meet, people can.' These were the words written on the front of a bus in the city of Port-au-Prince in Haiti. The saying sums up the nature of Haitian culture as a mixing of Africa, Europe and the New World. The syncretism has resulted in a rich variety of religious expression that has flourished and developed over the last three or four hundred years.

Today, many Afro-American religious movements meet in thousands of centres throughout Latin America. In the islands of the West Indies, Voodoo is a potent force especially in Haiti, and is practised by six million people on the island.[1] It extends to the mainland of Central America and the southern coastal regions of the United States. The term *Voodoo* derives from the Dahomean term *vodu*, meaning 'deity' or 'spirit'. Voodoo is a complex system of myths and rituals, which relates the life of the devotee to the deities that govern their life.

In Brazil, the Afro-American movements take on different expressions and go by various names: 'Macumba', 'Candomble' or 'Umbanda'. In 1991, there were estimated to be some thirty million people involved in Umbanda in Brazil out of a total population of 150 million with some 20,000 centres in the city of Rio alone.[2] However, the major ceremonies that used to take place on Copacabana Beach are no longer so visible as they were during the time of the 'Economic Miracle' of 1968–74. In recent years, Candomble, the movement most concerned with asserting authenticity in its African rituals, has shown greater growth. The Yoruba tradition has intensified, with initiates urged to study Yoruba language and rituals. The growth of Candomble compared to its rival Umbanda suggests a growing African cultural pride. These developments illustrate the continuing change of such movements and raise questions about the needs they meet.

From the complexity of religious beliefs of these movements, this chapter looks at two of the most significant: Umbanda in Brazil and Voodoo in Haiti. These illustrate not only the ways in which traditions have mixed, but also the role of spirit mediumship.

Slave religion

The origin of the Afro-American movements provide an important illustration of the interaction and development of religious beliefs and practices. It is especially important in showing how traditional beliefs may take on new forms within developing countries. Four main strands can be identified in the formation of the movement: West African traditional religion, indigenous Indian religion, Roman Catholicism, and European Spiritism.

When Christopher Columbus arrived in the West Indies in 1492, he found the islands inhabited by Taino Indians of South America, but the coming of the Europeans was to have a profound effect upon them. The Spanish were eager to seek gold and quickly subjected the Indians to hard labour in the quest for gold and also to till the new farms. Some of the Indians fled to the hills whilst others killed themselves in despair. The Europeans brought with them diseases to which the Indians had no immunity and many thousands died. The cruel treatment of the Indians by the settlers did not go unnoticed, and some years later Rome began to consider the discovery of the New World as a challenge to spread Christianity. By 1511 Pope Julian II had formed three bishoprics on the island of Haiti. Although the missionaries tried to stop the mistreatment of the Indians many died as slaves working in the growing plantations.

The need for new workers in the New World soon led to the development of the African slave trade. These people were torn from their homes in Africa, leaving most of their cultural heritage behind. In the USA initial high levels of slave importation rapidly gave way to an increasing reliance on the native born slave population, whilst in Brazil slave importations continued until 1851 when the slave trade was finally supressed. The new slaves provided a continuing replenishment of religious knowledge and skills among Brazil's African-descended population. These populations were also more densely concentrated in the large coastal cities than they were in the USA, and it is not surprising that it was in the coastal cities of Brazil that new movements grew. From the religious beliefs and rituals salvaged from the various peoples and languages of Africa, spirit possession was a common element accepted in America. When the drums sounded and the proper songs sung it was believed that the gods of Africa could hear their people across the sea and come and possess them.

Because the white masters were Roman Catholic they required their slaves to have at least the appearance of Roman Catholicism. Little real religious instruction was given, but the slaves did become familiar with the Roman rituals and saints. If their masters found slaves practising anything of their traditional religions they were beaten. Therefore to prevent interference, the slaves provided their gods with the identities of Roman Catholic saints. As long as the saints were venerated the masters did not enquire into the nature of the rituals and what was done. Many of the Yoruba gods thus became associated with a particular Catholic saint. For example, in Brazil, the Virgin Mary became associated with Yemanja, the Yoruba goddess of the sea. Shango the god of thunder and lightning was identified with St Jerome because of the fact that he dwelt in the desert with lions. Ogun, the Yoruba god of war, was identified with St George, and Jesus with Olorun the chief god.[3] Eshu, the master of divination, had already been associated by missionaries in Africa with Satan, and this was carried to Brazil. These new movements also adopted many of the Roman Catholic rituals and applied them in their distinctive ways.

In Haiti, slaves found possessing any of the symbols of voodoo were punished with lashings, imprisonment and even hanging. The cruelty of the white masters merely associated voodoo with a desire for independence, and in 1804 Haitian Black independence was gained. This gave freedom for the practice and development of Voodoo. In Brazil, such movements were criticised by the authoities, and even in the 1920s were portrayed in the national press as barbaric and depraved. The police often raided ritual centres and the leaders were jailed, with the result that many movements were driven underground. In 1965, Umbanda gained official recognition, and its centres of worship could be legalised by a simple process of civil registration. The 1970s therefore saw a rapid growth in Umbanda that was soon followed by over 10 per cent of the population of Brazil.

The final influence came from the writings of a French professor, Denizard Rivail, who wrote under the pseudonym of Allan Kardec. His book *The Book of Spirits* was first taken to Brazil in 1858 in the luggage of a Portuguese nobleman.[4] Kardecism has *alwa*ys claimed to be a science as well as a religion. He proposed the standard spiritualist teaching that human beings are considered to be spirits which take up a temporary abode in physical bodies. However, he also wrote of the possibility of successive reincarnations depending upon the moral choices made in life. The first spiritualist centre was opened in Salvador in 1865, and the movement quickly spread throughout the country. This literature had a special influence in the

Brazilian movements and resulted in a more refined expression that is still found in the country by the name of *Espiritismo*.

The isolation of Haiti from Europe after independence allowed the preservation of whole enclaves of African traditions in Voodoo. The shape of the religious practice depended on the particular blend of ethnic mix, and the Kardec tradition had little influence on the island.

Umbanda – Brazil

Umbanda appears to have started as a distinct movement in the 1920s in Rio.[5] One story is that around 1920, a young man called Zelio became paralysed. His father initially sought medical treatment before turning to Kardecism. Zelio was visited by the spirit of a Jesuit priest, who revealed to him that the sickness was spiritual and was the sign of a special mission. He was to be the founder of a new religion dedicated to the worship and propitiation of Brazilian spirits. He was also informed that he would shortly have a visitation from his own special spiritual mentor, who would give him further instruction. Zelio returned home and was soon cured. He then received the prophesied visit from his mentor who identified himself as the Caboclo of the Seven Crossroads. Zelio's mission was to found a new religion to be called Umbanda. The first Umbanda centre began in the mid-1920s, and eventually moved to a downtown area of Rio where it still flourishes today. Early in its history Umbanda acquired an explicit nationalist interpretation, which has served various purposes for the groups. This has given the movement increased appeal among the more educated Brazilians.

The emphasis in Umbanda is on experience rather than doctrine, and so one cannot find any fixed creed only a variety of religious ideas. Most Umbandists accept a cosmology consisting of three levels: the astral spaces, the earth and the underworld. God is the creator, but is distant and presides over the astral spirit world. Below him come other powerful personages in a complex hierarchical system. As mentioned earlier, these powerful personages have dual identities as African deities and Roman Catholic saints. The organisation is often based upon seven lines. The first line is headed by Jesus Christ and his counterpart Oxala, St Jerome/Xango the second; St George/Ogun the third; St Sebastian/Oxossi the fourth, etc. The seventh and lowest line is headed by St Michael, and has no African equivalent.

The next class of spirits is the Caboclos and Petros Velhos, or Brazilian spirits that have no African equivalent. These are known to Umbanistas through oral tradition, and through the texts of sacred songs sung at the ceremonies. Caboclos are collectively identified as unacculturated Indian inhabitants of the Amazonian forest. They are regarded as proud warrior leaders who are highly intelligent and talented specialists in curing and advising on a variety of problems. In contrast the Petros Velhos are polar opposites of the Caboclos: elderly, humble and patient. The songs for the Petros Velhos illustrate the difference in tone in being closer to the vernacular. The Petros Velhos are pictured as blacks, humbly dressed and seated on low benches leaning on canes.

Umbanda beliefs find their principal form of expression in the public ceremonies that take place in the evenings two or more times each week. The meeting places are usually decorated with paintings of the Caboclo and Petros Velho spirits. The room is divided with a fence, which separates the ritual area from the congregation. The ritual area consists of a dance floor, and at the far end facing the congregation is an altar. The initiates enter carrying smoking incense burners and begin to sing. The tempo of the meeting increases and members of the congregation begin to sing songs inviting the spirits to come down and work through the initiates. As the mediums dance, the spirits begin to appear, each spirit possessing the particular medium who is accustomed to receive him.

Mediums, as they become possessed, stop dancing, begin to perspire and often look slightly ill, sway, and then, bending over and giving a series of rapid jerks, receive their spirits. Upon straightening up, they have taken on the facial expressions, demeanour, and bodily motions characteristic of the particular spirit they have received. Caboclos wear stern, even fierce expressions and utter loud, piercing cries. They move vigorously around the dance floor in a kind of two-step, often dropping to one knee to draw an imaginary bow, and they smoke large cigars, whose smoke will be blown over their clients as a form of ritual cleansing and curing.[6]

Every person is thought to be a potential medium, and by means of divination one can find out which spirit is the potential possessor. However, not all spirits initiate such a relationship, but those who do may suddenly seize their donor. The relationship between the person and the spirit is simple and direct. The person makes his, or her, body periodically available to the spirit so that it may then manifest itself and take part in ceremonies, and in return the spirit provides various kinds of assistance. When a person is first seized by a spirit this may result in a fall, or the person staggers around the room making incoherent sounds. However, with the assistance of an experienced medium the person is helped to gain a control of their movements, and to allow the spirit to manifest its own particular character through their body. The mediums are aware of when they are possessed, or, in what they would call a 'pure' state – unpossessed.

When the Caboclo spirits first arrive at the ceremonies they kneel at the altar and pay respect to the saints represented there. They then ask for their accoutrements before beginning a series of elaborate ritual greetings, first embracing their fellow spirits and then leaving the ritual area to greet important visitors. The spirits then return to the ritual area, where they dance, sway, and puff on their cigars. In contrast, the Petros Velhos sit on a low bench and quietly smoke pipes.

The ritual area appears to be the scene of relentless activity with some remarkable displays of power. Some possessed mediums may ignite gunpowder on their bare hands, and others may pass a candle flame slowly over their body. One of the most important aspects of these ceremonies are the consultations with the spirits to whom people come for advice and healing.

> Caboclo Tupinamba, a much respected Indian warrior who works through a tiny white-haired woman of perhaps 60, commands in a loud voice for the servant attending him to fetch another of his favourite cigars. Puffing steadily and pausing to utter a long piercing cry, he turns to his first client and begins the consultation by giving him a big ritual hug. Next he gives him a ritual cleansing involving *passes*, in which he touches him lightly with his fingers, drawing off the evil fluids into his own hands, and shaking them off with a snapping sound. Then he anoints him with large puffs of smoke. 'Now, my child, what is your problem?' he asks. And the consultation begins.[7]

Umbanda has many rituals similar to those of the Roman Catholic Church. The ritual of baptism of infants follows that of the Catholic Church quite closely. The leader will recite the Christian formula: '"I baptise you in the name of the Father, and of the Son, and of the Holy Spirit" and everyone present shouts, "Baptised, baptised!".'[8] Infants are only baptised in such a way if it is felt that because of illness or some other reason the child is in need of special protection, and in such cases spirits can act as godparents.

Umbanda is composed of small groups of adherents organised around charismatic personalities. It varies greatly in ritual and in class composition, but is a common product of the rapid changes that have occurred in the southern cities of Brazil during the twentieth century. In so doing it has drawn together the main threads from Africa, Europe and the New World to form a distinctive religion that includes healing and gives guidance in a rapidly changing world.

Voodoo – Haiti

Like Umbanda, Voodoo has a variety of beliefs, but a common creed has been summarised by Leslie Desmangles:[9]

> I believe in Bondye, the Almighty Father of the sky, who manifests his spiritual nature in me; in a large number of spirits; and in all things visible and invisible.
>
> I believe in the *lwa*s, the gods of Africa, and all the saints of the Catholic Church. Masters of the universe, they are manifestations of Bondye, who see all things and direct the course of all things; that some have made themselves known to us through our ancestors in Africa, and others we have come to know, emulate, and serve in our new home in Haiti; that these *lwa*s are potent enough to mount us, their children, in spirit possession; and that through their mounting, they can inspire us as to the needs of our community; that our moral duty is to faithfully serve them; that the *lwa*s are capable, like us, of gentleness and mercy, but also of anger and revenge.
>
> I believe in the power of ancestors who watch over us and serve us before the *lwa*s; that they must be remembered and served faithfully.
>
> I believe that the *lwa*s interfere through magic in the normal flow of events as established by Bondye's will; in the efficacy of the medicines derived from the local fauna endowed to us by the *lwa*s. I believe in the Holy Roman Catholic Church, in the communion of saints, and in life everlasting.

Bondye is understood in a similar manner to the Supreme Being in most African traditional religions as described in chapter 2. Bondye is an impersonal deity who is identified with the forces of creation, and is manifest in the mountains and rivers. Bondye is considered to have fashioned the physical body of human beings from clay and water, and has infused his divine energy into this body as if it were a vessel. Humans are therefore like the world around them, and at death the body decays back to clay and the spirit (*espri*) is released.

The human spirit is conceived as consisting of two compartments. The first is the immortal, cosmic spirit of Bondye known as *gwo-bon-anj* ('big-good-angel'), which is the life force. This is the root of being and the source of physical motion identified with the flow of blood through the body, breathing, and the beat of the heart. *Gwo-bon-anj* is associated with varying degrees of creativity and intelligence. It is an immortal and divine spirit that manifests itself in human life. The other compartment of the soul is the *ti-bon-anj* ('little-good-angel'). It is personality, conscience, and reveals itself through individual behaviour. It mirrors the *gwo-bon-anj* in that it is able to make moral decisions. It is through this element that the individual is able to feel happiness or sadness, rightness or guilt with regards to one's relationship to others. These compartments are not understood as separate parts, but more that they must work together in harmony.

At death, the harmonious relationship between the two compartments is fractured and each follows its separate way. The expiration of the last breath is the expulsion of the *ti-bon-anj* from the body, and it is believed to enter into a heavenly state. This heavenly state roughly corresponds to the Roman Catholic doctrine in that the *ti-bon-anj* is believed to appear before Bondye and must suffer the appropriate penalties for its misdeeds. It is however believed to have no independent power and no further contact with the living.

In contrast, the *gwo-bon-anj* is of great importance to practitioners. The death rites performed by the priests are to send the *gwo-bon-anj* to join the ancestors in Ginen. There is no common agreement as to the location of Ginen, and some say it is under the sea, others in the bowels of the earth, and yet others above the sky. In this place the *gwo-bon-anj* takes the role of an ancestor. This is analogous to the death rite of the Fon where a priest comes to the house of the deceased with two goats and a rooster. He then sacrifices the animals to the gods and ancestors, and orders the soul and the protector deity residing in the head of the deceased to leave the body and enter the appropriate abodes: the deity to the sky and the soul to the ancestors.[10] The *gwo-bon-anj* will stay for one year and one day in Ginen, after which it will be absorbed into the family of the chief of ancestors. Then it may influence the human community through manifestations in the bodies of devotees by possession.

The body is by then an abandoned vessel separated from Bondye its life-force. It should disintegrate, return to the earth and never be animated again in the same form. There is a common belief that some sorcerers have raised bodies from the grave to make zombies. Because the body is now without a soul it is incapable of moral judgement, and is presumed to be under the control of the sorcerer. Vodouisants claim that zombies are often used for housework and labouring in the fields. Recently, there have been debates among anthropologists as to the possibility of zombification. Davis has argued that small doses of a concoction made from the backbone of the puffer fish create a state of profound lethargy in which the individual may be pronounced dead and then buried. If the body is soon raised from the grave, a state like that of zombie can be maintained through the administration of continuous small doses of the chemical.[11]

To ensure the body is not raised a number of ruses may be used. The priest may cut tufts of the dead man's hair and pieces of his fingernails, which are put in a jar to be buried with him later. This precaution hinders the possibility of a sorcerer tampering with the body before burial. A few branches of the sesame plant may be included in the coffin. A branch of sesame has a lot of seeds, and it is believed that a sorcerer would have to count all these seeds before being able to raise the body. The nose and ears of the deceased are stuffed with cotton wool so as to prevent the person from breathing again, or being awakened by a loud noise. Personal objects such as tools, toothbrush, and comb may also be included in the coffin to avoid the person returning to seek them.

Like many of the traditional religions of the world, Voodoo

believes that many invisible spirits or *lwas* populate the universe. The practitioners often group the *lwas* into families or nations, called *nanchons*. There are generally said to be seventeen *nanchons* of *lwas*, but most Haitians know only a few by name. They include the Wangol, Rada, Petro, Ginen, Kongo, Nago and Ibo.

As with Umbanda the *lwas* manifest themselves not only in material objects, but also in the lives of their devotees. Vodouisants come to know the *lwas* by drumming and dancing, singing and mimicking the personalities of the *lwas*. Voodoo is imitative rather than meditative. The *lwas* manifest themselves through the possessed devotee in a manner that the community envisages them in their local mythology. In the bodies of their devotees, the *lwas* take on the deportment and mannerisms of the *lwas*, and they ask for certain artefacts that identify them. In this way the community recognises which *lwas* have come to visit them in the meeting hall.

Milo Rigaud describes a typical possession.[12]

At a voodoo ceremony, someone in the company may be seated or walking around when all at once he seems to receive a terrible blow in a certain place on his body. Some initiates claim that it is at the nape of the neck; others that it is in the legs. Often he utters a cry or a moan, giving a clear impression that an invisible force means to or is trying to get control of him. He struggles, staggers, nearly always going around in circles, and throws his arms in all directions in an obvious effort to drive off the force that is trying to possess him . . .

But the moment the invisible power has mounted the 'horse', he becomes transformed, straightens himself up, and goes about the business of the mystere *who has taken his place in the person's own body.* The mystere gives his greetings, and usually asks for his special emblems.

These emblems consist of arms, costumes, kerchiefs to tie around the head, the waist, the wrist, or the ankles, magic wands, beverages and perfumes, which stand as symbols of the hermetic colours and forms of the invisibles. The symbolism in these objects permits the loas to perform their magic better.

Christian attitudes

The Afro-American religious movements have occurred during periods of rapid urban growth and social change amongst many people who felt alienated from the dominant Roman Catholic Church. This would illustrate Niebuhr's theory that all religious movements start life as sects amongst the poor, oppressed and underprivileged.[13] However, the growth of similar movements in many sections of Afro-American society shows a more complex process of development with the changing social context.

In general, the Roman Catholic Church has officially resisted these movements, and sought to safeguard orthodox Catholic traditions. As was mentioned earlier, this frequently resulted in denunciation and even persecution by the civil authorities. Today there is a more placid acceptance of these new religions. People like Desmangles are arguing that the Haitian Roman Catholic Church needs to become more flexible if it is to survive in the island. It can only do this by becoming more indigenous in both doctrine and practice.

It must allow the Haitians the opportunity to exercise their own resourcefulness in their religious practices, to take their destiny into their own hands, and to determine once and for all the fundamental choices necessary to ensure the formulations of, and adherence to, their own genuine religious traditions – whether these be purely Vodoo, or a Vodounized Catholicism.[14]

In contrast, the Protestant Church, which has shown significant growth throughout Latin America, has consistently opposed the various manifestations of Afro-American religious movements. Pentecostal churches especially draw large crowds with their emphasis on healing and deliverance. During their meetings, the spirits are asked to manifest themselves so that the church leaders may exorcise them. People are prayed for asking that God would heal them and give them guidance during difficult times. In their own way, these Pentecostal churches are addressing the same needs that attract people to the Afro-American churches. This in part accounts for the rapid growth these churches have shown during the twentieth century.

Notes

1 Desmangles, L. G., *The Faces of the Gods* (Chapel Hill: The University of North Carolina Press, 1992), p. 2.
2 Brown, D., *Umbanda: Religion and Politics in Urban Brazil* (New York: Columbia University Press, 1994), p. xvii.
3 McGregor, P., *The Moon and Two Mountains* (London: Souvenir Press, 1966) pp. 57–8, 187–92.
4 *Ibid*. p. 89.
5 The story is recounted in Brown, *op. cit.* pp. 38–49.
6 Brown, *op. cit.* p. 81.
7 *Ibid.* p. 82.
8 Leacock, Seth & Ruth, *Spirits of the Deep* (New York: Anchor Press, 1975), p. 298.
9 Desmangles, *op. cit.* p. 63.
10 Herskovits, M., *Dahomey: An Ancient West African Kingdom* (New York: Augustin, 1963), vol. 1, pp. 368–98.
11 Davis, W., *Passage of Darkness: The Ethnobiology of the Haitian Zombi* (Chapel Hill: University of North Carolina Press, 1988).
12 Rigaud, M., *Secrets of Voodoo* (San Francisco: City Light Books, 1985), p. 47.
13 Niebuhr, R. H., *The Social Sources of Denominationalism* (Hamden: Shoestring Press, 1954).
14 Desmangles, *op. cit.* p. 181.

Chapter Sixteen

DREAMS OF HOPE – RELIGIOUS MOVEMENTS

While all writers are in agreement that conversion on a larger scale is most likely to take place in times of rapid social and economic change, the local expressions are far more complex. The previous two chapters have considered the process of syncretism as traditional beliefs merged with various world religions. This has shown that people do not merely change their allegiance from one religious system to another. New religious ideas emerge as part of the continuous dynamic within such societies, and some of these may develop into coherent religious movements.

The movements have been variously named. Harold Turner proposed the term 'New Religious Movements from Primal Religions' known by the anachronism 'PRINERMs'.[1] He defined them as:

> A historically new development arising from the interaction between a primal society and its religion, and another culture and its major religion, and involving some substantial departure from the classical religious tradition of both the cultures concerned in order to find renewal by reworking the rejected traditions into a different religious system.[2]

Turner argued that as the major cultural impact upon traditional societies in recent centuries has come from the interaction with Europeans who were at least nominally Christian, the new religion was usually Christianity. This often occurred as a direct result of the European missionary endeavour, but may also result from a wider contact with Western society. With such a broad definition the examples of Umbanda and Voodoo mentioned in the previous chapter may be included.

These movements have sometimes been called 'Regional Cults' because they are more far-reaching than any traditional religion, yet less inclusive in belief and membership than a world religion in its most universal form.[3] Regional cults therefore come in the middle range, and their central places are shrines that are often important centres of pilgrimage to which people come from a variety of language and social groups. They would include cults of Muslim marabouts, Christian and non-Christian prophets, local and territorial mediums. Regional cults therefore flow across major political or ethnic boundaries, and show great flux in growth and decline.

Anthony Wallace proposed the term 'revitalisation movements', and was interested in the reasons as to the emergence of these movements. He proposed that they tend to occur when a society finds that day-to-day behaviour has deviated from the accepted norms such that individuals cannot sustain the traditional religious understanding.[4] During this period of cultural dislocation, a charismatic leader emerges who epitomises the crisis of the culture and proposes a new way forward. To these leaders are attracted members of the society who are willing to experiment with the new thought-patterns and lifestyle. There is often a collective retreat to a conservative and negative position before there is a sudden leap forward to a new and seemingly radical position. Finally, the innovators succeed in influencing the more passive members of the community and the past and the present shape a new religious culture. According to this theory the core issue is the need for people under stress to find a dynamic equilibrium in which they may achieve mutual harmony and dreams of a new tomorrow.

Millenarian movements

As many traditional societies faced the extreme pressures of the advance of European power, some of their people had dreams of a promised future paradise on earth. Some of these visions told of a renewal of the glories of the past.

Ghost dance of the North American Indians

Some of the most dramatic were the Ghost Dance cults that spread across Plains Indians in the nineteenth century following the loss of their independence and destruction of the buffalo herds. One of the oldest is the Handsome Lake Religion that was founded among the Iroquois as early as 1800, and later other movements emerged among the Paiute.

> In 1869, a Paiute prophet named Wodziwob had religious visions which foretold the end of the existing world, the ousting of the whites, the return of dead relatives, and the restoration of Indian lands and integrity. These doctrines spread rapidly among Plains tribes whose way of life had disintegrated under white pressure and the extermination of the buffalo. Though attempts at military resistance generated by cult doctrines were smashed, the cult spread widely and diversified into local versions.[5]

In 1892, James Mooney recounts meeting with another prophet, Jack Wilson, whose Paiute name was Wovoka. As a young man Jack Wilson began to develop a reputation as a healer like his father, and showed remarkable self-discipline and sound judgement. Jack led the circle dances through which the Paiute opened themselves to spiritual influences. As they danced they listened to Jack's songs about the wonders of the mountains, clouds, stars, trees and animals. The climax of his mystical experiences came on 1 January 1889 when there was a dramatic total eclipse of the sun. He was lying in his tent ill with fever when all became dark like night. Some Paiute began to shoot guns in the air to scare off the force that seemed to be devouring the sun. Some wailed as at a death. Jack lost consciousness. Later Jack told Mooney of his vision.

> He saw God, with all the people who had died long ago engaged in their old-time sport and occupations, all happy and forever young. It was a pleasant land and full of game. After showing him all, God told him he must go back and tell his people they must be good and love one another, have no quarrelling, and live in peace with the whites; that they must work, and not lie or steal; that they must put away all of the practices that savoured of war; that if they faithfully obeyed his instructions they would at last be reunited with their friends in the other world, where there would be no more death or sickness or old age.[6]

Confident of his mission he quickly became well and began to preach with passion. Indians came on pilgrimages to Mason Valley curious about the new prophet. Even members of the Mormon community came to explore if Jack Wilson was the fulfilment of a prophecy of their founder, Joseph Smith Jr that the Messiah would appear in human form in 1890. Jack Wilson himself consistently explained that he was a messiah *like* Jesus, but *not* the Christ of the Christians. The religion was quickly taken up by Jack's own people, the Northern Paiute, and then travelled west and south where it was adopted by many Indians. The mechanism by which the religion spread was either by people visiting other tribes, or visitors observing the circle dance. Although it was never an organised church, the religion spread by independent converts from Oklahoma to California.

The name often applied to the movement was 'Ghost Dance' because the prophet foresaw the resurrection of the recent dead with the hoped-for renewal on earth. The Paiute themselves simply called their faith 'dance in a circle'. It was a marvellous message for a suffering people who had lost their lands, their economic resources, and their political autonomy. To his last days in 1931, Jack Wilson served as father to the believers with a simple message of a clean, honest life.

Cargo cults of the Pacific

Among the Maori of New Zealand there have been a dozen or so religious movements, of which the largest is the Ratana Church. Prophet Wirenu Ratana founded this movement during the influenza epidemic of 1918. In Polynesia and Melanesia, there have been hundreds of similar movements generally called 'Cargo Cults' because of their emphasis upon material goods or cargo.[7] As the Melanesians observed the missions and successive governments, they were impressed by the amount and diversity of material goods and equated spiritual salvation with them. The 'cargo' brought by Europeans was perceived as an essential part of salvation as preached by the missionaries. The belief is that someday the people of that region will receive certain material goods now possessed by white people and denied to others.

Cargo cults first arose in the nineteenth century when Europeans began to enter the Pacific region in greater numbers. The growing sense of demoralisation and death due to alien diseases mentioned in chapter 12 caused disillusionment and despair. The arrival of American troops during the Second World War gave impetus to these movements. The sight of unlimited numbers of unknown goods such as washing machines, Nissen huts, eating utensils, cars, canned food, cigarettes, and canned drinks were beyond the imagination of these island people. Various messiahs arose everywhere, promising both the coming of the cargo by ship or plane and the end of white domination. Few of these prophets lasted for more than a few months, or two or three years at most. When the cargo did not come as promised, their followers lost faith and turned to other leaders or gave up the idea of cargo altogether. Some groups saw the solution in political action and organised political parties and co-operatives. However, in some cases the cargo movements took on a particularly religious expression, and continued much longer.

Tanna is an isolated island at the bottom of the New Hebrides chain. According to the Tannese, a mysterious figure by the name of John Frum appeared in about 1937. As Edward Rice shows it is not easy to answer the question, 'Who is John Frum?'[8] John Frum was first noticed by the British District Agent, Mr James Nicol, and it seemed to him that this was a person who was merely causing trouble. His solution was to arrest him, and send him to prison in Port Vila. It soon became apparent that this person was not John Frum, and a second man was arrested, and then a third and a fourth. All these men were arrested and jailed without any crimes being proven. Since that time many stories of the appearance of John Frum have been reported. Sometimes he is said to be white and other times brown. He is believed to often travel to America and even visit the President. It is believed that someday he will appear to all the islanders in a sacred field that has been denied to the Tannese by the white people.

Rice suggests that a clue to the identity of this mysterious figure comes from the observations of Codrington writing long before the emergence of stories of John Frum. 'The Melanesians believe in the existence of beings – personal, intelligent, full of *mana*, with a certain bodily form which is visible but not fleshly like the bodies of men. These they think to be more or less actively concerned in the affairs of men, and they invoke and otherwise approach them. These may be called spirits, but it is most important to distinguish between spirits who are beings of an order higher than mankind, and the disembodied spirits of men, which have become in the vulgar sense of the word ghosts.'[9] By this definition, John Frum for the Tannese would be spirit full of *mana* who has come to bring hope to a people disillusioned with their situation.

African independent churches

It has, however, been in Africa that the greatest number of new religious movements has occurred. As early as 1968, David

Barrett listed some six thousand in his book *Schism and Renewal in Africa*.[10] The Republic of South Africa alone has over three thousand such movements with over three million adherents. The largest of these movements in Africa is the Kimbanguists of Zaire who number over three million followers. These have generally been called African Independent Churches (AICs), or African Indigenous Churches.

Sundkler was the first writer to describe these movements in his book *Bantu Prophets in South Africa*.[11] Sundkler was a missionary working among the Zulus, and wanted to understand the new religious movements that were occurring among the people. He knew that the Zulus were a proud military people who had established a great state until they were finally defeated by the British. The first missionaries arrived in the region in the 1830s, and even though there had been a strong response to missionary work there were several breakaway religious movements.

Sundkler distinguished between what he called 'Ethiopian' and 'Zionist' type AICs.[12] Ethiopian churches are those which came out of the established mission churches primarily over a disagreement concerning the matter of leadership. They reacted against what appeared to them as dominant white leadership, and sought to establish an African-led church. These churches usually resemble the church or mission from which they divided, but are African in leadership and more African in certain cultural matters. Often these churches have had Ethiopia in their name following the Bible verse Psalm 61:31, 'Ethiopia shall stretch forth her hand unto God.' Others, however kept to more conventional names such as 'African Methodist Church', or 'Native Baptist Church', which still demonstrated their African character.

The second type of independent churches Sundkler called 'Zionist' because many were initially influenced by an American organisation founded by John Dowie with its headquarters at

Zion Illinois.[13] These churches have made a more radical transformation of missionary Christianity. Not only has there been a change to African leadership, but there is also a more African form of worship that was not always approved of by the American founders. Dance and drumming are common and healing always takes an important place.

In the first edition of his book, Sundkler considered these AIC as a 'bridge back to paganism'. In later editions he abandons this suggestion and considers them as protest movements against white domination in South Africa. This theory fitted in with Wallace's views, and the social turmoil that was taking place in the 1950s, which was the decade of independence for many African nations. Sundkler therefore proposed the view that Zionism was a precursor to nationalism. However, the Republic of South Africa has a different history to the rest of Africa, and there it appears that Zionism was more an alternative to nationalism than a precursor to it.

Similar movements occurred in West Africa, but here the emphasis was upon prophet-healers – many of whom modelled themselves on the charismatic Prophet Harris. Harris was a dynamic personality who burst upon the West African scene in 1914. He followed the coastline from Liberia, through the Ivory Coast into the Gold Coast, a distance of more than five hundred kilometres, before returning to the French colony. Everywhere he went there was a massive response to his simple message for the people to burn their fetishes and repent. Harris was accompanied by two women, Helen Valentine and Mary Pioka, who helped him with singing and using calabashes for the rhythm. They all wore white, the women in Western-style dresses and Harris in a cassock robe with a white turban. Harris carried a cross-topped staff in his right hand and a Bible in the other, and they all went barefoot. The two women were often referred to as his 'wives', which was for some a focus of criticism and for others an endorsement of polygamy.

The pattern of evangelism of the prophetic band was that

they would enter a village playing their calabash rattles and singing, and immediately they would go to the chief to explain their mission. Harris would then preach to the whole village, usually through an interpreter, and he would invite them to abandon their 'fetishes' and worship the one true God. Those who destroyed their fetishes were baptised, and were taught the Ten Commandments and the Lord's Prayer. The converts were encouraged to pray in their own language, and to keep Sunday for worship. If there were missions in the area the people were told to go to those churches whatever the denomination. If there was no mission, Harris often chose leaders, sometimes naming them 'twelve apostles', who were to supervise the building of places of worship from local materials. Often they were told to wait for the coming of the white men who would come with the Bible and teach them more. The reputation of the prophet seemed to go before him almost like a bow wave of heightened expectation with exaggerated stories of his power.

In May 1914, the prophetic group was going from village to village in the Nzima region of the Gold Coast which the missionaries had generally considered resistant. Both Methodists and Roman Catholics had some presence in the region, and the leaders of both churches initially appeared antagonistic to the prophetic group. The District Commissioner commented in 1916:

Apollonia before Harris's visit was steeped in fetishism and the towns and villages were in a most unsatisfactory condition. All this has now been changed, places of worship and schools are to be found in every village and the villages and towns are being remodelled on sanitary lines.[14]

Axim was the largest town in the region with a more mixed population than other areas. It was here that the group had some of their greatest successes, partly because Harris could now preach in English without an interpreter, and some of his most spectacular signs were reported. Harris's visit to the Gold Coast was not long, but he made an immense impact. Bruce reported that there was 'a general religious awakening throughout the length and breadth of the Apollonia (Nzima) district . . . Everywhere, bamboo chapels and churches were built. Their thirst for the Word of God and for the songs of Zion is insatiable.'[15] Sixteen months later the Wesleyan Methodists reported 160 new chapels with more than thirty-two thousand people on their church registers. The Rev. Charles Armstrong, a Methodist Missionary, visited Axim less than a week after Harris left, and reported:

> Hundreds of people are seeking admission to the church. They want to serve the living God and learn more of Christ their Saviour. They crowd in at our services, weekdays and Sundays, and attend Sunday School where they are learning the creeds etc. This is now the normal state of affairs and has been for three months. Whole villages have given up fetish and are asking for the gospel, chiefs are offering land for buildings and everywhere there is an awakening that we have prayed for, but scarcely expected, perhaps.[16]

On 4 August 1914 war broke out in Europe, which had an immediate effect on the economic situation of the region. The prophetic group was arrested and roughly treated before being deported to Liberia. It has been estimated that some two hundred thousand people were converted through the two year ministry of Prophet Harris and his group.[17]

Following the ministry of Prophet Harris many similar prophet-healers emerged throughout West Africa. Sampson Oppong was such a figure among the Asante of central Ghana. God called him when he was in prison, and during the period 1917-1935 directed thousands of converts to the Methodist Church. In western Nigeria, Joseph Babalola was a steamroller driver when he received a call to preach. Initially he resisted the call, but eventually he submitted and saw many thousands repent and become Christians. Garick Braide worked as an Anglican catechist in Eastern Nigeria when he was called to preach in 1917. He was just doing his job when things started to happen. People were saved, others healed, and many returned to the Lord. However, he came into conflict with his bishop and was turned out of the Anglican Church, so formed his own Christ's Army Church.

Bennetta Jules-Rosette traced the original impetus for the growth of African independent churches to six basic conditions:

(1) The disappointment of local converts with the premises and outcomes of Christianity led to the growth of prophetic and millenarian groups. (2) The translation of the Bible into local African vernaculars stimulated a reinterpretation of scripture and a spiritual renewal in mission-linked groups. (3) Reinterpretation of the scriptures also fuelled the development of new theologies that both criticised and incorporated the messages of Euro-Christianity. (4) The preconceived divisions in European and American denominational Christianity and its failure to meet local needs influenced the rise of separatist churches and community-based indigenous churches. (5) The weakness of Western medicine in the face of psychological disorders, epidemics, and natural disasters was a catalyst for concerns with spiritual healing in the new African religious movements. (6) The failure of mission churches to break down social, ethnic, and cultural barriers and generate a sense of community led by the strengthening of social ties in small, sectarian groups. In general, the African churches have tried to create a sense of community and continuity in multiethnic, urban environments and in rapidly changing rural villages.[18]

In all these cases people were looking for a wider salvation than was offered by the mission churches. Then in 1918 major pandemics swept through Africa. These were white man's illnesses such as influenza, for which the African healers had no remedies nor had the Western doctors. The prophet healing churches provided an answer through the power of prayer and the word of God.

The initial attitude of the missionaries was one of condemning the African Independent Churches as heretical and divisive. They were regarded as being the churches of the uneducated and allowing sexual immorality. Most Western missionaries therefore took little interest in such movements until the 1960s. Since that time a growing number of missionaries began to realise the relevance of these independent churches, and even began to work with them. The ministry of Edwin and Irene Weaver,[19] and Stan Nussbaum provide useful models.[20] These authors have understood these Independent churches as attempts at making Christianity relevant to the needs of the people of Africa. This is a process of syncretism, but one in which the essential principles of Christianity remain as the practice is africanised.

Movements within mission Christianity

The main focus of academic study in Africa has been upon movements of independent Christianity. These movements have seemed more authentically African, more exotic, and for this reason have received more attention. It is necessary to appreciate that the mission churches have not been without their own religious movements that have resulted in renewed religious enthusiasm. The noted African scholar Terence O. Ranger has appreciated the importance of revival movements within the mission churches. He writes:

> Many scholars have argued that African independent churches arose in reaction against the institutional rigidities of mission Christianity. What has been much less noticed is that movements of independency almost nowhere swept the mission churches away. There was a rallying by African mission Christians. In many places independency was countered by movements of revival from within

the mission churches, led by African Christians and expressive of the dynamic values of popular Christianity. Often these mission revivals were as enthusiastic as any prophetic movements, sweeping across wide areas like wild-fire and giving the colonial authorities the same anxieties as the Zionist and Apostolic movements.[21]

A notable example is that of the so-called East African revival. Ian Linden in his sociological study of the revival has stressed both its egalitarian character and opposition to traditional African religious movements.

> The centre of the movement was on the Rwanda–Uganda border, among the Kiga and in Ndorwa, in the very region that had for decades produced Nyabingi prophetesses. From the first, response . . . fell within the tradition of the shamans. As hundreds of Kiga flocked to church, some believing that the Second Coming was imminent, the revival became increasingly independent of mission control . . . The revival movement, which spread through eastern Rwanda to Burundi from 1937 to 1942 was a translation of the CMS teaching on the radical sinfulness of man . . . into the idiom of witch-calling and Nyabingi shamanism . . . Groups with a core of CMS members toured the hills, holding prayer meetings and seeking confessions.[22]

More recently the charismatic movement has had a major influence in many of the historic missionary denominations of Africa. From the emergence of this movement in West Africa in the 1970s it has grown rapidly, affecting many students of the major West African Universities. The doctrinal emphasis was initially placed on the baptism of the Holy Spirit and speaking in tongues to which healing, prophecy and visions became important elements. Today some of the largest congregations in Africa are part of this Charismatic movement.

For example, the Deeper Christian Life Ministry was established in the University of Lagos in 1973 amidst the enthusiastic evangelism of the Christian students.[23] The ministry began with William F. Kumuyi through a Bible study group, which rapidly grew so that by 1975 the group had to move to an auditorium in the near-by Redeemed Christian Church of God (an indigenous pentecostal church). In December 1975 Deeper Life held its first major public programme that brought the movement to the public knowledge. In 1982 the Deeper Life organisation moved from a Bible study group to become a denominational church. This transition also resulted in a shift in doctrinal emphasis from Bible study and evangelism in the seventies to healing, miracles and church planting in the eighties.

The meetings still consisted in the main of University educated young people who were fluent in English and aware of the global nature of Christianity. These are the new educated elite who appreciate singing the new songs from *Spring Harvest* conventions. They are eager to read the writings of Charismatic leaders from around the world and apply this teaching into their own situation. These Christian young people want to be the Africans of the twenty-first century. Here is Christianity being reworked by a new generation for a new social context.

Conclusion

During the twentieth century traditional societies have changed radically. There are few societies left in isolation from the modern world of Coca-Cola, McDonalds, MTV, radio and television. These societies that were once the primary focus of anthropological research have been drawn into the complex web of the world economic system. It is easy to lament the passing of lifestyles so different to those known and experienced by those of the modern urban world. There is a sense in which the loss of such divergent societies is to be regretted, but one should not slide into a romantic view that these were merely happy innocent people free from stress as is sometimes portrayed in popular magazines. Like all societies they struggled in their local environment to cope with issues of getting enough food, providing shelter for their families, and dealing with misfortune and sickness.

Mark Ritche recounts the conversation with a Yanomamo Indian in which a person remarks that many Western people say that they were happy living in the Amazonian forest and should be left alone. Ritche recounts the Indian named Hairy saying:

> I say to you, please don't listen to the people who say that. We need help so bad. We are so miserable here and our misery never stops. Night and day it goes on. Do those people think that we don't suffer pain when the bugs bite us? If they think this is such a happy place out here in the jungle, why aren't they moving out here to enjoy this beautiful life with us?[24]

In the struggle to cope these societies turned for assistance to the world of the spirits. During the nineteenth and twentieth centuries these societies have been drawn into the modern world, but they have often been stranded in the lowest class. The poverty and deprivation of the urban slums have often only replaced the harsh life of the forests. The people continue to look to the world of the spirits to help them cope with the continuing struggle of what is now a concrete jungle.

With the new order has come the great missionary religions, and especially Christianity which has introduced new symbols of spiritual power. Christianity has brought hope, but also confusion as people have struggled to relate new religious ideas within their traditional belief system. One of the major themes of this book has been to show the complexity of religious conversion. People do not merely change from one fixed religious system to another, and this applies equally to those religions that have here been called 'Traditional'. Even before the encounter with major world religions traditional religions were in a continual state of flux. A strong belief in an unseen world that impacts upon the empirical has been an important characteristic of all these religions.

Many societies have adapted Christianity to meet their own particular need, but it has been transformed out of all recognition. The new religion has often been woven with traditional beliefs and rituals into an original tapestry different than that brought by the foreign missionaries. This religious syncretism continues to draw upon powers from the world of the spirits to meet their needs. New religious movements are significant as new initiatives for 'making sense' of the world, and provide answers in the search for salvation. One thing that is certain is that in the midst of a rapidly changing world societies will continually see new expressions of old beliefs.

The study of traditional religions at the beginning of the twenty-first century is totally different from that at the beginning of the twentieth century. The hundred years has changed traditional societies, but the quest for assistance from the world of the spirits still continues in the urban slums. In the West, many are now turning back to try and discover old religious beliefs and practices, and out of the mist of time craft what they consider a close approximation. Christians continue to be faced with the issue of holding to the historic Christian tradition as preserved in the Bible, whilst relating to emerging religious ideas that are part of the contemporary world.

Notes

1 Turner, H. A. 'Religious movements in traditional (tribal) societies' *Mission Focus* 9 (1981), pp. 45–55.

2 *Ibid.*

3 Werbner, R. P., *Regional Cults* (London: Academic Press, 1977).

4 Wallace, A. F. C., 'Revitalization movements: some theoretical considerations for their comparative studies' *American Anthropologist* 58 (195), pp. 264–81.

5 Mooney, J., *The Ghost Dance Religion* (Washington: U.S. Government Printing Office, 1896).

6 *Ibid.* p. 771.

7 Steinbaur, F., *Melanesian Cargo Cults* (London: George Prior Publishers, 1979).

8 Rice, E., *John Frum He Come: Cargo Cults and Cargo Messiahs in the South Pacific* (New York: Doubleday, 1974).

9 Codrington, R. H., *The Melanesians* (Oxford: Clarendon Press, 1891).

10 Barrett, D. B., *Schism & Renewal in Africa* (Nairobi: OUP, 1968).

11 Sundkler, B. G. M., *Bantu Prophets in South Africa* (London: Oxford University Press, 1961).

12 *Ibid.* p. 39.

13 *Ibid.* p. 48.

14 Cited in Haliburton, G. M., *The Prophet Harris* (Longman: London, 1971), p. 90, (Letter dated 29 May 1916).

15 *Ibid.*, p. 7.

16 Armstrong to Griffin, 2 August 1914, WMMS, Box 14, microfiche 1386.

17 David A. Shank has given an important account as to how the life and ministry of Prophet Harris was reconstructed to make him more acceptable within the Wesleyan mission. 'The taming of the Prophet Harris', *Journal of Religion in Africa,* 27 (1997), pp. 59–95.

18 Jules-Rosette, B., 'Modern movements' in *The Encyclopedia of Religion* (New York: Macmillan, 1989), p. 82.

19 Weaver, E. & I., *The Uyo Story* (Mennonite Board of Missions: Elkhart Indiana, 1970).

20 Nussbaum, S. W., *Towards Theological Dialogue with Independent Churches* (University of South Africa doctoral thesis 1985).

21 Ranger, T., 'Religious movements and politics in Sub-Saharan Africa', *African Studies Review* 29 (1986) p. 35.

22 Linden, I., *Church and Revolution in Rwanda* (Manchester: Manchester University Press, 1977), pp. 203–6.

23 Ojo, M. A., 'Deeper Christian Life Ministry: a case study of the Charismatic movements in Western Nigerian', *Journal of Religion in Africa* 18 (1988), pp. 141–62.

24 Ritchie, M. A., *Spirit of the Rainforest* (Chicago: Island Lake Press, 1996), p. 183.

BIBLIOGRAPHY

Abbink, J., 'Reading the entrails: analysis of an African divination discourse', *Man* 28 (1993), pp. 705–26.

Achebe, C., *Things Fall Apart* (Nairobi: Heinemann, 1958).

Aguilar, M. I., 'African conversion from world religion: religious diversification by the Waso Boorana in Kenya', *Africa* 65 (1995), pp. 525–43.

Ahmed, S. A., & Hart, D., *Islam in Tribal Societies* (London: Routledge & Kegan Paul, 1984).

Allison, N., 'Make sure you're getting through', *Evangelical Missions Quarterly,* 20 (1984), pp. 167–8.

Bah, C. N., 'The Supreme Being, divinities and ancestors in Igbo Traditional Religion: evidence from Otanchara and Utanza', *Africa* 52 (1982), pp. 91–103.

Balzer, M. M., *Shamanism: Soviet Studies of Traditional Religion in Siberia and Central Asia* (London: M. E. Sharp, 1990).

Barker, J. 'We are *Ekelesia*: conversion in Uiaku, Papua New Guinea' in Hefner, R., *Conversion to Christianity* (Berkeley: University of California, 1993), pp. 199–230.

Barker, P., *Peoples, Languages, and Religion in Northern Ghana* (Accra: GEC, 1986).

Barrett, D. B., *Schism & Renewal in Africa* (Nairobi: OUP, 1968).

Bartle, P. F. W., 'The universe has three souls', *Journal of Religion in Africa* 14 (1983), pp. 85–112.

Bartolome, M. A., *et al.*, *Declaration of Barbados: For the Liberation of the Indians* (Copenhagen: International Work Group for Indigenous Affairs, 1971).

Bawa Yamba, C., 'Cosmologies in turmoil: witchfinding and AIDS in Chiawa, Zambia', *Africa* 67 (1997), pp. 200–23.

Beattie, J. H. M., 'The ghost cult in Bunyoro', in Middleton, J. (ed.), *Gods & Rituals* (Austin: University of Texas, 1967), pp. 255–87.

Beattie, J., 'Divination in Bunyoro, Uganda', in Middleton, J. (ed.), *Magic, Witchcraft and Curing* (Austin: University of Texas Press, 1967), pp. 211–31.

Benedict, R., *Patterns of Culture* (London: Routledge & Kegan Paul, 1934).

Bevan Jones, V., *Women in Islam* (Lucknow: Lucknow Publishing House, 1941).

Bloch, M., *Prey into Hunter* (Cambridge: CUP, 1992).

Boddy, J., *Wombs and Alien Spirits: Women, Men and the Zar Cult in Northern Sudan* (Madison: University of Wisconsin Press, 1989).

Bolaji Idowu, E., *African Traditional Religion* (London: SCM Press, 1973).

Bong Rin Ro, *Christian Alternatives to Ancestor Practices* (Taiwan: ATA: Taichung, 1985).

Bosman, W., *A New and Accurate Description of the Coast of Guinea Divided into the Gold, the Slave, and the Ivory Coasts* (London: Frank Cass, 1969). Original English edition published in 1705, and the Dutch edition in 1704.

Brain, J., 'Ancestors as elders in Africa: further thoughts', *Africa* 43 (1973), pp. 122–3.

Brown, D., *Umbanda: Religion and Politics in Urban Brazil* (New York: Columbia University Press, 1994).

Bruner, E. M., 'Mandan' in Spice, E. H. (ed.), *Perspectives in American Indian Cultural Change* (Chicago: Chicago University Press, 1961).

Burnett, D., *Dawning of the Pagan Moon* (Eastbourne: Monarch, 1991).

Burton, R. F., *A Mission to Gelele, King of Dahome* (London: Tinsley Bros., 1864).

Busia, K. A., *The Position of the Chief in the Modern Political System of Ashanti* (London: Frank Cass & Co., 1968).

Busia, K. A., 'The Ashanti of the Gold Coast' in Ford, D. (ed.), *African Worlds* (Oxford: OUP, 1954).

Campbell, J., *The Way of Animal Powers* (London: Time Books, 1984).

Chagnon, N. A., *Yanomamo: The Fierce People* (New York: Holt, Rinehart and Winston, 1983).

Clifton, C., 'Armchair shamanism: a Yankee way of knowledge' in Schultz, T. (ed.), *The Fringes of Reason* (New York : Harmony Books, 1989), pp. 43–9.

Codrington, R. H., *The Melanesians: studies in their anthropology and folk-lore* (Oxford: Clarendon Press, 1891).

Comaroff, J. & J., *Of Revelation and Revolution: Christianity, Colonialism and Consciousness in South Africa* (Chicago: Chicago University Press, 1991).

Comaroff, J. & J., *Modernity and Malcontents: Ritual and Power in Postcolonial Africa* (Chicago: University of Chicago Press, 1993).

Cook, R. R., 'Ghosts', *East Africa Journal of Evangelical Theology*, 4 (1985), pp. 35–48.

Covell, A., *Ecstasy: Shamanism in Korea* (NJ: Hollym International Corporation, 1983).

Craemer, W. de, Vansina, J. & Fox, R. C., 'Religious movements in Central Africa: a theoretical study', *Comparative Studies in Society and History* 18 (1976), pp. 458–75.

Danquah, J. B., *The Akan Doctrine of God: A Fragment of Gold Coast Ethics and Religion* (London: Lutterworth, 1944).

Danquah, J. B., *The Akan Doctrine of God* (London: Lutterworth, 1944).

Davis, W., *Passage of Darkness: The Ethnobiology of the Haitian Zombi* (Chapel Hill: University of North Carolina Press, 1988).

Derrett, J. D. M., 'Spirit-possession and the Gerasene Demonic', *Man* 14 (1979).

Desmangles, L. G., *The Faces of the Gods* (Chapel Hill: The University of North Carolina Press, 1992).

Douglas, M., *Witchcraft: Confessions and Accusations* (London: Tavistock Pub., 1970).

Douglas, M., *Purity and Danger* (London: Routledge & Kegan Paul, 1966).

Dundes, A., 'Wet and dry, the evil eye', in Dundes, A. (ed.), *The Evil Eye: a Casebook* (London: Garland, 1981), pp. 257–312.

Dye, T. W., 'Towards a cultural definition of sin', *Missiology* 4 (1976), pp. 26–41.

Eliade, M., *Shamanism: Archaic Techniques of Ecstasy* (London: Routledge & Kegan Paul, 1964).

Eliade, M., *A History of Religious Ideas*, vol. 3 (Chicago: University of Chicago Press, 1985).

Eliade, M. (ed.), *The Encyclopedia of Religion* (New York: Macmillan, 1987).

Endicott, K. M., *An Analysis of Malay Magic* (Oxford: Clarendon Press, 1970).

Eni, E., *Delivered from the Powers of Darkness* (Ibadan: Scripture Union, 1987).

Evans-Pritchard, E. E., *Nuer Religion* (New York: OUP, 1977).

Evans-Pritchard, E. E., *Theories of Primitive Religion* (Oxford: Clarendon Press, 1965).

Evans-Pritchard, E. E., *Witchcraft, Oracles and Magic among the Azande* (Oxford: Clarendon Press, 1976).

Fadiman, A., *The Spirit Catches You and You Fall Down* (New York: Noonday Press, 1999).

Field, M. J., *Religion and Medicine of the Ga People* (London: Oxford University Press, 1961)

Field, M. J., *Search for Security* (London: Faber and Faber, 1960).

Fisher, H., 'Conversion reconsidered: some historical aspects of religious conversion in Black Africa', *Africa* 43 (1973), pp. 27–40.

Fisher, H., 'The Juggernaut's Apologia: conversion to Islam in Black Africa', *Africa* 55 (1985), pp. 153–73.

Fortes, M., 'Some reflections on ancestor worship', in Fortes, M., & Dieterlen, G. (eds.), *African Systems of Thought* (London: OUP, 1965), pp. 122–42.

Fravret-Saada, J., *Deadly Word: Witchcraft in the Bocage* (Cambridge: CUP, 1980).

Frazer, J., *The Golden Bough* (London: Macmillan Press, 1978).

Friesen, J. S., *Missionary Responses to Tribal Religions at Edinburgh, 1910* (New York: Peter Lang Publishing, 1996).

Geertz, C., *The Religion of Java* (Glencoe: The Free Press, 1960).

Glucklich, A., *The End of Magic* (New York: OUP, 1997).

Gluckman, M., *Customs and Conflict in Africa* (Oxford: Blackwell, 1959).

Goode, W. J., *Religion Among the Primitives* (New York: Free Press, 1951).

Greene, S. A., 'Religion, history and the Supreme Gods of Africa: a contribution to the debate', *Journal of Religion in Africa* 26 (1996), pp. 122–38.

Guerber, H. A., *The Myths of Greece and Rome* (London: George G Harrap & Co., 1925).

Guthrie, D., *New Testament Introduction*, Vol. III (London: Tyndale Press, 1966).

Haliburton, G, M., *The Prophet Harris* (London: Longman, 1971).

Harner, M., *Hallucinogens and Shamanism* (London: OUP, 1973).

Harner, M., *The Way of the Shaman* (New York: Bantam, 1982).

Hayes, S., 'Christian responses to witchcraft and sorcery', *Missionalia* 23 (1995).

Hefner, R. W., *Conversion to Christianity* (Berkeley: University of California Press, 1993).

Herskovits, M., *Dahomey: An Ancient West African Kingdom* (New York: Augustin, 1963).

Hezel, F. X., 'Spirit possession in Chuuk: a socio-cultural interpretation', *The Micronesian Counsellor*, Occasional Papers, No. 11, July 1993.

Hicks, D., *Tetum Ghosts and Kin* (Palo Alto: Mayfield Publishing Company, 1976).

Hill, H., 'Witchcraft and the Gospel: insights from Africa', *Missiology* 24 (1996).

Hoebel, E. A., *The Cheyennes: Indians of the Great Plains* (Orlando: Holt, Reinhart & Winson Inc., 1978).

Holmberg, D. H., *Order in Paradox: Myth, Ritual, and Exchange Among Nepal's Tamang* (Ithaca: Cornell University Press, 1989).

Horton, R., *Patterns of Thought in Africa and the West* (Cambridge: CUP, 1994).

Horton, R., 'African conversion', *Africa* 41 (1971), pp. 85–108.

Horton, R., 'Judaeo-Christian spectacles: boon or bane to the study of African religions?' *Cahiers d'Etudes Africaines* 24 (1984), pp. 392–436.

Horton, R., 'On the rationality of conversion', *Africa* 4 (1975), pp. 219–35, 371–99.

Horton, R., 'The Kalabari world-view: an outline and interpretation', *Africa,* 32 (1962), pp. 197–220.

Hultkrantz, A., 'Shamanism: a religious phenomenon?' in Doore, G. (ed.), *The Shaman's Path* (Boston: Shambhala, 1988), pp. 35–7.

Hvalkof, S. & Aaby, P., *Is God an American? An Anthropological Perspective on the Missionary Work of the Summer Institute of Linguistics* (Copenhagen: IWGIA & SI, 1981).

Idowu, E. B., *African Traditional Religion: A Definition* (London: SCM, 1973).

Idowu, E. B., *Olodumare: God in Yoruba Belief* (London: Longmans, 1962).

Ikenga-Metuh, E., 'The shattered microcosm: a critical survey of explanations of conversion in Africa' in Petersen, K. H. (ed.), *Religion, Development and African Identity* (Uppsala: Scandinavian Institute of African Studies, 1987), pp. 11–27.

Irwin, J., *An Introduction to Maori Religion* (Bedford Park, S. Aust: Australian Association for the Study of Religion, 1984).

Jewsiewicki, B., 'The formation of the political culture of ethnicity in the Belgian Congo', in Vail, L. (ed.), *The Creation of Tribalism in Southern Africa* (London: Currey, 1988).

Keesing, R. M., *Cultural Anthropology* (New York: Holt, Rinehart and Winson, 1981).

Keesing, R. M., *Kwaio Religion: The Living and the dead in a Solomon Island Society* (1981).

Kendall, L., 'Healing thyself: a Korean shaman's afflictions', *Society of Scientific Medicine* 27 (1988).

Kenyatta, J., *Facing Mount Kenya* (Nairobi: Heinemann, 1982).

Kertzer, D. I., *Ritual, Politics and Power* (New Haven: Yale University Press, 1988).

Kiev, A., *Magic, Faith, and Healing* (New York: Free Press, 1964).

Kim, K., 'Rituals of resistance: the manipulation of shamanism in contemporary Korea', in Keyes, C. *et al.* (eds.), *Religion and the Modern States of East and Southeast Asia* (Honolulu: University of Hawaii Press, 1992).

Kopytoff, I., 'Ancestors as elders in Africa', *Africa* 43 (1971), pp. 129–42.

Krader, L., 'Buryat religion and society', in Middleton, J. (ed.), *Gods and Ritual* (Austin: University of Texas Press, 1967), pp. 103–32.

Kraft, C. H., 'Christian animism or God-given authority?' in Rommen, E. (ed.), *Spiritual Power and Mission: Raising the Issues* (Pasadena: William Carey Library, 1995).

Kramer, H. & Sprenger, J., *Malleus Maleficarum* (London: Arrow Books, 1986).

Kreamer, C. M., 'Transformation and power in Moba (northern Togo) initiation rites', *Africa* 65 (1995), pp. 58–78.

Kudadjie, J. N., 'How morality was enforced in Ga-Adangme society' in *Traditional Religion in West Africa* (Accra: Asempa Publishers, 1983).

Kunitz, S. J., 'Disease and the destruction of indigenous populations' in Ingold, T. (ed.), *Companion Encyclopedia of Anthropology* (London: Routledge, 1998), pp. 297–325.

Kuper, A., *The Invention of Primitive Society* (London: Routledge, 1988).

Lambek, M., 'Taboo as cultural practice among Malagasy speakers', *Man* 27 (1992), pp. 245–66.

Lamphear, J., *The Traditional History of the Jie of Uganda* (London: Clarendon Press, 1976).

Lan, D., *Guns and Rain: Guerrillas and Spirit Mediums in Zimbabwe* (London: James Curry, 1987).

Lang, A., *The Making of Religion* (London: Longman, 1898).

Last, M., 'Reform in West Africa: Jihad movements in the nineteenth century', Ajayi & Crowder (eds.), *History of West Africa*, vol. 2 (London: Longman, 1987), pp. 1–47.

Leacock, S. & R., *Spirits of the Deep* (New York: Anchor Press, 1975).

Levi-Strauss, C., *Structural Anthropology* (Harmondsworth: Penguin, 1973).

Lewis, I. M., *Ecstatic Religion* (London: Penguin Books, 1971).

Lewis, I. M., 'What is a shaman?' *Folk* 23 (1981), pp. 25–35.

Lewis, I. M., *Religion in Context: Cults and Charisma* (Cambridge: CUP, 1986).

Lewis, N., 'Manhunt' in *Sunday Times Magazine*, 26 January 1975.

Lewis, N., *The Missionaries* (Sekker & Warburg, 1988).

Lin Yutang, *My Country and My People* (London: Heinemann, 1962).

Linden, I., *Church and Revolution in Rwanda* (Manchester: Manchester University Press, 1977).

Linehardt, G., *Divinity and Experience: The Religion of the Dinka* (Oxford: Clarenden Press, 1987).

Livingstone, D., *Missionary Travels and Researches in South Africa* (New York: Harper & Brothers, 1958).

Luig, U., *Conversion as a Social Process: A History of Missionary Christianity among the Valley Tonga, Zambia* (Hamburg: LIT, 1996).

Madsen, W., 'Value conflicts and folk psychotherapy in South Texas' in Kiev, A. (ed.), *Magic Faith & Healing* (New York: Free Press, 1974).

Malinowski, B., *Magic, Science and Religion* (London: Sovereign Press, 1974).

Marwick, M. G., *Sorcery in its Social Setting* (Manchester: Manchester University Press, 1965).

Maupoil, B., *Le geomancie à l'ancienne Cote des Esclaves* (Paris, 1943).

Mbiti, J. S., *Concepts of God in Africa* (London: SPCK, 1970).

Mbiti, J. S., *African Religions and Philosophy* (London: Heinemann, 1969).

McCaskie, T. C., 'Anti-witchcraft cults in Asante: an essay in the social history of an African people', *History in Africa* 8 (1981), pp. 125–54.

McClelland, E., *The Cult of Ifa among the Yoruba* (London: Ethnographica, 1982).

McGavran, D., *Understanding Church Growth* (Grand Rapids: Eerdmans, 1970).

McKim, M., 'Little communities in an Indian civilisation', in Leslie, C. (ed.), *Anthropology of Folk Religion* (New York: Vintage Books, 1960), pp. 169–218.

Mead, M., 'Tabu' in *Encyclopedia of the Social Sciences* (London: Macmillan, 1937), vol. VII, pp. 502–5.

Mendonsa, E. L., 'Elders, office-holders and ancestors among the Sisala of Northern Ghana', *Africa* 46 (1976), pp. 57–61.

Meyer, B., 'If you are a devil, you are a witch, and if you are a witch, you are a devil': the integration of 'pagan' ideas into the conceptual universe of Ewe Christians in Southeast Ghana', *Journal of Religion in Africa* 22 (1992), pp. 98–132.

Milingo, E., *Healing : 'If I tell you, you will not believe me!'* (Lusaka, 1976).

Miller, Elmer S., 'The Christian missionary: agent of secularisation', *Missiology*, 1 (1973) pp. 99–107.

Mooney, J., *The Ghost Dance Religion* (Washington: U.S. Government Printing Office, 1896).

Morris, B., *The Anthropology of the Self: The Individual in Cultural Perspective* (London: Pluto Press, 1994).

Munzel, M., 'The Ache: Genocide in Paraguay', IWGIA document 1974.

Murphy, J. M., 'Psychotherapeutic aspects of Shamanism on St Lawrence Island, Alaska' in Kiev, A. (ed.), *Magic, Faith, and Healing* (New York: Free Press, 1974).

Musk, B., *The Unseen Face of Islam* (Eastbourne: Monarch 1992).

Mutiso-Mubinda, J., *Anthropology and the Paschal Mystery* (Eldoret: Gaba Publications, 1979).

Nadel, S. F., 'Witchcraft in four African societies: an essay in comparison', *American Anthropologist* 54 (1952), pp.18–29.

Niebuhr, R. H., *The Social Sources of Denominationalism* (Hamden: Shoestring Press, 1954).

Nussbaum, S. W., *Towards Theological Dialogue with Independent Churches* (University of South Africa doctoral thesis 1985).

Nyamiti, C., *Christ as our Ancestor* (Gweru: Mambo Press, 1984).

Obeyesekere, G., 'The Great Tradition and the Little in perspective of Sinhalese Buddhism', *Journal of Asian Studies,* 22 (1963), pp. 139–53.

Ojo, Matthews A., 'Deeper Christian Life Ministry: a case study of the Charismatic movements in Western Nigerian', *Journal of Religion in Africa* 18 (1988), pp. 141–62.

Park, G. K., 'Divination and its social context', in Middleton, J. (ed.), *Magic, Witchcraft and Curing* (Austin: University of Texas Press, 1967), pp. 233–54.

Parrinder, G., *African Mythology* (London: Paul Hamlyn, 1967).

Parrinder, G., *African Traditional Religion* (London: Sheldon Press, 1962).

Parrinder, G., *Witchcraft: European and African* (London: Faber & Faber, 1970).

Parrinder, G., *Africa's Three Religions* (London: Sheldon Press, 1962)

p'Bitek, Okot, *African Religions in Western Scholarship* (Nairobi: Kenya Literature Bureau, 1971).

McGregor, P., *The Moon and Two Mountains* (London: Souvenir Press, 1966).

Peel, J. D. Y., 'Religious change in Yorubaland', *Africa* 37 (1967), pp. 292–306.

Peel, J. D. Y., 'History, culture and the comparative method: a West African puzzle', in Holy, L. (ed.), *Comparative Anthropology* (Oxford: Blackwell, 1987), pp. 88–118.

Peel, J. D. Y., 'The cultural work of Yoruba ethnogenesis', in Tonkin, E., Chapman, M., McDonald M. (ed.), *History and Ethnicity*, (London: Routledge, 1989).

Porterfield, A., 'Shamanism: a psychosocial definition', *Journal of the American Academy of Religion* 55 (1987), pp. 721–39.

Prince, D., *Blessing or Curse: You Can Choose* (Milton Keynes: Word, 1990).

Prince, R., 'Indigenous Yoruba psychiatry' in Kiev, A. (ed.), *Magic, Faith, and Healing* (New York: Free Press, 1964).

Prince, R., 'Shamans and endorphins', *Ethos,* 10 (1982): Special edition.

Raj, Muthusami, 'Christianity and the Social Transformation of the Maltos People of Bihar, India' (MA thesis, ANCC, 1997).

Ranger, T., 'Religious movements and politics in Sub-Saharan Africa', *African Studies Review* 29 (1986).

Rasmussen, S. J., *Spirit Possession and Personhood among the Kel Ewey Tuareg* (Cambridge: CUP, 1995).

Rattray, R. S., *The Ashanti* (London: OUP, 1923).

Read, K. E., 'Morality and the concept of the Person among Gahuku-Gama' in Middleton, J. (ed.), *Myth and Cosmos* (New York: AMNH, 1967), pp. 185–229.

Redfield, R., *Peasant Society and Culture* (Chicago: University of Chicago Press, 1956).

Redfield, R., *The Little Tradition*, (Chicago: Chicago University Press, 1955).

Reid, J., *Sorcerers & Healing Spirits* (Canberra: Australian National University Press, 1983).

Rice, E., *John Frum He Come: Cargo Cults and Cargo Messiahs in the South Pacific* (New York: Doubleday, 1974).

Rigaud, M., *Secrets of Voodoo* (San Francisco: City Light Books, 1985).

Ritche, M. A., *Spirit of the Rainforest* (Chicago: Island Lake Press, 1996).

Rivers, W. H. R. (ed.), *Essays on the Depopulation of Melanesia* (Cambridge: CUP, 1922).

Robertson Smith, W., *Lectures on the Religion of the Semites* (London: A & C Black, 1927).

Roper, L., *Oedipus and the Devil: Witchcraft, Sexuality and Religion in Early Modern Europe* (London: Routledge, 1994).

Rosaldo, M. Z., *Knowledge and Passion: Ilongot Notions of Self and Social Life* (Cambridge: CUP, 1980).

Rose, H. J., 'Divination (Introduction)', *Encyclopaedia of Religion and Ethics,* Hastings (ed.) vol. 4, (Edinburgh, 1911).

Rouget, G., *Music and Trance: A Theory of the Relations between Music and Possession* (Chicago: University of Chicago, 1985).

Sanders, A., *A Deed without a Name* (Washington D.C.: Berg, 1995).

Sangree, W. H., 'Youths as elders and infants as ancestors: the complementarity of alternative generations, both living and dead, in Tiriki, Kenya, and Irigwe, Nigeria', *Africa* 44 (1974), pp. 65–70.

Sankar, S. S., *The Malers of the Rajmahal Hills* (Calcutta: Model Printing Works, 1974).

Sanneh, L., *Translating the Message* (Maryknoll: Orbis, 1989).

Shanin, T., *Peasants and Peasant Societies* (Harmondsworth: Penguin, 1971).

Shank D. A., 'The taming of the Prophet Harris', *Journal of Religion in Africa,* 27 (1997), pp. 59–95.

Sharp, L., 'Steel axes for stone-age Australians', *Human Organisation* 2 (1952), pp. 17–22.

Shaw, R., 'The invention of African traditional religion', *Religion* 20 (1990), pp. 339–53.

Simpson, J., 'Io as supreme being: intellectual colonization of the Maori', *History of Religion* 37 (1997), pp. 50–85.

Smith, E. W., *The Golden Stool* (London: Holborn Publishing House, 1926).

Spencer, H., *The Principles of Sociology*, vols. II & III (New York: Appleton, 1880–1896).

Spooner, B., 'The evil eye in the Middle East' in Maloney, C. (ed.), *Evil Eye* (New York: Columbia University Press, 1976), pp. 76–86.

Steinbauer, F., *Melanesian Cargo Cults* (London: George Prior, 1979).

Steiner, F., *Taboo* (Harmondsworth: Penguin, 1967).

Stewart C. & Shaw, R., *Syncretism/Anti-syncretism: The Politics of Religious Synthesis* (London: Routledge, 1994).

Stewart, K., 'Spirit-possession in native America', *Southwestern Journal of Anthropology* 2 (1946).

Strang, V., 'Familiar forms: homologues, culture and gender in Northern Australia', *Journal of the Royal Anthropological Institute* 5 (1999), pp. 75–95.

Sundkler, B. G. M., *Bantu Prophets in South Africa* (London: Oxford University Press, 1961).

Sutherland, A., *Face Values* (London: BBC Publications, 1978).

Tanner, M., *The Independent*, Thursday 29 October 1998.

Taylor, J. V., *The Primal Vision: Christian Presence and African Religion* (London: SCM Press, 1963).

Ter Haar, G. & Ellis, S., 'Spirit possession and healing in modern Zambia: an analysis of letters to Archbishop Milingo', *African Affairs* 87 (1988), pp. 185–206.

Ter Haar, G., *Spirit of Africa: The Healing Ministry of Archbishop Milingo of Zambia* (London: Hurst & Company, 1992).

Terwiel, B. J., *Monks and Magic: An Analysis of Religious Ceremonies in Central Thailand* (White Lotus: Bangkok, 1994).

Thomas, K., *Religion and the Decline of Magic* (London: Penguin Books, 1971).

Tienou, T., 'The invention of the "primitive" and stereotypes in mission', *Missiology* 19 (1991), pp. 293–303.

Tippett, A. R., *Solomon Islands Christianity* (Pasadena: William Carey Library, 1967).

Turner, E., *Experiencing Ritual: A New Interpretation of African Healing* (Philadelphia: University of Pennsylvania Press, 1992).

Turner, H. A., 'Religious movements in traditional (tribal) societies', *Mission Focus*, 9 (1981), pp. 45–55.

Turner, V. W., *The Drums of Affliction* (London: Hutchinson & Co. Ltd, 1981).

Turner, V., *The Forest of Symbols: Aspects of Ndembu Ritual* (Cornell: Cornell University Press, 1967).

Tylor, E. B., *Primitive Culture* (London: John Murray, 1871).

Van den Bersselaar, D., 'Creating "Union Ibo": missionaries and the Igbo Language', *Africa* 67 (1997), pp. 273–95.

Van Gennep, A., *Tabou et totemisme à Madagascar: étude descriptive et théorique* (Paris: Ernst Leroux, 1904).

Van Gennep, A., *The Rites of Passage* (London: Routledge & Kegan Paul, 1977).

Wagner, P., *Territorial Spirits* (Chichester: Sovereign Word, 1991).

Wallace, A. F. C., 'Revitalization movements: some theoretical considerations for their comparative studies', *American Anthropologist* 58 (1995), pp. 264–81.

Wallensteen, P., 'Scarce goods as political weapons: the case of food', in Harle, V. (ed.), *The Political Economy of Food* (Westmead: Saxon House, 1978).

Weaver, E. & I., *The Uyo Story* (Mennonite Board of Missions: Elkhart Indiana, 1970).

Weber, M., *The Protestant Ethic and the Spirit of Capitalism* (London: Allen and Unwin, 1930).

Werbner, R. P., *Regional Cults* (London: Academic Press, 1977).

Westermarck, *Pagan Survivals in Mohammedan Civilizations* (London: McMillan, 1933).

Whiteman, D., *Melanesians and Missionaries* (Pasadena: William Carey Library, 1983).

Winkelman, M. J., 'Trance states: a theoretical model and cross-cultural analysis', *Ethos* 14 (1986), pp. 174–204.

Wirz, P., *Kataragama: The Holiest Place in Ceylon* (Colombo: Lake House, 1972).

INDEX